KT-452-142

Competitive Retail Marketing

McGRAW-HILL MARKETING FOR PROFESSIONALS

Series Editor: Patrick Forsyth

Competitive Retail Marketing

Dynamic strategies for winning and keeping customers

Andrew Collins

McGraw-Hill Book Company

London • New York• St Louis • San Francisco • Auckland • Bogotá
Caracas • Hamburg • Lisbon • Madrid • Mexico • Milan • Montreal
New Delhi • Panama • Paris • San Juan • São Paulo • Singapore
Sydney • Tokyo • Toronto

Published by
McGraw-Hill Book Company Europe
Shoppenhangers Road, Maidenhead, Berkshire, SL6 2QL, England
Telephone 0628 23432
Fax 0628 770224

British Library Cataloguing in Publication Data
Collins, Andrew
    Competitive retail marketing : dynamic strategies for winning and
    keeping customers.
    I. Title
    658.87
    ISBN 0-07-707567-6

Library of Congress Cataloging-in-Publication Data
Collins, Andrew
    Competitive retail marketing : dynamic strategies for winning and
    keeping customers / Andrew Collins.
        p.   cm.
    Includes index.
    ISBN 0-07-707567-6
    1. Retail trade. 2. Marketing. I. Title.
    HF5429.C577 1991
    658.8'7–dc20   91-28123

1234 CUP 9432

Typeset by Focal Image Ltd, London
and printed and bound in Great Britain at the University Press,
Cambridge

To my children, Anna and Peter.
If they should go into business, I hope they will learn a little
from this book and avoid some of the mistakes the rest of us
have made already.

Contents

Foreword

Retailing is one of the most dynamic and competitive areas of business organization. It is also one in which British companies have often been world leaders in terms of quality and innovation. Effective marketing is the central dimension of successful retailing. Today, few retailers manufacture their own products; instead their key skills are in anticipating the wants of their target customers and in designing and sourcing an offer that will meet these needs more effectively than any offer by their competitors. This is the management activity we call marketing.

What makes a successful retailer? First, and most important, the business must 'fit' its market environment. This environment shapes what people will buy, how they will buy it and from whom they will buy it. It is a function of living standards, social conditions, consumer confidence and competition. For example, Woolworths, once the world's largest retail group, lost its market position because it failed to upgrade its merchandise and store environment to the increasing affluence and rising expectations of families in the 1960s and 1970s. Other retailers, such as Marks & Spencer and J. Sainsbury, forged ahead through understanding these changes and adapting to them. Successful retailing is therefore about change because the environment in which these organizations operate is changing continually and often dramatically.

The successful retailers of the future will be those that are alert to the emerging opportunities and threats caused by the environmental changes occurring now. Among these destabilizing forces are important demographic shifts, new retailing technologies, changing attitudes and tastes, the impact of the European Community on competition and new, emerging products and services. The tasks of management are to seek to understand the nature and implications of these changes for their business, develop strategic plans which adapt their market positioning to them and then to align the organization and its human resources policies so that competitive advantage can be secured.

Many retailers suffer because they lack a real understanding of what being marketing-orientated really means. Many are led by their buying departments rather than their customers. They have focused on seeking to buy better, to achieve lower prices or superior quality, believing that 'good value' merchandise will sell itself. Subsequently they have often been disappointed to find that customers had different views about what, for them, represented good value. Other retailers have sought success through dramatic advertising or aggressive promotion, again only to find that such 'selling' never builds a strong business foundation. Marketing-orientated retailers know that it is the customer who defines what 'quality' and 'value' mean.

Marketing means recognizing that success requires building an organization that can meet the needs of customers more effectively than competition. Crucial to this concept is developing an organization that is customer-orientated. Satisfying customers means encouraging people in the business—store management, buyers, distribution, but most of all the shop staff who directly interface with customers—to 'put the customer first'. Personnel will only do this if top management give the highest priority to their training and motivation.

Market positioning is at the heart of retail strategy. There are two core elements to strategic positioning. The first is choosing a clear target market segment, or group of customers. Management must understand these customers' needs and seek to meet them more effectively than competitors. It is through satisfying these customers that the business will generate its profit and growth. The second key positioning task is developing the firm's competitive advantage. All customers can buy from a variety of retailers; success depends upon giving them a reason for choosing your business rather than that of a competitor. By building a strong competitive advantage, retailers can raise profit margins and extend their catchment areas. Positioning strategy is the choice of target market segment, which defines where the business competes, and the choice of competitive advantage, which determines how it competes. In any market different positioning strategies are viable—for example, Sainsbury and Kwik Save pursue quite different strategies in grocery retailing, but both, so far, are highly successful.

Once a business has defined its positioning strategy it then needs to develop a marketing mix to implement it. This means designing a range of merchandise, pricing policies, services, location strategies and in-store environments. Finally, top management will need to put together an organization for running the business. People and organizations are, in the long run, the only sustainable sources of competitive advantage. Products, locations, pricing and store environments can normally be copied quickly by competitors, but it is much more difficult to emulate the commitment, knowledge and skills that some organizations have been able to build up over a long period. These attributes give the business the means to renew itself continually and make the adaptions that are inevitably necessary as its competitive environment evolves.

Andrew Collins' book covers in a highly effective way these issues of marketing and managing complex retail organizations. He comes to the tasks uniquely qualified with a strong academic background in business administration and twenty years' experience of senior management positions in both high street and mail order retailing. He provides a thorough treatment of this fascinating subject, which will provide new insights for managers and students of business.

Peter Doyle, BA, MA, MSc, PhD

Professor of Marketing and Strategic Management
Warwick Business School
University of Warwick

Acknowledgements

I should like to thank the many colleagues, friends and acquaintances in the retail and mail order business who have given advice, opinions, ideas and inspiration over the years, much of which has found its way on to the pages of this book.

Particular thanks are due to Peter Doyle, who encouraged me to publish this book, and kindly wrote the Foreword, and to the staff at McGraw-Hill who have guided me and my work through their own fascinating industry.

Introduction

The theme running through this book is that marketing matters to you, whatever discipline or function you manage.

Marketing and the retail business

For many shopkeepers the term 'marketing' invokes all sorts of complications to the essentially simple business of buying and selling goods and services. Why conduct market research when you meet customers every day, and the till tells you their reaction to the retailer's offer? Why think about advertising when the shop is its own advertisement? Why worry about such intangibles as strategy and market positioning when the only real facts that count are last Saturday night's takings?

The small shopkeepers who ask these questions can do so with some justification. They have intimate and personal contact with their market. They can talk to their customers, even those who choose not to buy, and they can see and hear how those customers react to new merchandise, changing prices, displays and the personal treatment they receive from both shopkeepers and staff. They are, in effect, continuously marketing and carrying out the functions of the marketing manager (and for that matter, buyer, personnel manager, training manager, sales manager, accountant and managing director as well). They are researching their market, organizing their sales promotion and planning their marketing strategy because it is second nature and an integral and essential part of the job.

Sadly, however, this level of understanding does not often survive the transition from owner/driver, where most of the nation's largest retailers began life, to the large-scale multiple retailer. Head office is no longer sited at the shop counter. Roles and responsibilities are no longer vested in one person, but are split among many. Chains of command grow longer. Branch managers report to area managers; area managers report to regional managers; regional managers report to national sales managers. A real understanding of the needs of the customers stands in danger of being lost within the bureaucracy.

Who looks after the customer?

Guardianship of the customers' interests can also disintegrate, with many different functions partly responsible for meeting the customers' needs. Sales managers, buyers, merchandisers, personnel and training departments, distribution management and information systems experts all share, knowingly or not, in the job of satisfying customers. In theory they are all playing in the same team, and all have a common goal in profitably meeting the needs of the customers. In practice, it is all too easy for the team members to be playing different games, to different sets of rules. Human nature is partly to blame. Most of us who have worked in large companies recognize that we have our own agenda of objectives, and satisfying the customers is not always the top priority. We are concerned with personal survival, raising and securing our living standards, pleasing the boss, making the next rung up the management ladder, or simply keeping a low profile in case the bullets start flying.

We also react to the objectives we have been set. Meeting these objectives does not always allow us to meet the customers' needs also. As buyers we might be judged on the level of gross margin achieved, and this will tempt us to use supply sources that do not have the best record for quality or supply continuity. As salespeople we may be under considerable pressure to meet this week's sales target, and we are more interested in getting customers out of the shop with carrier bags in their hands than with wondering whether they will ever have the enthusiasm to return in the future.

Successful marketing refocuses managers' minds, objectives and decisions towards customers—the people who pay all the bills and without whom no retailer can make profits. As the business grows, marketing may become more formal, more technical and even create its own bureaucracy, but the essential simplicity of purpose should remain intact. Sometimes it does not, however, if chief executives, or any other line managers, fail to recognize that marketing is an essential part of *their* job, and view marketing as an expensive accessory manipulated by young whizz-kids. Marketing then ceases to be the unifying and integrating force it should be, and becomes personally and operationally isolated: an attendant service to be used or disused at will, and a conspicuously separate budget item tempting the finance director's red pen at every budget review.

Why this book?

This book is designed to help you manage retail marketing more effectively. It will, I hope, help you to weave customer orientation into the fabric of the company. I fear that many books on marketing management serve only to isolate marketing, creating unnecessary barriers of technical language and theoretical concepts. While marketing managers and students may be enthralled, the rest of the management world usually decides to leave well alone and concentrate on the things they consider really matter to *them*.

But the theme running through this book is that marketing matters to *you*, whatever discipline or function you manage. More often than not, effective marketing is implemented through the actions of retail operations managers, accountants, buyers, personnel managers, trainers and, of course, chief executives, rather than through the direct actions of marketing managers. Thus most of the people who are responsible for marketing have no professional or technical knowledge of the discipline, and deserve a reasoned, simple explanation of how marketing integrates management decisions.

So where this book tackles 'technical' topics such as market research, advertising, public relations or location planning, no prior knowledge is presumed. You will be offered guidance on strategy and management and enough technical background to help you use and commission specialist resources.

A handful of essential themes run through this book:

● *Marketing is about* **people**. All too often we are misled by marketing textbooks into thinking that marketing is a toolbox to help you manipulate a marketing machine. Nothing could be further from the truth. Companies are operated by *people* with their own sensibilities, strengths, weaknesses, prejudices and opinions. The way people think controls their decisions, and the way people think about marketing will affect the company's marketing capability. On the other side of the trading fence, markets are not statistics but *people* who are not that dissimilar to company managers. Effective marketing happens when retailers understand market personalities as well as industry statistics.

● *Understanding the market and its structure is the key foundation of good marketing*. Management attitudes to the customer, the design and control of the retail offer, and the strategic direction of the company all stem from this understanding. If that knowledge is lacking, through absent research systems, or an unwillingness to listen and act on market information received, the management of the business at best depends on good luck.

● *Marketing management is every manager's business.* All managers
have marketing responsibilities, whether or not the scale of the
business justifies a full-time marketing manager. The specialist
manager can bring specialist skills and help to engender a
customer and market focus into the business, but the lack of a
marketing manager should not mean that the business needs no
marketing.

● *Customer orientation, quality, service and effective implementation are
the basic capabilities that will support competitiveness in the future.*
There are no 'quick fix' solutions: just a single-minded attention to
understanding and fulfilling the needs of the customer. High
profile, chromium-plated activities such as advertising and retail
design, almost synonymous with marketing management over the
last decade, give a misleading impression of the scope of
marketing and the sources of market competitiveness for the
future.

● *We live in a world that is changing continually and often unpredictably.*
Retailers have to design flexibility and responsiveness into the
business—a demanding and difficult requirement when people
fear change.

Who should read this book?

When I joined a part-time MBA programme the resulting weight of
course textbooks caused terminal damage to my bookshelf. Some of
these were, and remain impenetrable, witnessed by the pristine
condition they still retain. Others became very dog-eared. These were
the ones that were relevant to the 'real world'. They introduced
theories and ideas that the business academic world took for granted
years ago, but for my practitioner colleagues and me they often
revealed explanations and solutions for many business problems that
we had all been trying to cure for years. They provoked us into
thinking about our old business problems in new ways, in much the
same way this book is intended to provoke retail managers into
thinking about the way retail marketing is managed in *their*
organization.

It will be relevant to anyone responsible for retail management, and
not just to marketing specialists. It will be relevant, too, for managers
responsible for training and management development, providing a
source book of theory and practice directly related to the retail trade.

My experience as a grey-haired (well, slightly grey!), part-time
student also revealed the shortage of marketing books written by

practitioners. Theory can be a valuable catalyst for generating practical ideas, but only if you have the foundation of practical management experience to match ideas and experience. In this book I have aimed to integrate theory and advice on practical implementation, both to help the non-specialist but responsible manager, and to guide the less experienced student. Textbooks can be valuable in simplifying issues to black and white solutions, but the reality of most management decision making is much more grey and foggy. There is rarely enough information, money or time to make the 'right' decision. A book that introduces new marketers to some of the grey issues of marketing management must therefore have a useful role to play.

Part I
Key issues in marketing strategy

1

Customer orientation

> *Customer orientation should pervade both your strategy and your tactics: it becomes the backbone which supports, connects and integrates your management decisions and actions.*

Marketing is both an approach to the way you do business, and a set of management techniques. Good marketing should not differ in any way from good business practice: marketing simply recognizes that the customer comes first. This is not an altruistic assumption. In the end the customer is the only person who can deliver your profits, and wages for you and your employees. You have the best chance of achieving these two objectives if you satisfy your customers, and do so more effectively than other organizations who are competing for their attention and their money.

While you may think that this is rather obvious, it is remarkable how many firms lose sight of the obvious. Businesspeople may laugh about 'customers getting in the way of the smooth running of the business', yet this attitude is sufficiently common for the joke to retain a ring of truth to most managers who have worked in any large organization. The trouble is that as a firm grows managers become more isolated from the customer and become more orientated towards their own specific function and the demands of their colleagues. If you asked most managers whether their actions and objectives were orientated towards meeting the needs of the customer, or meeting the needs of the boss, few would honestly opt for the former.

In a Utopian world personal objectives and responsibilities should coincide with the general endeavour to meet the customers' needs profitably. We know that in practice this does not always happen. Here are just some of the reasons why other priorities over-shadow the prime objective.

1 The customers' needs have been forgotten.

2 The customers' needs have changed and the organization has not realized.

3 The company's objectives are cited solely in terms of financial or growth objectives, leading managers to pursue functional objectives that may be detrimental to the customers. (For example, cutting prices to improve short-term sales may destroy the firm's credibility among its customers.)

4 Organizational objectives are distorted by the will and personal objectives of powerful individuals.

In order to maintain customer orientation you need to achieve a balance between and perspective of:

● market and environmental awareness

● the human factor inside the organization (despite IBM's best endeavours, companies are still run, won and lost by people, not computers)

● the level and quality of resources (financial, human and physical) and the use to which these are put.

You need the mechanism to ensure that the market—people again—is fully understood by everyone working in the company so that they have the choice to relate (consciously or not) their actions to the ultimate objective: satisfying customers. I use the word 'choice' intentionally. People can and will set themselves other objectives: finishing early to go out for the evening, keeping the boss happy, stabbing the boss in the back—to name but three of the more common goals. The art of ensuring that most people choose customer-related objectives most of the time is critically important to good marketing management.

Marketing management

Marketing management is not just for marketing managers, it also highlights a critical and oft forgotten factor of good marketing. Marketing managers and marketing directors are not usually responsible for personnel selection and development; nor are they often responsible for setting corporate financial targets, or for organization structure outside their own departments. Nor do they control the objectives set by other functional managers. I am not arguing that omniscient marketing directors should be responsible for all this, but I am arguing that marketing management is part of *every* manager's job description.

The chief executives also have a marketing job to do. They have a role as both orchestrator and conductor. They need to read, understand and interpret the score (the information on the market and its needs). They have to plan and bring together the players and their instruments (the company's staff and their skills). They have to make sure that the players understand the score, must listen to the players' advice and experience, and get everyone playing the same tune at the same time, and with a common interpretation.

Yet if you look objectively at the marketing skills of some retailers, the managers appear not only to be playing different tunes, but also seem to be turning up at different concert halls.

Establishing customer orientation

I believe that customer orientation is not only useful but essential to the long-term viability of a company. It does not commit you to an ever-open cheque book, paying for customers' fanciful notions of ideal products that they would like but rarely buy. Marketing is, after all, essentially about profitable trading based on the recognition that, in the long term, everything depends on the customer *wanting* to buy your goods and services.

There will be times when cost cutting and retrenchment will be the order of the day, and this is bound to create some loss or dissatisfaction for the customer. But if your firm retains its market orientation, those costs will be cut in the areas which least damage your position in the market. Customer orientation should pervade both your strategy and your tactics: it becomes the backbone that supports, connects and integrates your management decisions and actions. There is a natural flow from customer orientation to the other activities of the business.

This flow, illustrated in Figure 1.1, needs a little explanation.

1 If you consider that customers are the most important people in your business, you will want to know more about their needs in relation to products, prices, quality, service, convenience, etc.

2 In carrying out this research you will quickly recognize that not all consumers are your customers, and start to identify why some are and others are not. It may be a question of accessibility, perception

Marketing is essentially about profitable trading based on the recognition that in the long run everything depends on the customer wanting to buy your goods and services.

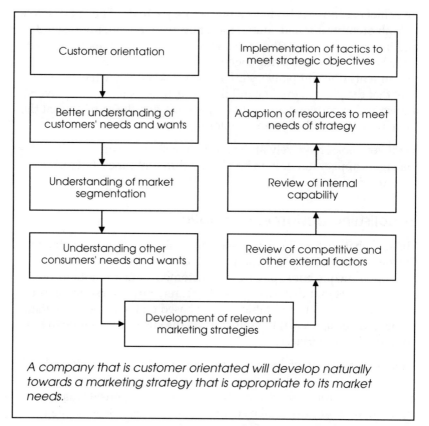

A company that is customer orientated will develop naturally towards a marketing strategy that is appropriate to its market needs.

Figure 1.1 Customer orientation and business strategy

of your offer, prior experience or subtle differences in the consumers' perceived needs, preferences and expectations.

3 You start to sort out the various segments of the market that exist: groups of people who have more or less compatible needs and opinions and who are likely to be satisfied by the same kind of retail offer.

4 Recognizing these differences, you start to consider those whom you are best able to target as prospective customers, and identify any changes you need to make to your existing offer to either meet more closely the needs of existing customers, or develop alternative offers for other people.

5 Before you start investing a lot of time and money, you look at the competition, the economy, the size of the market and changes in shopping habits that might affect your judgement of success, and the worth of your investment.

6 You then question whether you have the skills and resources on board to adapt and achieve these changes. You may need new finance, or buyers with a different background, or more highly trained branch managers, or a more efficient stock control system.

7 You work out how and when you can introduce or adapt the necessary resources.

8 You can then plan and put into effect the changes in trading methods that will give effect to your marketing strategy: the actions that will enable you to meet your target customers' needs more effectively than competitors.

9 Monitoring the effect on sales and profit performance, you also review customers' less visible reactions through market research, reinforcing and deepening your insight before reiterating the chain...

Are you non-customer orientated?

Customer orientation starts with a will to make it happen. Many retail companies do not have that will because they are orientated in other directions.

Traditional folklore has the buyer as king, a role still happily fulfilled by many buyers today. This should be good, because buyers—of all people—should have a keen vision of their customers' needs and wants. Unfortunately this is often not the case. Too frequently buyers are out of touch with their customer markets, focusing exclusively on supplier markets and on the physical product in isolation from the complex mixture of product, service and image that customers choose to buy. Buyers do have a difficult job, particularly in large multiples, because they have to predict what the customers will want, sometimes more than a year ahead. But too many have come to believe in their own folklore, and they do not always have their eyes open to the changing world.

Marketing myopia

The great danger in product-led organizations is the condition known as 'marketing myopia'. This is common in retail firms dominated by either buyers or salespeople, where the 'product' can be construed either in terms of merchandise or the store. There is undue focus on

Unless a company continues to be sensitive to the market, even the most visionary leaders can misdirect their businesses and become myopic.

the product rather than the need. While vision is limited to the product, which may indeed be excellent, the world outside changes unnoticed.

The classic example of this problem in the retail industry must be Burton's, which in its pre-Halpern tailoring days had lost touch completely with the changes in the clothing market. While customers wanted reasonably priced, well-made clothes Burton's interpreted this as a continuing demand for its traditional strengths in making made-to-measure suits for the mass market. The public was not really interested in 'made to measure' which made instant satisfaction impossible and increased risk, since they never quite knew how a new suit would appear and fit at the time of order. When European manufacturing technology improved, creating the opportunity to buy off-the-peg suits that fitted well and looked good, the buying public bought them without hesitation, leaving the giant Burton network beached like a whale.

Combined with an increasing trend to more fashionable and casual clothes, this lack of vision nearly destroyed the group. It had also become production orientated rather than market orientated, setting out to sell what it could make—an enormous fund of both financial and emotional capital was tied up in its Leeds production facilities.

Unless a company continues to be sensitive to the market, even the most visionary leaders can misdirect their businesses and become myopic. The qualities which turn visions into reality—determination and single-mindedness—can easily turn to inflexibility, and more modern retailers have suffered too. Both 'Next' and 'Sock Shop', for example, have suffered rapid collapse as the market and environment, which originally supported their rise in popularity, moved against the original vision.

Retailers: the ultimate followers of fashion?

Retailers' essential sensitivity to fashion can cause problems too. The industry follows fashions in trading just as much as its customers follow fashions in product choice. Let me give you an example from the clothing business, with which we are all familiar as users if not as managers. When overseas production markets started to open up in the 1960s, multiple retailers enjoyed tremendous growth on the back of the public demand for plentiful and cheap clothing. Many of these retailers missed the market's change of direction towards higher fashion, until belatedly scrambling to fulfil the demands of a rising and prosperous generation of young people.

Style and presentation became the order of the day, with millions of pounds invested in new retail designs. New shop interiors for a time became the principal source of sales growth, delivering an instant boost in turnover of 10–20 per cent in each revamped unit. Yet relatively little attention was paid to differentiating product ranges, and it did not take long for the customers to discover that underneath the fresh new paint there was still little to choose between one retailer and another.

The uniformity was broken by 'Next', which perhaps for the first time produced a shop that almost totally integrated the elements of the retail marketing mix. It offered a coherent package of merchandise, style and character which, in total, resembled no other High Street outlet. 'Next' made an enviable success of meeting the needs of its market better than its competitors. It satisfied customers who were looking for the fundamental qualities of the staid Marks & Spencer, yet offered a touch of difference that appealed to many young-at-heart customers who did not yet feel ready to be pigeon-holed by mass marketing. Sadly, though, the 'Next' vision contained the seeds of its own downfall. Success created growth which ensured that it became an institution rather than a challenge to the establishment. Quality never quite kept in step with the overall image of the business, creating a gap between customers' expectations and experience. And of course every other retail group tried to emulate 'Next', usually restricting their attentions only to the design elements of the store, which slowly devalued the original differentiation, often without even achieving clear positioning for new competitors.

The mid 1980s produced huge growth in non-food retail sales, fuelled by an expanding economy and falling inflation. Multiple retailers fell over themselves in the race to expand their chains, often negotiating the purchase of new outlets within hours of their coming on the market. The enthusiasm fuelled take-overs to expand the network, and a new enthusiasm for out-of-town shopping centres. Partly this was justified by the greater mobility of customers who could now travel to the less frenetic centres created with proper parking facilities, but the restricted availability of High Street units proved to be the main cause of demand. Now the estate directors took command in retail boardrooms. More money could be made from property than from satisfying retail customers. Retailers began to look like estate agents, buying and selling property, and became property developers. A little astute accounting could demonstrate that property departments created profit rather than customers. A new fashion trend had been born.

The economic downturn of 1989–91 brought this new trend to an abrupt halt, leaving retailers wondering where their future really lay. The answer is just the same as it has always been—identifying and satisfying customers' needs.

Future prosperity continues to depend, as it has always done, on retaining customer orientation. You have to lock this into the business, partly through changing and maintaining the attitudes of your staff, and partly by ensuring the systems are in place that make customer orientation possible. You need:

- information about your market

- a clear strategy, which stems from this knowledge

- the right resources to implement your strategy

- information feedback so that you can monitor your performance

- flexibility in both attitude and resources to react and adapt to this information.

2

Planning marketing strategy

> *The discipline of strategic planning helps you determine how the outside world is likely to influence your business, the options you have to progress the business, and the resources you are going to need to pursue these options.*

'Strategy' has become rather an over-worked word, often used just to dress up and give a specious authority to decisions made on the hoof. It is a word used, even by the largest public companies, to tie together in retrospect a series of quite unconnected and arbitrary decisions. You will often find this sort of 'strategy' concocted for a chairman's statement in an annual report. (If you want to find out whether a company really understands strategy, read through five or six successive chairman's statements. Clearly most chairmen do not do this, or they would have died of embarrassment. Great new ideas are launched one year and dismissed as a test marketing exercise the following year. 'Strategically vital' bids reported one year are quickly followed by the sale or closure of the new business 'which no longer fitted with our long-term aims'.)

Strategy is actually a very simple idea: it is the way you intend to match your company with its environment.

All change, please

The 'environment' is everything happening in the world outside that is relevant to your business (see Ideas 2.1). In the environment you will find your customers, the wider market of potential customers, competitors, the economy, politicians and tax people. None of these categories is well known for consistency. They are apt to change. Indeed, recognition that everything around you will change is about the only safe prediction you can make.

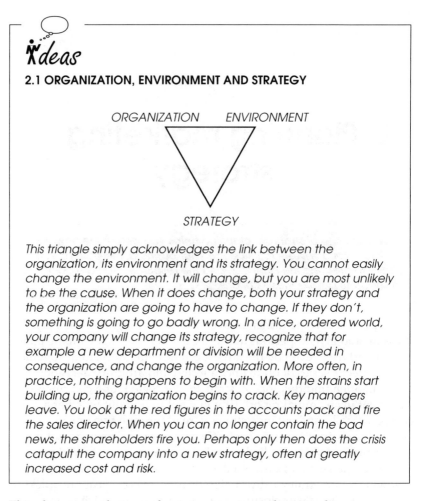

2.1 ORGANIZATION, ENVIRONMENT AND STRATEGY

ORGANIZATION   ENVIRONMENT

STRATEGY

This triangle simply acknowledges the link between the organization, its environment and its strategy. You cannot easily change the environment. It will change, but you are most unlikely to be the cause. When it does change, both your strategy and the organization are going to have to change. If they don't, something is going to go badly wrong. In a nice, ordered world, your company will change its strategy, recognize that for example a new department or division will be needed in consequence, and change the organization. More often, in practice, nothing happens to begin with. When the strains start building up, the organization begins to crack. Key managers leave. You look at the red figures in the accounts pack and fire the sales director. When you can no longer contain the bad news, the shareholders fire you. Perhaps only then does the crisis catapult the company into a new strategy, often at greatly increased cost and risk.

This also means that your business is going to have to change, constantly, if it is to stay in step with the changes in its trading environment. Of course, this presumes that you keep your senses alert to changes and their significance, and maintain enough flexibility to react. When you are a very small business this is straightforward. Walk down Oxford Street when it's starting to rain, and you can see displays of umbrellas springing from nowhere onto the street traders' stalls. Find a hot, sunny morning on your local High Street and the greengrocers will be moving strawberry punnets to the front of their window displays.

Bigger companies find it less easy to change. Flexibility disappears beneath bureaucracy and dulled, unresponsive senses. You will find there are many reasons why this happens, and most companies of

any size and tradition can offer evidence of at least some of the
following:

1 The decision makers are too remote (both literally and
   metaphorically) from the customers to see the changes happening.

2 Given that this is inevitable when the company grows large, it still
   fails to introduce market research systems to make sure that
   market information *is* received.

3 Market information is available in abundance, but management
   does not understand its significance, or sometimes does not *want* to
   recognize bad news.

4 In any case, change is bad news in most companies because it
   means that established ideas, systems and resources must also
   change.

5 It can actually be very difficult to change the direction of large
   organizations, not only because of inflexible personal attitudes, but
   because it can take a long time to alter any kind of resource
   allocation. Changing your range may mean recruiting buyers with
   different skills and waiting perhaps a year for their first purchases
   to reach the shops. Changing shops takes much longer and is very
   expensive.

Thus, you can be sure that there will be resistance to change. This is a
fact of life in corporate business. Resistance will come about through
human nature and existing or needed resources limiting your room
for manoeuvre. It can be very tempting to forget the whole thing, and
plough on regardless. Unfortunately this is a slow but certain way of
destroying the business. Things *have* to change in line with the
external changes that *will* be going on continuously.

Planning or reacting?

There used to be a system called 'corporate planning'. Huge
departments of corporate planners were set up, and the subject
spawned dozens of books, courses and conferences. The idea was that
companies planned and plotted their future for years ahead, and
every self-respecting company had its 5- and 10-year plans sitting on
the managing director's bookshelf (which is where many of these
plans remained). Sales, profits, stocks and marketing activities were
planned in amazing and specific detail. Then the world was thrown

> *Change is bad news in most companies because it means
> established ideas, systems and resources must also change.*

into its first oil crisis, discovered hyperinflation, and companies realized that their corporate plans were suddenly so out of date they could only be used for scrap paper.

Nursing a black eye, planning crawled into a corner to consider its future. It re-emerged as 'strategic planning' to lukewarm applause. We had all seen it before, and knew it would never work. However, this time there is—or should be—a major difference in approach. Without doubt planning has lost its certainty, but it has a new emphasis. Strategic planning is about planning for change.

The strategy that you should plan must presume change. The act of planning is still very worth while, because it will make you think about the future, consider how things are changing and the probable changes you will need to make inside your business. As Eisenhower said of the Normandy invasion preparations: 'Plans are nothing; planning is everything.' Thinking about strategy is not 'cloud nine' stuff because it will make you much more ready and willing to adapt, to avoid potentially fatal pitfalls, and grasp at new trading opportunities.

If you want to see the value of strategic planning in another context, cast your mind back to the days when you learnt to drive. Everything seemed to happen very quickly, so you drove very slowly. Trees, cars and pedestrians sprang out just in front of you. You noticed road signs (if at all) at the last minute, and lurched round traffic islands for a second try. You had to make snap judgements and decisions and hoped none of them would be fatal to your car or to other road users. You did all these strange things because your eyes were focused just 20 or 30 yards in front of you. But as your experience grew, you looked further ahead and gave yourself the time to prepare, and most importantly the *free time* to look for potential hazards and the real but unpredictable hazards of loose dogs and children. Then you could react to both the predictable and the unpredictable event.

Do the same with your business. And ask yourself whether you could pass your corporate driving test. Are you looking far enough ahead? Are you giving yourself time to evaluate risks and opportunities? Do you need marketing research spectacles so that you can see your trading environment more clearly? Have you switched onto 'autopilot' because you think the road ahead is so familiar?

Tha's nowt so strange as folk

You will find that I constantly return to the theme of people, because people, rather than inanimate assets, are at the heart of business. Good business strategy is linked to the successful management of people, and we are not particularly rational beings. There are many times when, as a senior manager in large retailing firms, I have asked myself why we were so crazy to do this or that, or to take this or that decision. Often it defied all logical explanation. No one, insofar as I knew, was actually trying to kick out the foundations of the business, yet this seemed to be the risk we were running in some of the self-defeating decisions that were made.

The answer is simply that the actions and reactions were entirely predictable if human nature is taken into account. My eyes were opened when I started reading some of the books on organizational culture and behaviour that the academics had been hiding from us for so many years. Not only did I have an explanation for our sometimes bizarre behaviour, but I could now see much more clearly how to avoid some of the pitfalls in the future. By telling you about some of their ideas, with the added relevance of experience, I can at least leave you fore-warned and fore-armed.

Setting objectives

A great many people, both practical businesspeople and 'experts', like to start the whole strategic planning process by setting objectives. Usually these are on the lines of:

- 'We're going to be the biggest retailer of bicycles in the country.'

- 'Sales must be up 25 per cent by this time next year.'

- 'We won't entertain a return on capital of less than 24 per cent.'

- 'We are going to reduce costs by 15 per cent.'

These are all very laudable aims, but in isolation they take no account of circumstances or practicality. Such statements tend to be made by chief executives rather than line managers, who look instinctively at the practical issues of turning such objectives into reality. The property manager who has just received a pile of uniform business rate increases averaging 20 per cent will wonder who is going to find the cost savings to compensate. The sales manager ponders over a 25 per cent uplift target in the light of a market so depressed that the previous year's sales figures can only just be matched. And if the chief executive comes from the tub-thumping school of management, he or she may never be told about many of these impracticalities until it is too late.

You must distinguish between missions and objectives. Good leaders *are* missionary. They take their people a few steps further than they would go of their own accord. It would be out of character if they did not have a mission to become the biggest, the best, or the most profitable. But they are wise enough to achieve their mission in stages. While always making sure that the company knows where it is aiming in the long run, objectives are set that are closer, visibly achievable, and take account of current realities.

Badly thought out objectives can also misdirect a company. Demand high sales targets in isolation, and you may find these obtained at the expense of margin, as Sale follows Sale, and a change (not necessarily beneficial in the long run) in the market's perception of your company and its offer. Demand cost reductions, and you will find the company reducing the costs that *can* be cut rather than the costs that *should* be cut. These are not necessarily the same thing. The health service is very good at this because of the way their objectives are set. If their cash flow budgets are wrong, hospitals find themselves running out of money in the last weeks of the financial year. They cut the costs they *can*. They close wards, halt operating programmes and leave surgeons and nursing staff contemplating vitally needed and unused resources.

So while you need objectives, make sure that these are set in the light of circumstances rather than set in the isolation of the boardroom. They come nearer the end than the beginning of the strategic planning process. First you need to know how the outside world is likely to influence your business, the options you have to progress the business, and the resources you are going to need to pursue these options. Once you have this information (or are at least in a position to make informed guesses) you can filter the alternative budgets through your financial objectives. You can make a better choice between growth now or growth tomorrow, between profit now or profit tomorrow, or indeed recognize with clarity that survival is the only item on the agenda. Your objectives will be very much clearer, and related closely to the actions you are going to take. And if you have worked through these issues with your staff and management, you can be sure they will be much more likely to work with you than against you.

The basic strategic choices

Marketing objectives resolve to a single issue—finding the best way to add value to the products and services you buy into the firm. The

> *Demand immediate cost reductions, and you will find the company reducing the costs that can be cut rather than the costs that should be cut.*

greater the level of added value (as perceived by the customers) the greater the potential for profit. You can tackle this problem from two directions: by reducing the unit cost structure of your company, relative to the competition, and by increasing the relative price that customers are prepared to pay. You can obtain higher prices by differentiating your retail offer from that of competitors, providing those differences are valued by customers. They may believe, for example, that your service is better, your shops more accessible and convenient, or that the quality of your merchandise is higher. Alternatively, you can lower your relative costs. This increases your flexibility to compete by differentiating on price (lowering prices relative to the competition), but does not force you to adopt this stance. If you differentiate successfully, and as a result increase sales volume, this may provide the opportunity to reduce the base cost structure while maintaining price levels.

The important factor for success is not necessarily the choice, but the extent to which you are single minded in following your chosen strategy through to its conclusion. The biggest risk is falling down a hole in the middle—failing to achieve real cost leadership, failing to achieve a level of differentiation that customers recognize as clearly as the company would wish, or failing to be consistent in focusing on one particular area of expertise. Unfortunately there are many retail companies who have fallen into one or more of these traps.

Cost leadership

You can only achieve cost leadership if you pursue this objective relentlessly through the business: the only reason for costs is to create the foundation for adding value, and every cost needs to be incurred with a clear and directly attributable goal in increasing the margin of added value.

You are going to need economies of scale so that, for example, you can negotiate low prices from your suppliers. Negotiating skill alone is not enough. When demand is low you may get good deals, but so will your competitors. You must be buying enough through the good times and the bad for the supplier to obtain his own economies of scale through long batch runs, or a production line devoted exclusively and continuously to your orders. If you are going to offer large orders you may also need to keep the number of suppliers to a minimum, but never so small that you have no buyer's leverage.

Your product range also needs to reflect your commitment to low costs. There is a fact of economic life known as the 'Pareto Rule' which, as you probably know, predicts that 80 per cent of your sales

Ideas

2.2 KWIK SAVE

Food retailers Kwik Save have a well-established cost leadership strategy carried through consistently in retail sites (secondary but convenient), shopfitting (utilitarian), information systems (basic but effective), and merchandise policies (a small range of fast-moving top sellers). The approach is enshrined in the statement of 'beliefs' posted in the window of each shop:

- The more efficiently we operate, the more you benefit from the best prices.

- We sell only top brands and top sellers, and never compromise on quality.

- We always use our buying power to set the keenest prices, and pass on the savings through our everyday low prices.

- We will only operate smaller, efficient stores that are easy to shop and easy to get to.

- We will not insult you with frills or gimmicks that you the customer end up paying for.

will come from 20 per cent of your stock lines. You will never beat this rule, however much you carve away at your product range, but essentially you need to recognize that a significant part of your range is unlikely to be contributing profit, and therefore is increasing your overall cost structure. This means that you are unlikely to be able to combine low costs and wide ranges. In a sense this focuses your product offer: because customers will not use you for your breadth of range, they will be looking for other benefits—principally relatively lower prices (see Ideas 2.2).

It is also essential to keep the cost of your infrastructure at a minimum. You cannot afford palatial head offices. You need a tight, short management structure. You need cost-efficient retail locations that keep fixed costs to a minimum. Choosing 'secondary' sites is not necessarily a bad thing. They may not be good for retailers who have chosen a differentiation strategy, but for you they may be 'primary', perhaps closer to where your customers live or work and thus reducing *their* cost structure.

Cost leadership is not a 'minimal investment' strategy. Indeed, you will have to invest very heavily to obtain scale economies and, for example, to provide you with top-quality management information. A great deal of investment cash is consumed in stock, and highly sophisticated management information systems may be necessary to make your working capital work harder. If you retain this single-minded approach you should achieve the margins necessary to deliver above-average profits.

Cost leadership is not the same as price leadership. Low relative costs certainly provide the potential for implementing a price leadership strategy and some measure of comfort if market or economic conditions force price competition to the fore. If your cost structure is more efficient, you will be able to absorb lower prices and still retain higher relative profitability.

In some markets cost leadership may reduce the potential for differentiating on other factors that are just as important to the customers, such as personal service and range variety. To remain competitive you need to have some differential to offer to paying customers, and lower prices may be the only available option. Some retailers recognize this strategy and apply it ruthlessly. The latest and one of the most successful entrants to this field is the German firm Aldi, whose supermarkets are located in undistinguished industrial suburbs and sell a limited range of branded goods at very low prices.

Watch your back!

Price leadership is a dangerous game in retailing. If you play, you *have* to win. There are few prizes for the second cheapest store in the High Street, particularly if you have no other cards up your sleeve. It is also a difficult and expensive game to get into, because at the start there is no way you can achieve cost leadership from a small trading base. Big companies with other sources of revenue can do it, providing they are willing to sit and wait.

You are also susceptible to competition from retailers who achieved lower cost structures through other routes. For example, a retailer that differentiates on quality (which I shall define here as 'all the other non-price benefits') in the long run stands a good chance of building market share. With high market shares come the opportunities for scale economies and the consequent chance to compete on quality *and* price—in other words, excellent value for money. They will be moving very close to your territory with a more sustainable competitive position.

Differentiation

Most retailers in the UK, large or small, follow a differentiation strategy with greater or lesser clarity. The strategy works solely because consumers differ in their needs and preferences. A

differentiated retailer can succeed by providing a package that meets
these requirements more closely than the offers of other competitors.
Hidden behind the strategy is the recognition that one of these
retailers is not attempting to be 'all things to all people'. Many
retailers move much too closely to this generalist approach, and
suffer as a result. It is true that some of their product will appeal to
some of the people some of the time, but these people are going to
have to hunt for what they want, and consumers have neither the
time nor the inclination to do this.

Know your market

So differentiation requires special skills and dedication from the
retailer to deliver the greatest potential. Because there is an implicit
assumption that the market is not homogeneous, retailers must know
how parts of the market differ. They need a deep and accurate
understanding of the market. In larger firms, which inevitably
become distanced from their market, this means that effective market
research is vital. Much of this information can come from internal
sources—particularly their sales information—but this offers
guidance primarily about existing customers. It says little about the
retailer's position in the market, its relevance to the market, and the
potential that may be being missed. You will have to use external
research to obtain this information.

Be consistent

The retailer must also deliver a consistent and coherent message.
Everything the retailer does must be focused on the group of
customers being targeted. Inappropriate store locations, store designs,
staff, merchandise, prices, and so on, that give out any contradictory
messages will be diluting the saliency of the offer. We have all seen
examples of inconsistency. 'Next' slipped up on product quality,
which failed to match the standard implied by the advertising and
retail style of the shop. Horne Brothers, another 'up-market' men's
wear retailer, confused its customers by offering cheap and poor-
quality casual clothing alongside expensive, top-quality designer
suits. For years, their customers deserted in droves, unwilling to act
as the company's quality control clerks.

There is an infinite number of ways to differentiate, especially in the
retail industry. Even companies selling identical product ranges can
differentiate through the many other factors that customers take into
account in making their choice of shop. Location, convenience, service
and design style are all part of the 'product'. This, of course, is one of
the dangers of any one function—such as merchandise buyers—

becoming dominant in the organization. This gives the firm a perspective on the product offer and source of differentiation that is not shared by its potential customers. So organization structure and culture are just as important in determining your offer's coherence as any more obvious factor. Again—as with cost leadership strategies— it is essential that the whole firm and its staff are able and willing to play the same game under the same rules.

I know of one retailer, for example, whose entire retail culture was dominated for decades by the presumed need to compete on price. From time to time other marketing philosophies made an appearance. The need for more fashion, or more quality, or more sophistication was argued. Yet the offer was translated into the stores in the same old way, with only minor concessions to the latest policies. 'Spring Events' followed 'January Sales' and 'February Clear-Outs'. 'Holiday Fashion Offers' preceded 'July Sales', chased hot foot by 'Sophisticated Suit Saver' price reductions in the run up to Christmas. Sadly this clear and probably justifiable preference for price leadership was not followed through with any meaningful strategy for cost leadership. This was a classic case of a company caught in the strategy trap, not knowing which horse to put its money on.

Niche retailing

In the retail context, this is an extension of the differentiated approach. It is the marketing opposite of 'Jack of all trades, master of none'. A highly focused strategy implies a small and highly defined market. Buyers in such a market expect a very close match between their expectations and the retailer's offer.

You can focus through any of the elements of the retail mix. Sock Shop and Tie Rack are product specialists in the clothing field, as are Holland & Barrett in food retailing. Savile Row tailors use location to signal their specialist position, and their top of market pricing ensures a very focused price, quality and product position. Mothercare and Adams Childrenswear focus on a particular group of customers— mothers and children—but within this category do not focus on any particular product line.

Focus strategies do hold a number of traps for the unwary. The more focused the offer, the more limited becomes the market. Sock Shop, or more properly their unwary investors, thought they had uncovered a pot of gold. No one seemed to reflect on the fact that the market for socks is really very small, largely utilitarian, and dominated by Marks & Spencer. The scope for growth was limited and totally out of line with the expectations of an optimistic financial market. Certainly there are some attractive nuggets of gold in niche markets, which can make a few people very rich, but there is not enough to share among a wide circle of 'friends'.

The instinct or need (perhaps to repay investors) to grow can also create problems. Once a niche demand has been satisfied, growth has to come from elsewhere. There is always a temptation to develop the offer, especially when demand is slack. You will see ties in Sock Shop and socks in Tie Rack. There is a great danger of losing the original focus and simply becoming a rather inadequate shadow of the multi-product stores.

Most new concepts also have some novelty value that will attract customers. However, you must ensure that there is an enduring reason for customers to continue dealing with you. If you are following a focus strategy, this means that you will need to do more than uproot the tie department from your local outfitter. You must become *dominant* in your trade, and become the only sensible place for women to buy their husbands' ties. If you do not do this, sooner or later people will retreat to their traditional sources, where at least they can find a shirt to match the tie.

3

The marketing strategy options

> *Fundamentally, you are setting out to make an offer that is different from and better than that of your competitors. The only valid judgement of these benefits is made by your potential customers.*

It's not easy to keep your eye on the ball when you are juggling with half a dozen. Yet this is an essential skill of management. There are plenty of opportunities to become distracted from the basic decisions and policies that really matter. You must avoid making decisions that seem appropriate in isolation, but leave you with an overall strategy that lacks any clear direction.

One of the essentials for successful long-term management is the ability, therefore, to focus on the underlying direction in which you are going to take the business. Work out where you are going, and then pin the map, so to speak, above your desk so that at every decisive junction you can check your ideas against your intended route. It helps to have a framework to set out the basic options open to you. I have found the framework shown in Figure 3.1 to be particularly helpful.

Long term, improving profitability is the goal of most businesses. Ultimately that goal is achieved only by satisfying customers, but the way in which you do this is important. You have to decide which customers you intend to satisfy, how you are going to do this, and how you are going to structure and manage the business. There are many choices you can make; however, they resolve to just two basic solutions. You can make improvements in profitability by:

● increasing sales volume

 and

● improving productivity.

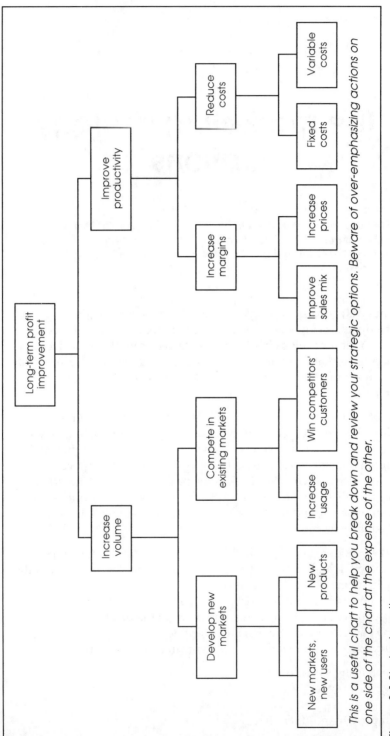

This is a useful chart to help you break down and review your strategic options. Beware of over-emphasizing actions on one side of the chart at the expense of the other.

Figure 3.1 Strategic options

Of course these are not mutually exclusive options. You can work on both at the same time. But, as you will see from Figure 3.1, they have a different focus. Your sales director's instinctive choice will be the former. Your finance director is more likely to focus attention on productivity, because he or she is the person who can measure, and therefore control, costs and operational efficiencies. Many retailers tend to be dominated by one faction or the other. This can be dangerous, because you throw the strategic push out of balance. The sales-orientated company is likely to push forward its plans to increase turnover and pay insufficient attention to the cost and productivity implications of its plans (see Ideas 3.1). Conversely, the company dominated by financial accountants can focus all its efforts on margin improvement and ignore the customers. But if sales growth disappears, margin becomes irrelevant: it is a concept that only becomes tangible as cash goes into the till.

Ïdeas

3.1 ALLOCATION OF STRATEGIC DECISIONS

Try allocating your own company's strategic decisions to the appropriate box in Figure 3.1. Does this highlight areas where you should focus more attention? Is your strategy balanced or one-sided?

In the long run you have to achieve a balance, otherwise the company will be pushed inexorably towards a one-sided and financially disastrous strategy. Any retailer who focuses exclusively on sales development, without proper regard to the financial consequences, will run into trouble sooner or later. It is equally dangerous to focus on financial targets without paying due consideration to the market viability of the retail offer, and the sources of future sales growth. At its simplest, adequate margins are essential to survival, but margins become tangible only when sales are made in response to customer demand. If you pay exclusive attention to cutting the costs of the business and improving the notional margin, you run the risk of altering the market appeal of the offer to the point where cost savings are negated by declining sales.

Any retailer who focuses exclusively on sales development, without proper regard to the financial consequences, will run into trouble sooner or later.

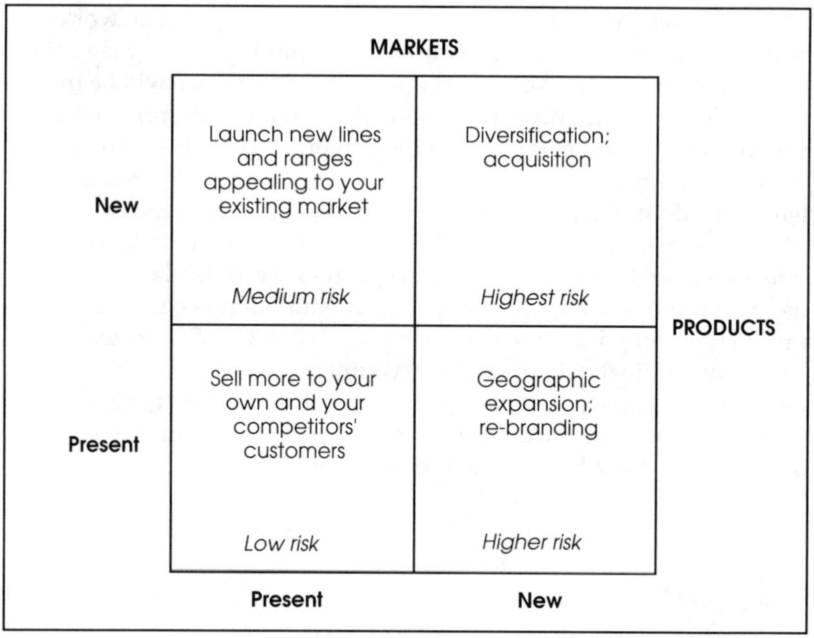

	MARKETS		
	Present	New	
New	Launch new lines and ranges appealing to your existing market	Diversification; acquisition	
	Medium risk	*Highest risk*	**PRODUCTS**
Present	Sell more to your own and your competitors' customers	Geographic expansion; re-branding	
	Low risk	*Higher risk*	

Figure 3.2 Sources of new sales volume

Increasing sales volume

The little matrix shown in Figure 3.2 neatly summarizes your choices. You can:

● develop sales of existing products to existing markets: *sell more to your own and your competitors' customers*

● develop sales of new products to existing markets: *launch new lines and ranges appealing to your existing market*

● develop sales of existing products to new markets: *extend the branch network or re-position/re-brand your existing offer*

● develop sales of new products to new markets: *diversification, acquisition, international development.*

Compete in existing markets

I have listed these options in risk order, from the lowest to the highest. It has often been said, and indeed it is a fundamental rule in the direct marketing industry, that your existing customers are *always* your best prospects. This is sound common sense, because you have

Your existing customers are always your best prospects.

already established a relationship with them. You know them, you understand their needs and preferences, and they know and trust you. Even more importantly, you do not have to pay anything to find them. So improving your existing market penetration offers the lowest risk route to sales expansion.

Because there is an established relationship you are in a good position to introduce new products. This can be achieved both through range extension and sales promotion. This strategy worked superbly well for Marks & Spencer when they introduced food halls a few years ago. Their reputation in clothing was already well established, with a huge body of regular and enthusiastic customers. By applying the same product attributes of quality and dependability to their new food ranges, they were able to move customers into this new product range with little difficulty. Tactical sales promotion can be used to bring customers' attention to new lines, such as cook-chill dishes, and build the productivity of a regular customer flow.

There has to be a synergy between the new product range and the market you are already addressing. Marks & Spencer achieved this in launching both food and home-furnishing ranges. If they had launched a cheaper range of furniture, for example, that was positioned closer to, say, MFI, they would have confused their customers. The success that MFI has enjoyed over the years in selling huge quantities of cheap furniture would not have been repeated by M&S, and indeed they would have risked their reputation in their core product ranges.

Everything depends on how the customer views the retailer. Mothercare built their reputation on the slogan 'Everything for the mother-to-be and children under 5', and translated this policy into their product range with dedication. They never succeeded in extending their range to include children up to, at one stage, 14-year-old girls, and finally abandoned any attempt. It is difficult to say whether this amounted to range extension or market extension, though I believe that Mothercare thought they were pursuing a strategy of range extension, reasoning that mothers remained the primary customer. They failed to recognize that their new customer prospects included children who, from an early age, have significant control over the buying decision. I know from personal experience that even eight year olds will put their foot down: 'Mummy, I am *not* going into a baby shop.' And they didn't.

Figure 3.2 identifies two ways of expanding your market: one is to convert non-users; the other is to enter new segments of your market. This latter option is covered by my comments on product and target market extension. Some retailers can bring in new users, while others—such as food and clothing retailers—will find it difficult to discover anyone in this country who is not already a regular user of the generic product! Yet even these companies can find opportunities if they dig a little deeper. Food retailers put substantial advertising and PR effort into promoting interest in exotic and continental foods, with 'new' fruits, vegetables and dairy products gaining more widespread acceptance. A prime objective of brown goods retailers has been to convert non-users to new products such as CD players and satellite television. Think about your own product ranges. Are there ways in which you can bring in new customers who are not buying your product at all, either from you or from your competitors? Do they represent a significant growth opportunity?

If you are not selling more goods to your own customers, you can achieve greater market penetration only by increasing your market share. You are going to steal someone else's customers, or—more likely—persuade customers who already deal with you *and* your competitors to spend more of their money with you.

There are many ways you can set out to achieve this. You can advertise to make yourself better known, and hopefully better understood. You can offer a better service. You can offer a wider choice. You can offer your merchandise at lower prices. Fundamentally, you are setting out to make an offer that is different from and better than that of your competitors. You cannot be the judge of these benefits however. The only valid judgement is made by your potential customers. If *they* perceive an advantage to *them* in shopping with you they will do so. Simply telling them that they *ought* to buy from you is not enough.

So what makes *you* different?

This is the principle of 'differential advantage', the asset you must possess in order to build a secure customer base. Sometimes you may be lucky. If you are the only butcher in town, consumers have only one choice: to buy from you or not to buy at all. But as soon as they have a choice they will start considering which of the butchers has something to offer that most closely matches their preferences. If there are no differences between two butchers, and all other factors are equal, they are likely to share the market equally. Things are unlikely to stay like that for long. If one butcher has lower costs, or is prepared to sacrifice income, then that butcher may choose to invest in more attractive shop fittings, or offer lower prices, or buy a new counter to display cooked meats. Soon one butcher will achieve a higher market share, and will remain intent on keeping or increasing that share. Consciously or not, that butcher will be trying to create a package of benefits that customers perceive to be more attractive and even worth paying for.

Successful large-scale retailing depends on cultivating exactly the same reactions from customers. The only way you will improve your like-for-like market share is to improve your consumers' perception of the positive advantages offered by your company.

I return to an early premise of this book: to do this you must understand exactly what your customers want. Whatever its source, you must have accurate and complete market research information so that you can define your target customers and know what they value most highly. Then you have to deliver it competently and profitably.

Getting on the shopping list

Shoppers in this country have a very wide choice. In most shopping centres the choice is so wide in almost any product sector that an individual shopper will never visit all the possible outlets. As shoppers we develop an informal 'preference list' of stores we visit. This is based on our perception of the store, gained not just from experience but from a collection of images we have garnered from advertising, glances through the shop window, the experience of friends and half-remembered glimpses of other shoppers coming out of the shop. We mentally sort shops into two piles: 'my kind of shop' and 'the rest' (see Figures 3.3–3.5).

Shopkeepers expect and indeed hope that we will do this if they are pursuing a strategy of differentiation. By targeting a certain sort of customer, retailers know (but often forget) that many more shoppers will never consider going there. However, imperfect marketing causes problems. Some customers' perceptions of each retailer will be inaccurate or prejudiced, and suitable retail outlets will be consigned to the 'reject list' untried. We are also a generally busy bunch. Mostly we only consider the top two or three retailers on our list of possibles. These are the shops in which we have found the greatest satisfaction; they also offer the quickest and best service, and have—or we presume they have—the most appropriate merchandise for our needs.

If you want to gain market share you *must* get onto that top slice of shoppers' preference lists. Get stranded further down that list and you will only see customers when all the other competitors have fallen down on their service (see Ideas 3.2 on page 33). To expect one store to be out of stock, say, is not unreasonable. But to rely on three stores to run out of stock at the same time before you have a chance to sell something is to play a very dangerous game.

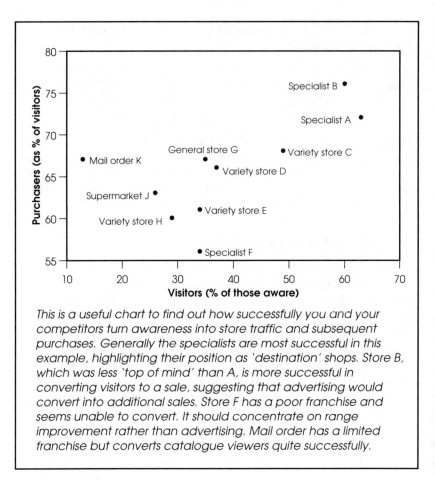

This is a useful chart to find out how successfully you and your competitors turn awareness into store traffic and subsequent purchases. Generally the specialists are most successful in this example, highlighting their position as 'destination' shops. Store B, which was less 'top of mind' than A, is more successful in converting visitors to a sale, suggesting that advertising would convert into additional sales. Store F has a poor franchise and seems unable to convert. It should concentrate on range improvement rather than advertising. Mail order has a limited franchise but converts catalogue viewers quite successfully.

Figure 3.3 Building and converting store traffic

People do not like taking too many risks with their money. This inertia helps market leaders and hinders challengers. A shop that has previously satisfied you consistently has got to get things very wrong before you abandon them and try elsewhere. Yet at the same time there are risks in venturing into the unknown territory of an untried competitor. Certainly we all like to experiment a little, especially if a shop appears to be new or different, or looks as though it might match our needs more closely. But I suspect that conservatism prevails in habit if not in taste.

All this means that market share gains have to be earned, partly through inspiration (getting the market positioning right), but mainly through sheer perspiration. Quality, consistency and coherence are the primary foundations of share growth. Advertising can help you, but it can only communicate and support the positive facts of your

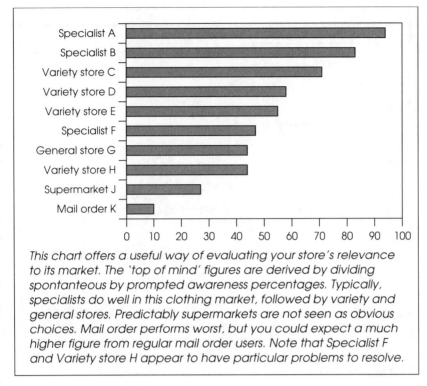

This chart offers a useful way of evaluating your store's relevance
to its market. The 'top of mind' figures are derived by dividing
spontanteous by prompted awareness percentages. Typically,
specialists do well in this clothing market, followed by variety and
general stores. Predictably supermarkets are not seen as obvious
choices. Mail order performs worst, but you could expect a much
higher figure from regular mail order users. Note that Specialist F
and Variety store H appear to have particular problems to resolve.

Figure 3.4 'Top of mind' retailers

on-the-ground activity. If you over-sell your offer through glossy
advertising you will in fact damage rather than enhance your
reputation.

Developing new markets

The simplest way for most retailers to develop new markets is to
extend the branch network. This is an option open to the vast
majority of multiple retailers, and a primary source of growth. Even a
retail chain with over 100 branches might cater only for the 20 per
cent of the population who have realistic access to the high streets
where that operator is represented. The key to success lies in the
choice of location. New branches represent heavy and long-term
investment decisions. If you get too many of these decisions wrong
you will cease to be financially viable, for no amount of branch
management skill can recover the losses that can result from a poor
siting decision. You must ensure that the 'product' you offer is
relevant to sufficient numbers of the *local* shopping population. Some
retailers who prosper in neighbourhood shopping centres look totally

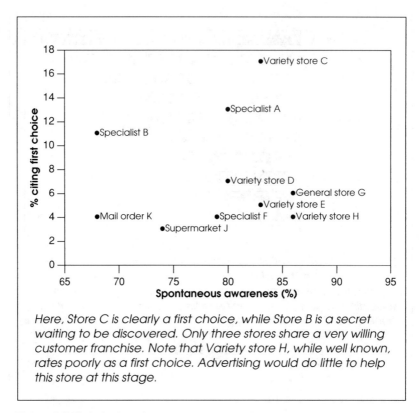

Here, Store C is clearly a first choice, while Store B is a secret
waiting to be discovered. Only three stores share a very willing
customer franchise. Note that Variety store H, while well known,
rates poorly as a first choice. Advertising would do little to help
this store at this stage.

Figure 3.5 First choice stores

out of place and remain uncompetitive in major city centre locations.
Similarly up-market operations will fail in down–market centres.

Your success in any particular locality will depend on:

- your market position as perceived by potential customers

- the level of relevant competition (i.e. retailers with a similar
  positioning)

- the type of shopping centre (where you are looking for a match
  between the profile of local shoppers and your target customer)

- the costs of operating your chosen site.

Fortunately retailers can now get a great deal of help from specialist
companies offering geo-demographic data on local markets. Skilfully
applied, this information can both reduce the risks attached to
individual location decisions, and identify new opportunities for
geographic expansion. The entire topic of retail location strategy is
examined in more detail in a later chapter.

ideas

3.2 FIRST CHOICE OR LAST RESORT?

You can use some very straightforward research to find out whether you are a first choice or last resort retailer. Do this in towns where you and your competitors have shops; even if you are a national retailer you will get false results if you use a random sample of shoppers, since some may not have direct experience of each store.

- Interview people within and around your target market, however you can best define this.

- Ask for the names of retailers who compete in your market. (This is known as 'spontaneous awareness'.)

- Show them a list of these retailers, and ask which they have heard of. (This is 'prompted awareness' in market research jargon.)

- Ask which shop they usually visit first.

- Ask which shops they have visited, say, in the last three months.

- Lastly, ask which shops they have bought from in the same period.

Diversification: the critical issues

Your second expansionist option is to diversify into new products and new markets. When you diversify you can take nothing for granted. You are travelling uncharted territory. Everything is different. You should be wary of falling into the trap of believing that at heart retailing is a simple business that differs little from trade to trade. The only common ground you will find is that all retailers aim to sell goods at more than the price they paid for them. Specialist skills, contacts, suppliers and cultures all vary. Markets, of course, also differ in their needs and preferences.

Therefore you must be realistic about the extent to which you can diversify, and the investment in time, knowledge and money you will need to make. The first step is to examine your motifs. Work through Checklist 3.1 and make sure that your reasons for wanting to diversify are really genuine.

Once you are completely convinced by the veracity of your motifs you can move on to consider how far you should diversify. My instinct is to recommend the minimum level of change. You are more likely to succeed if you diversify from leather shoes to trainers than from shoes to bicycles.

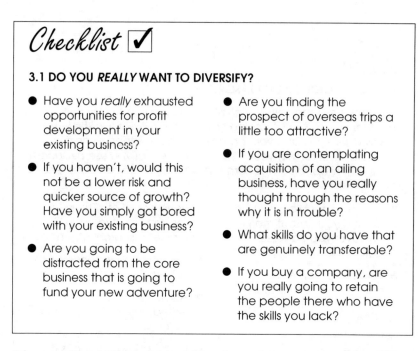

Checklist ☑

3.1 DO YOU *REALLY* WANT TO DIVERSIFY?

- Have you *really* exhausted opportunities for profit development in your existing business?

- If you haven't, would this not be a lower risk and quicker source of growth? Have you simply got bored with your existing business?

- Are you going to be distracted from the core business that is going to fund your new adventure?

- Are you finding the prospect of overseas trips a little too attractive?

- If you are contemplating acquisition of an ailing business, have you really thought through the reasons why it is in trouble?

- What skills do you have that are genuinely transferable?

- If you buy a company, are you really going to retain the people there who have the skills you lack?

Of course Ward White did just this when a few years ago the group sold out its shoe retailing interests and bought Halfords. They may not have been the first to recognize an impending collapse in the shoe market, but they were certainly the first company to have the courage to do something about it. But I also suspect that Ward White could contribute little direct retail skill to their new acquisition. Ward White's undoubted skill was their ability to buy and sell companies with impeccable timing, and this was the primary cause of a laudable record of growth in earnings per share.

This highlights another factor you should consider. Think deep and hard about your core skills. What are you going to bring to the party? What are you distinctly competent at doing in your present situation that can be applied appropriately within the new venture? Do you have superb systems for cash control? Do you have unusually effective management information systems? Can you research and implement marketing strategy better than others? Do you have special skills in physical distribution? If you cannot put an honest finger on such a distinctive capability, then do not risk diversification. Concentrate instead on building your own competences.

International expansion

You would be wise to regard international expansion as a high-risk diversification strategy even if you intend to introduce overseas an existing retail brand.

Many UK retailers have tinkered with geographic expansion overseas, and virtually all have failed. The fundamental cause is, I believe, the mistaken belief that this is a strategy of market extension through existing products. Any product, including a retail offer, is successful because it meets the needs and preferences of an adequately large group of consumers. But we also know that needs and preferences vary with local economic and cultural conditions. We accept that these variations exist within the UK, and of course they are just as visible overseas. In practice we are dealing therefore with new markets and new products—pure, high-risk diversification.

UK retailers have not had much success in international markets. Recent history is littered with failed exploits overseas by some of the largest and most famous British retail groups. Witness, for example, Marks & Spencer's mounting problems in the United States, Boots' withdrawal from the Canadian market, Sears' sale of its US footwear retailers and the terminal impact of Sock Shop's adventure across the Atlantic.

Failures in Europe have not been so dramatic because often less investment has been put at risk. Indeed, British retailers have moved into Europe with such caution that one must question whether many of them were ever really serious. While the names of Paris, Vienna and Milan may look impressive emblazoned on a carrier bag, the handful of branches opened in Europe by retailers such as Laura Ashley and Mothercare hardly formed the basis for sustainable growth.

If we are to accept the evidence that this country has one of the most advanced and concentrated retail sectors in the world, why can we not succeed abroad, and how should the nation's retailers approach the opportunities to internationalize their trade?

Part of the answer lies not in overseas markets but in our own retailers' approach to business development at home, where lack of understanding of the consumers' needs and preferences has certainly caused problems. Market research foresaw the prospect of Mothercare's fall from its pre-eminent position years before the facts became apparent in financial statements. Their present troubles could have been avoided. And in spite of a dominant market share, Sears' British Shoe Corporation failed to understand changes in shoe buying behaviour and introduced simplistic notions of market segmentation that failed to address the real problems of competing in that market.

So if there are such clear signs that retailers are not always learning from the markets they know best, it is not surprising that they should encounter problems in totally new markets with differing social and shopping habits, different economies, different trading methods, distribution channels and, of course, different languages.

Getting things right in overseas markets requires an approach no different from doing things right in the UK. The central problem is that too often UK retailers do not address the key factors for success at home, and then apply the same inadequate standards—often more thinly—as soon as they move into international markets. Of course there are many things that determine long-term success for retailers, but quite a short list lies at the heart of effective retailing, as can be seen in Checklist 3.2.

When retailers consider a move into Europe or elsewhere they should be ready to work through this checklist and make sure that they can fulfil the criteria for success not only at home, but in new and relatively unknown markets. For example, both consumer and industry research will be needed in every market under review. Local management and management advisers will need to understand your business, and do this well enough to advise you on the essential differences between your existing value chain and the adaption you take overseas. Remember, you must learn the vital minutiae of doing business abroad: letters and memos that the British would regard as businesslike would be seen as downright rude in southern Europe. You will need to consider whether the cost structures that work at home can be replicated elsewhere, and question whether these will be eroded or less competitive in a new trading environment. You will need to understand what your product offer really represents at home: is it based purely on distinctive merchandise (which is unlikely) or customer service, rapid replenishment or convenient store locations? Are these distinctive factors relevant in new markets and, indeed, can they be replicated in a new situation?

Most vitally, are you *committed* to international trade and able to support this commitment through adequate finance and manpower? You cannot diversify without proper funding and by leaving management to an over-stretched sales director to fit into Friday afternoons. This is where you must examine your motives. There must be conviction that international retailing is essential to the company's long-term goals and a proper use of shareholders' funds. Justifications—and these may be both explicit and implicit—should *not* include:

- We had better do something about 1992.
- We ought to follow our competitors.
- It sounds like fun (except the prospect of learning Spanish).
- If it works here, it ought to be successful anywhere.
- We're having trouble competing in the home market.

Checklist ✔

3.2 KEY FACTORS FOR SUCCESS IN RETAILING—AT HOME OR OVERSEAS

There are some essential factors that underpin successful retailing, and these are just as necessary in overseas markets as they are at home. Remember that the resources and industry infrastructure that support your home business may be different or lacking in overseas territories. This may undermine a successful formula and ensure its failure in a new market.

- Effective information: about the market, competitive structure and intentions, customers and their preferences and prejudices; about merchandise throughout its journey from source to point of sale; about the financial measures of business performance.

- The will and flexibility to react to and use this information in a timely manner.

- Good quality and appropriate management, working towards goals centred on customer satisfaction. Profit, sales and cost objectives are fine, but sooner or later they are quite irrelevant if the customers are not satisfied.

- Effective management of the supply chain, keeping this in line with the customers' needs.

- Relative cost advantage, brought about by ensuring that supply sources, physical distribution, stock management systems, head office resources and branch assets are consistently and coherently directed towards delivering a clear offer.

- A retail offer of product, service, quality and price that is more attractive in the eyes of the target consumers.

- These last two items provide the key to competitive strength: customers perceive that they are getting more value per pound from you than from your competitors. Higher relative added value will give you the capacity to raise volume market share or improve margins.

- Lastly, you will get none of these things unless you have the determination to avoid distractions and focus on the customers' needs with single mindedness.

This last justification raises the key question: should you stay at home and ensure that the core business is working as efficiently and effectively as possible? If the business is not wholly successful, it is probable that the key factors for success are not properly managed. If they cannot be managed in the market you know best, what real chance have you to implement a successful new business in another country? Remember also that the biggest danger is not the risk of trading abroad, but being distracted from the home business that is fuelling your international investment. Assume that the new international business will absorb twice the amount of time you expect.

Improving productivity

Productivity improvements should be of just as much concern to those planning marketing strategy as they are to the accountant. Indeed, marketing tactics can often be designed expressly to improve productivity. Multi-packs—whether of socks or yoghurt pots—are but one example of techniques designed to increase volume sales while containing packaging costs.

Customer productivity

In the mail order world, the cost of recruiting new customers is critically important because it has to be balanced against the revenue stream customers generate in subsequent months and years. Pay too much, and eventually you go out of business. All new customers always cost money; in direct marketing businesses this cost is simply more measurable than it is in shopkeeping.

Because you have to make an investment in every new customer (whether this is a visible cost or not), the longer you retain a customer, the more profitable he or she will become. It is therefore worth investing in customer retention. Handle complainants with care—they are fragile and valuable commodities. Focus on product and service quality improvements, because this will increase the chances of retaining customers. It is worth noting that recent research has demonstrated that cash investment in customer retention improves profitability more than any alternative investments in sales development.

> *Because you have to make an investment in every new customer, the longer you retain a customer, the more profitable he or she will become.*

Fixed costs

While accountants have often been accused of being unworldly, boring people who cannot see beyond the balance sheet, marketing men have also been guilty of taking too little notice of the financial implications of their ideas. Financial and marketing plans should be developed in concert.

In retailing, the two main items of fixed cost are the capital investment in retail outlets associated shopfitting costs, and the period costs of rent, rates and services associated with those outlets. Marketing strategy should aim to keep these in check. The most practical step is to ensure that the investment in retail property is yielding an optimum return. This requires a consistent branch location strategy—one that ensures that each location is matched with the market positioning adopted by the retailer. For example, if Garrards (the Crown Jewellers) opened a branch in Brixton they would not do much business. This may be rather an extreme and obvious example, but it underlines the point that all retailers need to match their disposition of outlets to the demands of local shopping populations. Anything less than perfection (which you will not achieve) is nibbling away at efficiency.

You need to be *effective* in positioning the total retail offer to meet the needs of the target market. You must also be *efficient* in placing the offer in front of the right people, in the right location.

Marketers and retail operations management also have their part to play in the design of shop interiors. Retail designers can and should be enthusiastic in their search for new and appropriate images. These need to be carefully matched to the needs of customers and the demands of your market positioning. But designers are not usually accountants, and unless you constantly monitor their progress you can finish up with shopfittings that are both expensive to buy and difficult to maintain.

Variable costs

Control of variable costs is not limited to housekeeping tasks. While these are essential, corporate strategy is going to lever these costs up or down. For example, the approach you take to quality management will have a direct bearing on costs.

1 Implementing a 'quick response' strategy within the distribution chain will make a heavy call on capital investment initially, but it can dramatically reduce working capital requirements through faster stock turnround, and produce increased sales through service level improvement.

2 More consistent product specifications will generate more repeat business.

3 Word-of-mouth publicity will lead to more new customers introduced through recommendation, thus reducing the cost of market development.

4 The costs of handling returns and complaints will be reduced.

5 Increased sales will lead to opportunities to improve margins as well as marginal contribution (since central overheads need not increase).

Increase prices

What? Increase prices in a competitive field like mine? You must be joking.

This is not such a derisory idea as you may think. I recall hearing that the job of a marketing manager is to make customers pay more. It is a rather over-simplified statement, but it contains a strong element of truth. The fundamental task of marketing is to maximize added value. If customers perceive that one retailer offers greater value than another, they will pay more if they can afford to. How often have you heard people say: 'I know they cost a bit more, but I know it will last' or 'They're not quite so cheap but those people are *so* helpful'?

You must find out what the consumers in your market value most highly, and then see if you can adapt your offer to meet these requirements. The products you sell are not the only factors to consider. Look at your personal service, after sales service, till queues, displays and changing room facilities. If any of these can be improved in a direction that brings you nearer to the customers' ideal, you will be adding value to the basic proposition you make. You then have the leeway to make a strategic choice between increasing prices (because your customers value your offer more highly) or maintaining your price and putting yourself in a good position to increase sales volume and market share (Figure 3.6).

Apart from using your own judgement there are other techniques that can be used to find out the particular features of your offer that are valued most highly by customers. One of the most useful is a market research technique known as 'trade off analysis'. We are all someone's customers, and we all make trade-offs in deciding where to buy. We choose between convenience, price, perceived product quality, expected service quality, and so on. This particular technique enables you to measure these trade-offs for your market and yields a list of their priorities. Quality, incidentally, appears to be the most important requirement in many retail markets. Other priorities will

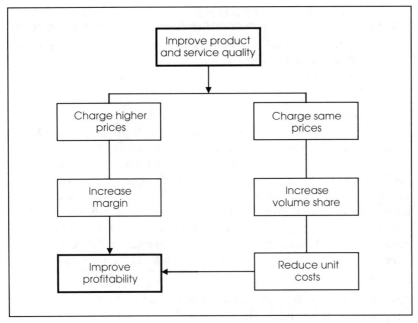

Figure 3.6 Adding value

depend on individual markets. For example, people who buy clothing for children rate very highly the ability to return goods without hassle. This is not surprising given the problems we all find in getting clothing to fit *our* children, and in a style they are prepared to wear.

Surprisingly, low prices are often a long way down the list of priorities. People value non-price benefits more highly, and this fact in itself underlines the point that many products are not sensitive to price, provided that you recognize, as the customer does, that you sell a product that encompasses much more than tangible goods.

Changes in the sales mix can have dramatic effects on overall performance. The first step you should take is to review the range you offer in relation to your target market. Almost always you will find lines, and sometimes entire ranges, that are quite inconsistent with the requirements of your target customers. Quite often you will find that customers simply do not recognize you as a serious option for some of the products you sell. I can give you an illustration from the time I worked for a chain selling children's clothes. We had always offered ranges for children from birth to about 12 years old. Sales of goods for the older children had always been significant, but never outstanding. When we started researching the market, we learned that the mothers who handed over their money were not necessarily the decision makers—the children themselves had a strong and often decisive influence, and older children did not like our shop. We scrapped our ranges for 9 to 12 year olds completely, used the space to expand our offer for younger children, and created an immediate and substantial boost in turnover. We not only focused our offer more closely, but improved its appeal and usefulness to our core customer base.

Even when these major strategic shifts have been accomplished, there are continual opportunities to refine the product range. The key to winning these improvements is good quality management information on individual product lines. Your objective must be to establish the profit contribution of each item of merchandise. The gross margin is only part of the story; real profitability depends also on the cost of capital invested in stock, the cost of distribution, and the cost of disposing of excess stock. With the cost of computing continuing to fall, and with EPoS systems coming within reach of even small retailers, product profitability calculations are now feasible for many businesses.

However, even without these tools you can achieve improvements simply by critically analysing your range.

1 Does it come together as a coherent offer? Are there 'odd ball' items that stand out in style or price? If you need help, ask a few customers.

2 Do you have an excessive number of close substitutes? Excessive choice is not only likely to confuse the customer but will slow stock turn, increase the cost of disposal and lead to more broken ranges if your business is seasonal.

3 Put yourself in a customer's place, coming into the shop with a specific need. Forget what you *should* have in stock. Forget how good the range looked in the sample room when it was planned. What is there available *now*, to meet your immediate need? Do you have *any* choice? If there is no choice, look carefully for the reasons. It could be a gap in the range, or—more likely—your range is spread too widely and too thinly.

4 Consider how your ranges are planned. They need to be constructed logically around the needs of your customers. Map out what you need, and then try to find the merchandise that fits each requirement. This sounds obvious, but too often I have seen ranges that are constructed 'on the hoof' and result in gaps, near-duplicates and items that contradict the retailer's intended positioning in the market. Nothing is better guaranteed to put off customers. They have neither the time nor the inclination to do your range planning for you.

Part II

Understanding the environment

4

Using market research

Treat market research in the same way you would treat management accounting information. It provides insight into the welfare of your business, and signals areas of concern and opportunity.

Retailers should consider themselves lucky. They have daily, face-to-face contact with the people who use the products they sell. Most other businesses are not as privileged and have to content themselves with much more indirect access to their end-users. Small retailers, and branch managers working in multiple operations, can get a healthy understanding of their customers' reactions to their products, services and shops. In effect they are continually conducting their own market research. They ought to be able to put this information to good use, subtly altering the offer to meet the needs of the customers.

Owner/drivers will do this, but branch managers have less freedom. Most of their actions are constrained by head office policy, central buying, rigidly defined procedures and, yes, a marketing strategy which the chain wishes to see replicated consistently across the whole multiple chain. The trouble with head office, most branch managers will tell you, is that they have lost contact with their customers, and furthermore 'they' rarely seem to take any notice of what the local management is trying to tell them about the customers' needs and opinions.

Retail companies should use customer and consumer market research to remove such barriers, which big retail companies seem to have spent most of their history constructing between themselves and their customers. Growth can be a terrible thing. Each new layer of management, and every extra mile between head office and the shop's front door, increases the opportunities for feedback from the customers to be distorted or lost. This is an inevitable result of growth, and the management problem we need to address is: how can we minimize the 'fog' that will rise between the grass-roots and the exalted heights of the boardroom?

Market research should be a positive aid to your management decision making. Treat it in the same way you would treat management accounting information. It provides insight into the welfare of your business, and signals areas of concern and opportunity. It allows you to plot the progress of your business at regular intervals. Think about this. You receive regular sales figures and a monthly accounts pack that you use to monitor progress and feed back the results of earlier actions. Do you take the same approach to market research, or do you just assume that you know what is going on out there in the marketplace until—at rare and random intervals—guilt, a frustrated marketing manager, or a fast-talking salesperson persuades you to buy in some research data?

The benefits of marketing research are much the same as those provided by good accounting information: they enable you to limit risks and evaluate opportunities. The only difference is the manner in which the information is collected. And this leads to one of the hazards met by new users of research. Too many research companies only talk about the *manner* of collection when they should be talking about the *use* of their information (see Checklist 4.1). They forget that research is there to enlighten you. But too often their speech and proposals are littered with impenetrable language—talk of hall tests, exit interviews, focus groups, sampling techniques and confidence intervals. Later in this chapter you will read a layman's translation of these phrases, which are far less alarming than they may sound.

Is market research relevant to *me*?

The simple answer is 'Yes'. The retail industry is littered with corporate and leadership casualties, more often than not brought down by a lack of understanding of the market. Usually this has happened because market knowledge was assumed—taken for granted—an easy trap for an established retailer to fall into but potentially very dangerous. It is very easy for retailers' perceptions of their customers' needs to diverge from the consumers' own views. You should take this danger seriously, even if you are an experienced shopkeeper.

Good market research delivers *insight*, a magic ingredient that is increasingly necessary as the industry becomes more competitive. Obvious market gaps do not usually stand around unexploited. In

> **Good market research delivers insight, a magic ingredient which is increasingly necessary as the industry becomes more competitive.**

Checklist ☑

4.1 INFORMATION MARKET RESEARCH CAN DELIVER

Check which of the following questions you can answer:

Your performance in the market
- What is my share of the market, and is it changing?
- What sort of people use my shops, and where else do they shop?
- Why do they buy from me, and why do they buy from my competitors?
- Do I get a reasonable share of their spending?
- Do my customers come to me as a first resort or as a last resort?
- Do I need to change my offer (merchandise, prices, range, image)?
- If I do, will I gain more business than I lose?
- Is there any growth potential in the market?
- Am I in a position to get an increasing share of this growth, and how can I get it?

Your shops
- Are my shops sited in the right shopping centres and the right positions?
- Are my unprofitable shops beyond redemption?
- In what other towns would it be best to open new shops?
- What is the best size of shop for my business and my type of locations?
- What reactions do my actual and potential customers have to my shop layout and design?
- What retail design would they prefer?
- Would their preferences make any difference to my sales performance?

Your merchandise
- What do they think of my merchandise and my service?
- How do my sales by merchandise category compare with competitors; where am I gaining and losing?
- How do my prices compare with the competition?
- What do people think of the quality of my merchandise?
- Do perceptions of quality equate with reality?
- Do these perceptions differ between customers and potential customers: is this stopping me building the business?

Your service
- How important is my service quality in determining whether people use my shops?
- Is service an important part of my total 'product offer'?
- Do I meet or exceed people's expectations?
- What can I do to improve the situation?

order to provide something different and relevant for the consumer you must have a deep understanding of customers' needs and motivations. Achieve this and you have real competitive advantage.

Even the simplest research can steer you away from disaster. It costs very little to find out what your customers think of your retail offer, and you are almost guaranteed to discover improvements that could pay for the research in a matter of days. And if you ever consider an acquisition, do your research *before* you complete the purchase. This simple act so often is ignored in the flurry of activity that surrounds a bid. Basic but sufficient research into market size, growth prospects and most importantly the target company's customers can be completed in a few days or even hours. Yet many acquisitions at home and abroad are completed without market research of any kind, relying on financial data, which—because it is retrospective—can be wholly misleading. Don't marry in haste and regret at leisure!

Sadly there are some large retail companies who should know better, have access to almost unlimited market information and yet still fail to act on it. Simply conducting research is not enough. The information must be used to steer and manage the company. Market research budgets are useless unless there is a commitment, from the top down, to *use* the information. Market information should be spread through the company as widely as possible. It should not be locked in the cupboard of the managing director or the marketing director. Everyone who works for you in the company is paid by the customer, and is in the business of satisfying customers better. You will achieve more if everyone knows where and how to target their personal efforts.

'Need to know' and 'nice to know'...

Your first step must be to work out your business's priorities. Before you commission research you must be very clear about how you intend to use the new information. Not only does this help you to focus on priorities, but it also helps to ensure that you ask the right questions. You will avoid getting lost in a fog of information which, while interesting, fails to help you make the right decisions.

How much to pay?

Secondly, cost is an important consideration. There are usually several ways of providing research answers to business questions. There is a trade-off to be made between significance, accuracy and completeness. Inevitably you will have to make compromises. You may find an adequate answer to your questions by stopping to talk to a few customers in your shops or, if you know their addresses, by telephoning them at home. After all, most people are genuinely flattered to have their views sought, particularly from a senior manager of a company they use regularly. This approach costs very little, but you need to be conscious of the pitfalls. If people are critical of your offer, they may be naturally reticent to criticize you to your face. There is also the usual danger of straw polls—you do not know whether the views being expressed are representative or untypical. Larger scale, professionally organized polls are designed to eliminate this risk. So cost can vary from almost nothing to £40 000 or more for a major survey.

Thirdly, you must consider what the information is worth to you as an investment. What is the payback? To be honest, it is not always easy to calculate the payback of research when you do something positive, such as launching a new shop design. If increased sales result, you will never know how much resulted from integrating research into the design development, and how much arose simply from the introduction of a new and fresh design that attracted the attention of customers. Comparative pre- and post-testing will draw good guidelines but it can never be conclusive.

Contrarily, much research has its greatest payback in a negative sense. It reduces the risks of decision making and *stops* you taking expensive actions that you may well have taken in the absence of research data. For example, let us assume that you have decided to open a branch in a new town. You are making a very expensive, long-term investment, where shopfitting costs alone may exceed £100 000. If you get the town or the location wrong, you may not even know this—believing perhaps that the management of the store is inadequate. In practice even the best branch management cannot compensate for a poor siting decision that could have been foreseen for the want of a few hundred pounds worth of location research. You will have traded long-term profitability for a one-off cost amounting to, say, a single advertisement in your local newspaper.

Continuity

A further issue in determining your market research strategy is that of *continuity*. Some research problems are unique, and once the problem is solved there is no need to conduct any further research. However, the value of much useful marketing information rises as you become more experienced in evaluating successive batches of

---

Contrarily, much research has its greatest payback in a negative sense. It reduces the risks of decision making and stops you making expensive mistakes.

information. If you take a photograph at the races, you do not know, from that single snapshot, whether the leading horse is going to win. If you take a series of snapshots, you may notice that one of the runners in the pack is edging towards the front and is likely to overtake the front runner.

So it is with market research. For example, a single measure of your market share performance can quickly be relegated to the 'nice to know' pile in your pending tray. But regular feedback tells you much more about your performance trends, and leads you to think strategically about how you are going to recover, or maintain, your market share. It also serves to give you early warning of impending problems, alerting you to corrective action before they become terminal. Market research can give you insight into problems months and sometimes years before they manifest themselves on your profit and loss account. Research will also tell you where to look for a solution—your accounts pack often simply confirms that you have a problem without prescribing a solution.

The language of market research

Every business has its jargon, including your own, so you should forgive the market research industry for developing its own language. A good research firm should translate for you, but inevitably some of their research-speak will punctuate your discussions. The researcher should be trying to understand your business, as you would expect, but your discussions will progress faster and more pertinently if you have a working knowledge of the more common market research methods. This section gives you a guided tour of the retail research world.

The basic research categories

There are three basic pairs of research categories, which are explained below. They are:

1 Desk research v Field research

2 Quantitative v Qualitative methods

3 Continuous v *Ad hoc* studies

Desk and field research

Desk research encompasses any research information that can be drawn from published sources. It has its place even in the most sophisticated research programmes, but it is also a form of research that you or your staff can conduct yourselves. Research companies might be able to find information more quickly, because their accumulated experience tells them where to look. (You should be aware that a lot of general consultancies—even the major management consulting groups—and advertising agencies often rely heavily on desk research and invest their findings with a degree of credibility and independence that is not always justified by the original data source.)

Large public libraries can be very helpful in guiding you towards the right source of information, and carry a wide variety of directories, statistical reports and surveys. You can also buy published market research reports on both products and distribution channels from a number of companies such as Euromonitor, Mintel and Keynote. Some of these publications are usually available in the reference sections of large public libraries. They can provide you with a useful introduction to a new market, but remember that they cannot be tailored to your needs and are produced to a budget. The level of insight and accuracy is not always as high as it might be. You should also check the publication date. Most of these organizations revisit a topic every few years. If you are unlucky the data and commentary provided will be very out of date in this fast-changing world.

Desk research can be a very useful preliminary stage to identify primary sources of information, and the areas on which you should focus more detailed attention.

Field research covers every other form of research, especially in relation to data gathered through personal visits, questionnaires and interviews. The most common forms of field research are outlined later in this review.

Qualitative and quantitative research

Your first problem is learning how to spell and pronounce these words. The most eloquent tongue can easily stumble. For this reason, you will often hear research industry people referring simply to 'qual' and 'quant'.

Quantitative research

Quantitative methods are concerned with numerical measurement. If a research company asks a representative sample of women how many pairs of tights they have bought during the last month, it can derive an estimate of total market sales volume for the month. By asking the price, and where each respondent bought her tights, market value and market shares can be derived. These results will be expressed as units, pounds or percentages. The information is *quantified*, but it is not *qualified*. It does not tell you *why* a customer chose one shop rather than another. It does not tell you if she thought the price paid was good value for money. Neither does it tell you whether she was satisfied with the quality. It is quite possible to measure these qualitative judgements, perceptions and attitudes, yielding quantified information—but more of this later.

Many of the large-scale retail trade surveys run by research companies such as Nielsen, AGB or the TMS Partnership are quantitative surveys. They can provide very detailed information about a company's actual performance in the market, and the survey's continuity allows you to measure long-term trends and compare competitors' performances with your own. But remember also that they record history—how customers have voted with their feet and their purses—and are not always a safe guide to future intentions. This is both a strength and a weakness. You cannot be deluded by wishful thinking—you are looking at hard facts—but you are still left to judge whether recorded trends will continue or reverse in the future.

Virtually all quantitative research is based on analysis of the actions of a sample of the people who make up the market. Certainly in the retail business it is difficult to obtain data from every customer, let alone everyone in the market. (Direct marketing businesses are different, however, since they have—or should have—transactional data on *every* customer by name.) Research companies take great care to ensure that their sample (or at least the grossed-up market data) accurately represents that market as a whole. If they tell you that the market is worth £230.3m, it will be a fair figure that you can use confidently in your decision making. It remains an estimate—the actual expenditure will be £230.3m plus or minus a bit, and statisticians can calculate what that 'bit'—called the confidence interval—is in each case. Nevertheless, your judgements and actions will be based on quantified, representative information.

Qualitative research

Qualitative research still aims to deliver information that is *representative*, but it makes no claims to be quantifiable. This type of research is concerned much more with the important but intangible aspects of your marketplace. It deals with attitudes, opinions, feelings, perceptions, habits, intentions and expectations. The fact that such things are intangible does not mean that they cannot be usefully and accurately researched. The techniques and the methods of data gathering differ from quantitative surveys. Generally the time spent by a researcher on each interview is much longer. The size of the sample is therefore much smaller. Apart from the benefit of containing costs to acceptable levels, this does not necessarily devalue the accuracy of the results because the researcher is not aiming to quantify the respondents' responses.

Do not be tempted to write off qualitative surveys as the unrepresentative ramblings of pseudo-psychologists and frustrated social workers. In my experience it can yield insight that identifies both major risks and opportunities. Just occasionally you will learn nothing new, but this is often because the purpose of the research was not thought out properly by the researcher or the client in advance. Much the most common reaction from working managers is typically 'My goodness, I'd never thought about it like that before'. (Usually the exclamation is less printable; I remember one senior manager who left the interview session ready to jump off the nearby Nelson's Column. But she had learned a new and important lesson about what her customers really wanted.)

Historically most research companies have tended to specialize in either quantitative research (which is more capital and information systems intensive) or qualitative research (which relies more on individual skill). It was, and often still is, the task of the commissioning manager to integrate the two jobs, which requires a great deal of experience. But more companies now accommodate both skills, and some marketing consultants can help a non-specialist manager to arrange and manage a research programme that draws on work from more than one research source.

Continuous and *ad hoc* research

The third pair of basic research methods are usually described as continuous surveys and *ad hoc* surveys. Continuous surveys are sponsored and managed by a research company. Such programmes are generally syndicated to a number of regular customers who buy the research at regular intervals—usually weekly or monthly, but with some surveys producing yearly or twice yearly results. Normally these surveys will happen irrespective of whether you choose to buy into the results, though clearly they need a sufficient number of regular buyers to stay in business. For this reason, and also to ensure continuity and comparability over time, the fieldwork cannot be varied to suit your own needs of the moment. (However, there is a special category of continuous research surveys—called omnibus surveys—that allow this: see below).

Although the basic questions and methods of the survey cannot be adapted easily to individual client needs, the way the results are presented can be adapted to meet your particular needs. This will allow you to focus on issues that are of particular interest to you, or to buy only the survey data that is relevant—thus avoiding the need to pay for information that has been gathered but is not strictly relevant to your problems.

The term *ad hoc* is used to describe any piece of research that is designed and commissioned simply to meet your own needs. You are the sole customer of the research programme, and you will be the only client to have access to its results. It can be tailored to fit your needs exactly and does not have to make any compromises to satisfy a variety of clients. On the other hand, because the costs cannot be split among a number of interested parties, *ad hoc* research can be expensive. Qualitative surveys are usually produced on an *ad hoc* basis, dictated by the needs of individual clients.

Use of different research methods

Quantitative research

Omnibus surveys

Most of the major market and opinion research firms offer omnibus research facilities. It's quite an apt description. All the clients clamber on together, and the omnibus takes them to a variety of destinations. Basically, the research company provides the vehicle for conducting research in the form of a regular personal or telephone interviewing programme, usually conducted each week or each month. The content of the questionnaire varies each time. You buy 'time' and 'space' on the survey and pay an agreed amount for each question. The price includes the cost of all the fieldwork, data processing, analysis and reports. Because a number of different clients share the overhead cost of running the survey, omnibus research is usually cheaper than the cost of commissioning an exclusive survey.

Apart from low cost, the main advantage of an omnibus survey is speed. With a telephone survey, you could get results within a week or two, but don't aim to do anything very ambitious. The system is suited to handling two or three questions. If you want to know who has seen your new television advertisement, and find out who has bought from your shops in the last two weeks, omnibus surveys will deliver economical answers for under £1000 per question. But if you become over-enthusiastic for information, the costs can rapidly escalate to the point where it might be more economic to commission your own *ad hoc* survey. If your questions require any deep thought from the respondents, remember that they may have just answered other questions on any topic from the brand of toothpaste they use through to their voting intentions in the next election.

Remember also that you pay a rate per insertion. If you need to track usage of your shops over, say, the ten weeks of an advertising campaign, you will pay a charge for each question each week. Multiple insertions may also be necessary if you operate in a niche market, simply so that you can build up a sufficient number of respondents to give you a valid result. I remember once working in the formal dress hire market (toppers and tails for weddings) and needing six insertions simply to find enough people to yield useful data for some basic market analysis.

Syndicated research

Syndicated research can be much more wide ranging and detailed than would be feasible for a single client to commission, since the overhead costs of conducting the research programme are shared by a number of clients. Although they are often in competition with one another, they implicitly recognize that there is a benefit in cooperating (through the research company) to obtain more detailed information about their market than would be possible if each acted independently.

In the non-food sector of retailing, one of the biggest surveys is run by The TMS Partnership, covering clothing and footwear. This firm also runs parallel surveys dealing with household textiles, lighting and ceramics. Its customers include a wide range of manufacturers and retailers. The TMS survey provides a good example of a syndicated survey and is described in more detail below.

EXAMPLE   The clothing and footwear survey is based around some 80 000 interviews with a sample of adults (mothers answer on behalf of their dependent children). Most of the interviews take place in respondents' homes and are conducted throughout the year. In essence the survey is very simple. Each respondent is asked what clothing or footwear they have bought recently. The definition of 'recent', usually called the 'recall period' by researchers, is normally four weeks, or twice this time for some high-value items such as men's suits. By grossing up the known purchases of this representative sample of customers, TMS can calculate accurate estimates of overall market expenditure.

In practice this simple process is made more complex by the variety of information which the research company's clients like to see, resulting in interviews which last some 45 minutes, with all the information recorded by the interviewer on complex questionnaires that are subsequently processed onto a computer database.

● An exact description of each garment is recorded, including its basic product category (say shirt or tie), its colour, fabric, construction, fibre content, country of origin, etc.

● The interviewer finds out where (which shop and which town) the product was bought, by whom and for whom, how much was paid, and whether it was bought in a sale or at a discounted price.

● Lastly all the relevant information about the respondent is gathered: location, age, sex, occupation, marital and family status and so on.

All this information provides a very flexible database, allowing clients to look at the data from almost any angle. You could, for example:

● Look at market share trends over the past five years, for individual retailers (such as Miss Selfridge), for retail groups (e.g. Sears), for retail channels (e.g. multiples), or manufacturers' brands (such as Levi's).

● Find out the market value of different products, from broad categories such as blouses, down to more precise analyses by colour, fabric and sleeve length.

● Look at volumes rather than values. This might be appropriate if, for example, you were a manufacturer of packaging materials and needed to evaluate the market for shirt bags.

● Check to see how your prices compared with those of your competitors over a range of different products.

● Discover the demographic profile of your customers, and see how this compared with competitive retailers' profiles.

The list of possible permutations is endless, and limited only by your needs and your budget. The TMS Partnership publish a small range of standard reports which provide an overview of various market sectors. This enables you to buy a useful view of the market for a few hundred pounds. But because clients' needs vary so much, most of the Company's reports are individually prepared. The cost to you will depend on the amount and detail of the information you want, and whether you are looking for a 'one-off' view or regular reporting. Certainly one of the benefits of this kind of survey is that you can build up trends over time which will deliver a degree of insight missing from 'snapshot' research. You are unlikely to get anything very useful for less than a couple of hundred pounds, and you could spend £20 000 or more for a wide-ranging and detailed analysis of the market. Although this is a significant amount of money, it is vastly cheaper than the cost of trying to obtain the data independently.

Ad hoc quantitative surveys

If you are contemplating national rather than local research, check first to see if there is a suitable syndicated survey into which you could buy, because quantitative research can be very expensive. Most of the cost goes into finding and interviewing the right people, rather than in subsequent analysis of the results. If you can get all the information you need from an interview lasting no more than five minutes you can use street interviews or telephone interviews. Expect to pay around £5 for each one. If the interview will last much longer than this, you either have to invite people off-the-street into more comfortable surroundings (cf. 'hall tests') or conduct the interview in the respondent's home. A home interview can easily cost £25.

Given that you are likely to need at least 200 interviews to obtain reliable results, you will see that you have already run up a bill for £5000. Furthermore, most people need to compare the answers for different groups of respondents—for example, five different age groups and a number of socio-economic backgrounds. You must remember that the minimum 200 interview figure applies, roughly speaking, to each group you want to analyse separately. So if you wanted to compare three age groups, and single versus married respondents in each age group, you will be faced with 3×6 or 18 cells of 200 interviews, giving rise to a cost of some £30 000 for in-home interviews.

The research company will be able to advise you on the minimum safe number of interviews. The exact number will depend on individual circumstances and the degree of uncertainty you are prepared to accept. As usual there is a trade-off between accuracy and cost, but do not be tempted to buy more accuracy than you really need. For example, you may be trying to find out whether customers are dissatisfied with your product quality. If the answer is 'most of them', you already have grounds for concern and should act to improve the product. (That research should have been designed to indicate how customers would like you to improve the position, too.) Knowing that the figure is 70–80 per cent may help you to estimate the amount of business at risk and justify new investment in quality assurance procedures. Knowing that the figure is 73.6 per cent adds little to either your knowledge or your decision-making capability.

Other forms of qualitative interviewing

I have described focus groups in some detail because they form one of the most common and effective methods of obtaining information from the public. However, there are other approaches that can be more appropriate. Ask your research company, consultants or marketing managers to justify their choice. Some of the alternative methods are summarized below.

Hall tests

These are personal interviews conducted in a 'hall' adjacent to a shopping centre. Respondents are recruited off-the-street and taken to the interview location, often a conveniently placed hotel lounge, to take part in an interview. Because it is warmer and more comfortable than the street, hall-test interviews can last longer than the four or five minute maximum for a street interview, but because they are unplanned (from the respondents' viewpoints) you will still be limited to perhaps ten minutes. With a limited length, and usually with several interviewers taking part, the discussion has to be fairly structured and is based on a pre-defined questionnaire. As with all questionnaire research, you have to make some pre-judgements about both the issues and the kind of answers you might expect. This method can therefore be useful to add some quantitative strength to the deductions made from earlier discussion groups. Costs are naturally higher than for street interviews, but less than in-home interviews. Exact costs will depend on the length of the interview, the degree of structuring (unstructured interviews need more experienced and expensive researchers) and the ease with which target respondents can be found.

Exit interviews

These are street interviews with people who are just leaving your store. They must be brief, but can be a useful way of locating people who have, clearly, recent experience of buying or browsing in your shop. It is a very good way of getting data on customer profiles, reactions to the store and its stock and service levels, and reasons for buying or rejecting the offer. You can compare different store locations and design styles effectively.

In-home interviews

These can be very expensive, in a range from £25 to £50 each but occasionally justified when you need detailed answers from your respondents. You will be using subcontracted interviewers who should be well briefed, but will not have in-depth knowledge of your company. They will therefore be working from structured questionnaires which should enable you to derive quantifiable information. If you intend to make practical use of quantified research, you can expect to complete perhaps 700 interviews and to run up a bill in the region of £20 000—not for the faint hearted, but justifiable in analysing important strategic issues. Syndicated research programmes can justify home interviews because the overhead costs are shared among many clients.

Telephone and postal interviews

You really need to have an existing database of contact names and addresses to make good use of these methods. Random contacts are possible, but this can be a very hit-and-miss affair and will achieve low response rates. If there is an existing relationship between you and the contact, perhaps as an account customer, he or she will be more willing to help. Telephone interviews are more invasive, and you must reach your own conclusions on whether this will harm your relationship with the contact. Both methods use structured questionnaires, and these need to be very carefully prepared and tested. There is nothing more annoying than trying to answer questions that are confusing or are clearly becoming irrelevant. Although the costs of contacting a respondent are low, remember that you can only use the information of those who make the effort to respond. Response rates for a postal questionnaire may be as low as 2–3 per cent, rising to perhaps 25–30 per cent where the contacts are very interested in either the topic or their relationship with the sponsoring company. At the *upper* end of the response rate range, the cost of each usable interview will be four to five times the cost of the original contact.

Qualitative research

Group discussions/focus groups

This is a method of research that has become almost synonymous with qualitative research, but is certainly not the only way of extracting the less measurable but vital details of a market's attitudes and perceptions. 'Group discussions' tends to be the most widely used terminology in the UK, but the American phrase 'focus groups' is becoming more widely used. They describe exactly the same methodology. The British sense describes what they are; the American term tells you what they do.

Focus groups provide a very effective way of gaining insight into your marketplace. The trouble with plain statistical data is that, while they describe who your market is and what they do, it is very much a black and white medium. Often it is very difficult to explain what the data show. You may see documentary evidence of a falling market share, but probably you will still not know *why* it is happening. Qualitative research, and in my experience focus groups in particular, add those missing shades of grey because you are confronted by real live people with opinions, ideas, misgivings, prejudices and experiences. You will not necessarily get a direct answer to your problem. It is unlikely you will hear someone say 'Their market share is going down because...'; but you will discover causes. 'Oh, I don't go in there any more, because they're always chopping and changing... If you see something you like one time, it won't be there next week.' Or, 'I think their quality's gone down the tube lately; it looks great on the hanger, but when you've washed it, it just looks like a rag.'

What happens in discussion groups? The first step, which the research company will talk over with you, is to decide the sort of people you want to interview. Let's say that you sell women's clothing, mainly to people in an age range of 18–35. You will often want to know what your own customers think, and also other women who fit the age profile but for some reason do not shop with you. Your best guess is that your prices may be too high for some, since you stock fairly high-quality clothing. So you might frame several groups covering a relevant spectrum of actual and potential customers, such as that shown in the panel.

The research company will use a simple questionnaire, and some of those famous ladies with clipboards, to find people who fit the specification for each group—either through street interviews or house-to-house calls. The recruits are invited to meet, usually at a private home, in a few days' time. They are normally given an indication of the topic for discussion and offered a nominal fee for

---

A TYPICAL FOCUS GROUP RECRUITMENT PROFILE

- A group of 18–24-year-old single working women, skilled jobs.
- The same 18–24 age group, but in clerical and semi-skilled jobs.
- 25–32-year old married, working women, without children, more 'up-market' (BC1s).
- 27–35 year olds, with children, up-market background but not now working.
- 25–32 year olds, married and working part time, children, middle market (C1/C2s).
- 25–32 year olds, children, not earning independently (C1/C2s).

---

their time and expense—usually around £10–£15. You might be surprised to discover how willing people are to become involved; I have seen everyone from teenage 'yobbos' to company managing directors join in with enthusiasm and enjoyment.

Normally around six to eight people attend each focus group. Their discussions are led by a researcher, or 'moderator', who leads them through a conversation covering all the topics that you will have previously agreed with the research company. The interview is taped for later transcription and analysis so that the moderator does not have to rely on his or her memory. Individual circumstances will dictate whether the name of the commissioning company is released. To do so may make your respondents less likely to be critical, but in my experience they are still unlikely to hold back, welcoming a rare opportunity to say what they really think about the service you provide.

After all the groups have been conducted, the researcher will prepare a verbal and written report for you. Common themes and differences quickly become apparent, emerging (perhaps from a different perspective) in group after group. The good researcher will pick these up and translate them into commercial problems and opportunities on which you can take action. The report should *not* be just a catalogue of consumer statements, unqualified and undigested. You are paying for the researchers' abilities to interpret the consumers' views into a commercial perspective.

Try to attend some of the discussion groups yourself. Although there are some drawbacks, not least of which are the late night drives back from difficult-to-find housing estates, the impact of listening to your market in such a direct way is not to be missed. It may well alter your perceptions of your customers for ever. If you do attend groups, there are some basic rules to follow. The researcher will probably allow only one visitor, and you are likely to be introduced as 'a colleague' listening in. Do not arrive late. Not only is this discourteous, but you will disturb the flow of the conversation. Dress conventionally, and do not wear your best Savile Row suit. Do not speak unless spoken to. Resist every temptation to interrupt or explain that the respondent does not really understand what your company is trying to do. You are there to learn from them, not the other way round. Lastly, be wary of putting too much credence on a single opinion. The dynamics of groups vary, and occasionally you will meet one highly opinionated individual who tries to influence the group. This happens everywhere, even in your own management meetings. The moderator has an advantage you will probably lack—attendance at *all* the groups—and in consequence can filter out untypical reactions more easily than you can.

But is it really representative?

Many managers are initially suspicious of this kind of research. Even at the best of times they are suspicious of samples, and question whether 1000 people are truly representative of over 40 million adults. They can be reassured in this respect, even though they will have to rely on the evidence of a statistician. But what of discussion groups, where you may be depending on the opinions of a mere 40 people? Researchers make no claims here to statistical validity, so you are going to have to rely on the researcher's experience and that of many other practitioners. The results can be staggeringly accurate, and if you do increase the number of groups, you quickly discover that successive groups add little other than confirm that early deductions were correct. You will also find that the output from qualitative and quantitative methods tend to complement, explain and reinforce each other. Indeed, it is better to mix both types of research where time and budgets allow.

How much does it cost?

The average rate for each group is about £1100. If this seems expensive for an hour and a half's conversation, remember that there are many less visible costs. These include the cost of recruiting and paying respondents, travel, the host's time and space, typing of verbatim transcriptions, and the researcher's time in analysing and reporting the results. The number of groups necessary depends on the complexity of your problem and your market. Anything less than four groups may introduce a high risk of bias, but few research programmes would justify more than 16 groups. So you may expect costs to range from £4500 to £20 000 for more complex national research.

Variations on the theme

You can run groups in your own stores. This can be very effective when you want to research reactions to store designs, merchandise layouts, or merchandise ranges, prices and quality. However, you will get reactions to what people *see*, rather than what they *perceive*. Away from the High Street respondents will be relying more on memory and perceptions, which can be very important if, for example, they avoid visiting your store because of bad experiences in the past. Their attitudes will not be changed easily even if you have solved the problem, because without the enthusiasm to visit your shop again, they will not be aware of the improvement. Changes in attitudes and perceptions generally lag a long way behind changes in reality.

If you want to discover the importance of perceptions, try removing or swapping the retailer brand labels on your products. See how perceptions of quality and value change, even when consumers can freely handle and compare the goods.

Naturally inside a store it is not possible to hide the sponsoring company's identity, but this is not usually a problem when researching those topics best suited to in-store groups. People will not be more complimentary just because the discussion takes place on home territory. Make sure that there is some reasonably comfortable seating. The broken and coffee-stained chairs found in most staff rest rooms will not encourage conversation. And, for that matter, why should you even expect your staff to put up with this standard?

There are a few locations around the country where discussions can be arranged in special rooms that have one-way mirrors, allowing more of the sponsoring company's staff to eavesdrop on the conversation from an adjoining room. This can be a wonderfully instructive method of bringing buyers and company directors closer to their customers. If you harbour a suspicion that 'head office' is getting out of touch, do not hesitate to pay for a couple of groups one evening. The cost will be covered handsomely by the improvement in understanding. The respondents will be told that you are watching, but because you are invisible it is a classic case of 'out of sight, out of mind'.

Working with market research suppliers

The market research industry is well developed in Europe and particularly well established in the UK where you can find several hundred research businesses. They vary in size from international operations such as Research International through to many single-operator businesses. The quality of work from the smallest businesses can be just as high as that delivered by the giants. Scope of activity and capacity rather than effectiveness mark out the major companies.

Research companies, and the separate divisions of the major research groups, can usually be classified under one of the following:

● Market research publishers

● Industry specialists

● Technique specialists.

The publishers—such as Mintel, Euromonitor and Verdict—research and publish regular written reports on many different products and markets. If you do not know a market well, these reports can provide a good starting point that will provide you with a useful overview of a business that is new to you. However, you should not expect to find profound observations. Most of the reports rely primarily on secondary research: government statistics and reviews of other published material. Some are seasoned with small-scale primary research gathered from omnibus survey questions, but this will do little more than indicate customer and user demographic profiles. While Mintel can offer you research on every subject from toothpaste to mail order, Verdict Research specializes in retail sectors and consequently provide a greater level of inside knowledge and interpretation.

Therefore it is fair to regard Verdict as an industry specialist, albeit specializing also in published research. Each sector of the retail trade tends to attract its own specialist research businesses, which often become dominant suppliers because the depth of specialist research required, combined with a relatively small customer base, prevails against new research competitors entering the arena.

The last classification is that of research technique. Broadly this divides between quantitative and qualitative research. Quantitative research tends to demand a bigger 'back office' infrastructure to handle the mass of detailed work involved in managing field research workers and processing questionnaires. Qualitative research requires fewer personnel, but the quality of the researchers conducting and analysing interviews is of paramount importance. There is no 'safety in numbers' because an individual project will be relying on the skill and experience of just one or two people.

When you work with research companies you must be prepared to spend time briefing them fully, and you should expect the research project manager to be very persistent in asking *you* questions about your business and your objectives. Detailed discussions are necessary because often you begin with a very imprecise idea of your problem: you probably *feel* that there is a problem with your range or your service, or *feel* that there is a new opportunity to exploit; and although you invite a research company to find solutions, they are also aware that imprecise questions lead to imprecise answers. Preliminary discussions will not lead directly to answers, but they will help to frame the scope of the research, the inherent risks and the best methodology. It is often sensible to plan for the research to be undertaken in stages, providing the researcher with the opportunity to feed back early results so that you can confirm, amend or abort the project in the light of new information as it becomes available.

When you are commissioning discussion groups you should agree a 'discussion guide' with the researcher who will be conducting the groups, specifying the areas that will be covered in discussion and the objectives of the research. This will provide both parties with some measure of protection; it is difficult to argue that important ideas were not pursued if they were never discussed beforehand. Even so, the researcher will trip over unexpected opinions from time to time as the research gets under way. A good moderator (the technical name for the researcher conducting the groups) will alter the course of discussions when this happens. But he or she should also report back to you immediately so that you can discuss how the project should be altered in the light of new information.

Good written questionnaires are very difficult to design. They have to be constructed in a way that is easy for the respondent to understand and must be relevant to his or her interests. There is nothing more irritating than being confronted with a question for which there is no feasible answer, and which appears only to demonstrate the enquirer's lack of understanding. To some extent, therefore, you have to anticipate possible answers and this demands at least some knowledge of the market—somewhat perversely—before you begin your enquiries. You can get round this problem by conducting a small-scale qualitative project before compiling the questionnaire, which will provide insight into the consumers' priorities and points of view, and by testing the questionnaire with a trial sample of respondents. This is good professional practice that will save you time and money in the end, but you must allow sufficient time for these preliminary stages.

Discuss the importance of timing with your research company in the early stages of planning, and remember to distinguish, in your own mind, between enthusiasm to get things done and the real needs of the situation. If a quick response from the market is really vital, this will dictate the scale of research and the methods used, and ultimately the most appropriate research company for the job. If you want to find out about market positioning, telephone research could give you some kind of answer within hours, but a full investigation that might uncover more subtle niche opportunities for your business could take several months to conclude.

You must also decide on the level of interpretation you want or need. Do you simply want a pile of statistics to analyse yourself, or do you want someone to guide you through strategic analysis and recommend management action? Good research companies should be capable of delivering either option, but you will avoid the risks of animosity and disappointment if you agree at the start the nature of the research response. Research companies with specialist industry knowledge should be able to provide a deep insight into interpretation, which you should use. But do not expect them to talk in detail about your competitors beyond the scope of the research information you have bought. After all, you would be appalled if you felt that your confidential discussions were being retailed elsewhere.

I believe that you should look for full interpretation in the presentation of qualitative research. Less experienced moderators may be tempted just to catalogue the opinions they uncovered. Expect the presenter to ask and attempt to answer the rhetorical question 'why?' people said or thought or felt as they did. You may not always agree with all their conclusions, but they provide an invaluable basis for discussion.

5

Environmental research

The best way to avoid being taken by surprise is to set up a system to continually review competitor activity.

No business operates in a vacuum. All companies are subject to environmental pressures that can lift profits on the crest of a propitious economic or market wave, and just as easily dash future prospects against the rocks. It would be wrong to suggest that retail performance rests entirely at the mercy of the prevailing economic climate: managing a changing environment is what good strategic management is all about. But this consistently good management depends on maintaining a clear awareness of the external changes that can influence the prosperity and competitiveness of the business.

Retailers must assume that change will be continuous. Consequently, retail companies must establish the processes and culture that try to anticipate and adapt to change. This is not always easy to do, particularly from within businesses that have been successful in the past. Attitudes, skills and systems are constructed over the years in response to a successful formula. However, if that formula becomes redundant in the marketplace, all the internal mechanisms—and sometimes the people operating in the firm—will need to adapt. The wrench of having to suddenly reposition retail brands and all the 'back office' resources that support brand positions can sometimes be too much for a company to support.

Awareness of the sources of change provides the conditions that make a flexible management response possible. Retailers are certainly renowned for their ability to apply 'Monday morning management': the flexibility to respond to the latest store performance figures with changes in price, promotion and merchandise. But essentially these are short-term responses to short-term fluctuations in the market-place. This focus on today's problems can create tunnel vision, leaving policy decision making unprotected from the less noticeable but insidious changes that can, over time, corrupt the retailer's competitive position.

So how, as a retail manager, do you ensure that an understanding of the world outside your shops and office doors is brought into your business and decision making? There are three essential steps:

1 Ensure that the business culture is looking outward rather than inward, and is willing to take on board information that may dictate changes to 'the way we do things around here'. (This topic is explored more deeply in the next chapter.)

2 Establish systems to obtain and digest the abundant information on economic, market and social changes that could affect the business. This information appears everywhere: in newspapers, trade magazines, bank and economic specialist business forecasts, and market research reports. Some of it carries a price tag, but much of this material is freely available.

3 Perhaps most importantly, learn how to assess the significance of this information and decide how external changes might affect the future direction of the business.

This last topic forms the focus of attention in this chapter. Because the trading and economic situation is in a constant state of flux, a book such as this is can never be an effective source of reference data. Some examples of environmental changes and trends are included, but they are likely to be out of date within weeks or months of publication. They are intended to illustrate how you should approach the analysis and evaluation of your particular trading situation.

Social and consumer trends

Social trends can alter markets fundamentally, but because they emerge slowly their significance is not always noticeable to an individual business until it starts to search for an explanation of already deteriorating performance. Despite bouts of inflation and recession, western economies have become progressively richer over the past few decades.

This new wealth has affected consumer expectations and demands in many ways. Until the end of the 1950s the privilege of consumer choice was immaterial to many of us. After deep depression of the 1930s and a world war we were more concerned with finding adequate supplies at affordable prices. The widening skills of multiple retailing firms satisfied our needs through, for example, the development of Far East supply sources. Little by little the acquisition of consumer goods became a practical proposition for most people. Refrigerators, televisions, freezers, microwaves and an expanding selection of clothes in the wardrobe first became a goal and then an accepted necessity in the home. Certainly within the UK, the need to 'keep up with the Jones's' became a national pastime.

However, as wealth increased attitudes slowly changed. As the Henley Centre put it so neatly, our goals moved to new horizons: we started wanting to 'keep *away* from the Jones's'. Wealth had granted us the privilege of individualism. More than ever we wanted to be ourselves and do our own thing, and had the money to pay for this service.

This has certainly proved to be something of a problem for the retail businesses that grew up in the comfort of a suppliers' market. Merchandise was bought and distributed in large quantities and limited choice. Identical branches stocking identical merchandise appeared in every shopping centre. And now the consumer wanted something *different*!

As a retailer you have been left with the problem of trying to reconcile the competing interests of efficient distribution and splintering demand. The industry has found a partial solution in creating differentiated retail brands. Large groups have split their property portfolio into several chains, each catering for a specific group within the market. Others have launched niche market operations specializing in focused product markets and increased range depth within these markets. While target marketing of this sort has now become accepted wisdom, some major retailers nearly collapsed because they were not quick enough to recognize a fundamental shift in consumer attitudes.

Consumer *expectations* seem to rise inexorably ahead of the retailers' ability to meet them. In the 1950s we would have been happy to have a television in the house (which, naturally, would have been black and white.) In the 1980s we assumed this would be a colour set. Now we want two or even three sets in the home, together with at least one video recorder. Our expectations of quality are changing too. As I recall, the early colour televisions were renowned for their unreliability and high maintenance costs. People routinely took out insurance policies to cover the cost of replacing the cathode ray tube. In Britain, the television rental business leapt ahead because rental ensured protection against breakdown and offered access to a fashionable product whose capital cost was still beyond the reach of most households.

And when did *your* television (which, naturally, is a colour model) last break down? In this area, and many others besides, you now presume that goods will be reliable—and the real cost of owning them has dropped dramatically. This is good news; but it was very bad news for the TV rental retailers. Technological change, and its consequent effect on consumer attitudes, has knocked the foundations out of the rental proposition: spreading the cost of ownership and insurance against unreliability. The two main players who remain in this market, Thorn EMI and Granada, are fighting to change their competitive stance. Although a significant cash-restrained customer base remains, they focus on a new benefit—the opportunity to keep up with the latest technical innovations without frequent recourse to the second-hand market or the local rubbish tip.

Product quality has become a major tool for levering competitive advantage from the market because consumers can now afford to be more selective. It will continue to affect the retail arena, I believe, for some years to come and a later chapter in this book is devoted to this subject. Consistently competitive quality requires both structural and technical changes within retail businesses, and those companies that learn to adapt successfully to this area of change will gain a competitive edge.

Quality is revealed not only in the reliability of the merchandise you sell but in the service you offer. Service is an integral part of retail products. Often this intangible benefit is more important than the physical product itself, and as the technical merits of merchandise improve, service provides an increasingly important source of retail differentiation. We have all experienced the frustrations of poor service. Sales assistants who patently do not understand their products; barely disguised irritation at having to serve a customer; unending queues at checkouts; and delays while salespeople search for a floor manager to authorize credit cards.

As individuals, if not always as retail managers, we all want better service, and increasingly customers are in a position to demand it. Firstly, it is something we are prepared to pay for, because it makes us feel good. Secondly, as retailers fulfil our rising demands for more choice and better product quality, we are starting to focus our reasons for choosing one retailer rather than another on our perception of their service quality. Thirdly, good service allows us to feel more like individuals, and less like a retailer's 'cannon fodder', processed through the store with the minimum of contact and the maximum convenience to the retailer.

Retailers will need to react to changing demands for service standards. These changes have been apparent for some time, but many retail groups appear to be inconsistently introducing the fundamental changes that will be needed. Some of the technically

> **Quality is revealed not only in the reliability of the merchandise you sell, but in the service you offer.**

based changes, such as the introduction of EPoS and EFT systems, are bringing improvements in customer service, but training and changes in staff and management attitudes to customers as individuals are emerging much more slowly.

The economy

One of the natural hazards of trying to plan reaction to future economic circumstances is that economists rarely agree on their forecasts of the future state of play. However, there is no shortage of advice. Virtually every day newspapers carry reports and comments on prospects and the state of the economy. There are also a number of well-reputed economic forecasts produced by commercial, academic and government institutions.

Naturally the economic state of the day affects both sales and costs. Retail sales are affected by the amount of money people have in their pockets, which in turn gets there from income, savings or loans. The economy can affect your costs in every department. Just as important as the current state of affairs is people's expectations of the future state of the economy. Few people outside business and political circles actually read economic forecasts in detail, but everyone maintains a 'gut feel' about how the economy will affect them personally. You can be sure, for example, that whenever a state of uncertainty prevails customers will pull back on their spending.

More direct events, such as rising unemployment, have an effect on spending. The extent to which this will affect an individual retailer will depend on circumstances. Unemployment rarely falls equally across the working population. Some types of business will be more affected than others. Local conditions are certainly measurable in their impact on sales. Redundancies at a local employer can have immediate and sometimes devastating effects on local shops.

Predicting such local and even national changes brought about by the economic situation is a difficult task for most retail managers, particularly as few are likely to have specialist training in economics. We rely on common sense. Even without specialist knowledge we can develop foresight. It is not too difficult to develop a number of 'what if…?' scenarios, and then to forecast the impact on the business and management reaction to different circumstances. This way we are at least aware of the risks and opportunities arising from economic change and are ready to react as soon as new trends emerge.

This approach can go some way towards helping us avoid the risk of getting carried away by 'bandwagon' opinions. The 1980s saw a tremendous acceleration of consumer spending in the UK economy as optimism displaced the despondency created by the political climate and inflation of the late 1970s and the worldwide recession of 1981. Spending was supported by rises in real disposable income and easy access to credit. All retailers, I suspect, presumed that this glorious state of affairs would continue indefinitely. Managers certainly acted as if this were so. Retailers started refitting shops every three or four years. They fought for sites and demanded yet more. Property developers responded and built new out-of-town centres, if only because there was no room for expansion in town centres. Competition for sites pushed rents to the point where only the major chains could afford to stay in business, and many smaller retailers were forced to close.

Consumers extended their lines of credit from willing lenders attracted by the prospects of rising interest payments. The booming housing market further stretched their financial commitments as house prices rose, but also created a retail demand for related consumer durables.

Common sense should have told us that the risk of a downturn in economic activity remained just as real as ever before. You need not be an economist to recognize that there are economic cycles. They may not be entirely predictable, but it is certain that the progressive increase in wealth within the developed countries has not been achieved through consistent, straight line growth. There are ups and downs. Likewise common sense tells us that debts have to be repaid sometime, and there will come a moment when people start using income to pay off credit card balances rather than spend more money in the shops.

In spite of this, no one seemed ready for the downturn when it became totally self-evident in 1990. The signs were already present, probably as early as 1988, and visible to many retailers through falling sales growth and upward pressure on costs. But at the same time many retailers seemed to have left themselves with little capacity to react with sufficient flexibility. They, like their customers, had extended their credit gearing too far. An uncomfortably large proportion of trading income was diverted straight from the business to lenders. Sales growth vanished while operating costs continued to rise. Highly geared management buy-outs collapsed. Demand for property dissolved.

The message is straightforward. You cannot control the economy, but you must not allow the economy to control you absolutely. History tells us that the economy can be both munificent and treacherous to businesses, if only because of its unpredictability. If you are not blessed with the foresight that would make you richer as an economist than as a retailer, you have to make do with caution and as much flexibility as you can muster.

Demographic changes

Sooner or later demographic changes can affect the performance and competitive position of most retail operations, but it is also important not to allow popular misconceptions to dictate strategy. In the UK there is a clear swing towards older age groups, with the young adult market becoming less dominant than it was in the early 1980s (Figure 5.1). There is a temptation to abandon retail formats targeted at this younger age group, but you should remember that while the numbers may be in decline, there is still a very substantial and free-spending market. Only the largest retailers with nationally developed chains are likely to find that demographic trends are directly affecting their capacity for growth.

The main demographic trends affecting retailers are the age profile of

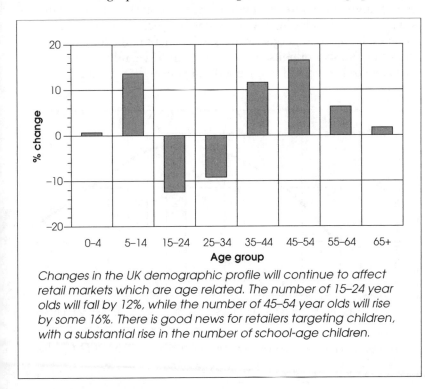

Changes in the UK demographic profile will continue to affect retail markets which are age related. The number of 15–24 year olds will fall by 12%, while the number of 45–54 year olds will rise by some 16%. There is good news for retailers targeting children, with a substantial rise in the number of school-age children.

Figure 5.1 Change in UK population age structure, 1991–2001
(*Source*: OPCS)

the population and the household structure. The principal trends in the UK are leading to:

- a rising population of school age children
- a falling population of young adults
- growth in the number of 35–54 year olds
- in the longer term, growth in the older 'grey market'
- a rising number of households, brought about through young people leaving home to set up their own households, higher divorce rates and higher numbers of old people continuing to live independently
- overlaying regional and local trends that can have a material effect on individual retail branches and regional retail companies.

Some retailers will be more affected by these trends than others. This depends on the degree of product and market focus developed by each retailer. Specialist baby and children's shops are quickly and significantly affected by changes in the birth rate (Figure 5.2). But even a falling birth rate need not incapacitate such a chain if branches are located in developing towns that have a local influx of new families. Household goods retailers will benefit in the long term from the rising number of households, raising the demand for furniture, furnishings, brown and white goods. However, bear in mind that

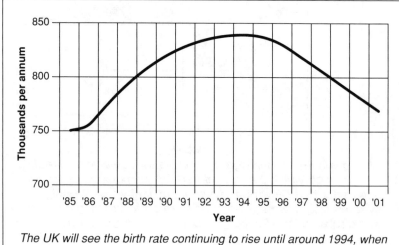

The UK will see the birth rate continuing to rise until around 1994, when the rate will start to decline over the ensuing ten years.

Figure 5.2 UK birth rate projections
(*Source*: OPCS)

shorter term movements, such as a slowdown in the housing market, can have far greater effects on demand.

As with all environmental changes, there is no hard and fast rule to tell you how your business should react to demographic shifts. The essential steps start with an analysis of the predicted changes; demographic forecasts are widely available from government information held at public libraries. Secondly, you must consider how much these changes are likely to affect your business, and determine whether you can or should react to them in planning your future strategy.

A common strategic marketing decision is whether to maintain a fixed market position, for example targeting 18–25 year olds, or to let the brand appeal drift towards an older market as the original customer base itself grows older. Many of the fashion retailers who grew up with the early 1980s bulge in the number of young adults have been facing this problem. Certainly it is not possible to stand still, freezing an originally successful formula in a market 'time warp' untouched by changing market preferences. Even if the original target customer profile is maintained, you must recognize that customers are changing their preferences and expectations. My own view, arising from the experience of monitoring both strategies, is that it is very difficult and expensive to attempt a substantial repositioning of any well-established retail brand. It is too easy to lose the core customer base, who become disillusioned by the diminishing focus on their specific interests, and too difficult to attract new users.

The changing age structure has also affected the human resource policies of retail companies. Traditionally many retailers have relied on recruiting and training young people to manage their stores. With a rapid reduction in the number of school leavers, it is becoming much more difficult to maintain an adequate flow of recruits, and many retailers are now turning to older staff. While there is realistic concern that 50 year olds would not fit comfortably into a fashion clothing environment, it is becoming widely recognized that older people can bring the maturity that ensures higher levels of customer service. Fortuitously, customers are demanding higher levels of customer care and service.

Technology

Progressive advances in technology are affecting every retailer, both in terms of the product and back-office systems. Earlier, the example of a TV rental business was used to illustrate how technology can affect demand for a retail service. As the real price of televisions fell and their reliability increased, the rental companies' *raison d'être* melted away. The profusion of new products and new technical innovations has also made staff product knowledge more difficult and more important as customers search for more specific advice from sales staff.

Rapid technological change, affecting both markets and systems, can make planning more difficult. I recall working with my colleagues on a corporate plan in 1979. We had identified economies of scale as a source of competitive edge, and in particular the use of our group's computer systems, which most of us believed would ensure that we would maintain cost and efficiency benefits over the many, mainly small, retail competitors in the market. Somewhat nervously I put forward the thought that within a few years every retailer could afford a computer and programs to manage its stock. This idea was demolished fairly quickly. Ten years ago stock control meant mainframe computers and tailor-made software. PCs had yet to be launched. A computer in every shop seems a pretty unlikely scenario. Of course, as we know now, this is totally realistic. You can buy off-the-shelf stock control and EPoS packages to run on microcomputers and shopkeepers can even bar code their own merchandise for a capital investment of a few hundred pounds.

Back-office systems are famous for anchoring your business to the past. In another more recent incident a mail order company discovered that its computer systems assumed that no product would ever be sold at a price exceeding £999.99. A few years ago, when the most expensive products would not have cost more than perhaps £200, this was a reasonable assumption. But rising prices and prosperity saw widespread demand for video camcorders at £1100 and £1200. This particular company was quite unable to satisfy this demand because the three figure price limit was locked so deeply into its systems and file structures. They had to wait until prices fell below £1000.

Electronic point of sale systems are now becoming well established in all retail sectors and are changing both economics and marketing opportunities. These systems allow more efficient stock management, which certainly saves working capital but in time will also raise customer service expectations. No longer will salespeople and customers shrug their shoulders and blame absent stock on the computer. Further down the High Street other retailers will have worked on their systems and ensured that stock *was* available to meet

---

Back-office systems are famous for anchoring your business to the past.

demand, and the customer will not be content to wait to find out if 'the computer might send us some on Friday'.

The increasing capacity to hold and manipulate data will also change the way in which retail businesses are managed. There is an old adage that 'information is power'. In the past the various streams of management information on sales, costs and stock has tended to merge only at the top of the organization structure. However, as systems have become more open and integrated, people at all levels of the business potentially have access to management information. Early computerization in retail multiples took decision making away from branch management; now technology is going to put that capacity back into branches. Likewise, specialist head office functions will be better able to make decisions in the light of the *whole* business position, previously the reserve of senior general management. These changes are going to require shifts in organization structure, responsibilities and human resource policy.

Legal and government

We are all affected by the legal constraints on trade imposed through government legislation. Over time these constraints change, even if rather slowly, to reflect—more or less—the social attitudes of the nation. Generally, the legal framework in which retailers trade is predictable. Changes are debated in the newspapers, and in industry and parliamentary circles long before they take legal effect. So while we may not like or agree with new legal arrangements there is usually some opportunity to adjust the strategy of the business.

Issues such as Sunday trading excite public debate. Both sides hold strong views and the first government attempts to amend the law in England and Wales have failed; but in the end I suspect that public opinion and the laws of supply and demand will hold sway. You need only visit the DIY superstores, garden stores and booksellers that are opening on Sundays (regardless of the legal position) to discover that there is widespread public demand for Sunday trading. However, I doubt that this will become universal even if legalized. The relaxation of the country's law on licensing hours brought about less fundamental change than many people expected. In effect the changes merely broadened the scope for differentiated service, with some pubs opening for extended hours to meet local demand and

> *Early computerization in retail multiples took decision making away from branch management; now technology is going to put that capacity back into branches.*

others finding a pattern similar to the original, legally defined arrangements to be the only economic solution. Some UK retail groups have assumed that extended trading hours will be detrimental to the economics of the retail business. They argue that the present level of trade will be spread over seven days rather than six, while the costs of personnel, heating and lighting will be increased. While this logic is hard to defeat, I cannot see that seven-day trading will become universal and it will simply increase the scope for service differentiation. Local convenience stores have certainly demonstrated that consumers will pay premium prices for longer trading hours.

Similar changes to shop trading hours in other European countries may take place but, as in the UK, this will depend on the strength of local pressure groups. Despite (or perhaps because of) a booming retail economy, Germany is held to be one of the most conservative nations in this respect. Even Saturday afternoon trading is restricted and the retail staff lobby is strongly resisting any pressure to extend trading hours.

Fiscal changes, such as the UK's introduction of the uniform business rate, can have a dramatic, one-time effect on retail economics. The introduction of this new rating system has ensured that some retail branches, particularly in the south-east, have moved from profit to loss because the method of calculating rating liabilities has changed. This is one example of an environmental change that impacts on strategy but leaves the retailer with little immediate scope for manoeuvre. Even if branch costs do rise, retail branches are long-term investments and the costs and practicalities of disinvestment can be substantial, particularly if property markets are depressed.

Demand for greater personal privacy is sweeping across Europe, and is reflected in the data protection legislation that is now operating throughout the EC and is indeed likely to be strengthened. Legal restrictions on the collection and use of personal data are increasing just as the retail industry's ability to use this information is improving. Direct contact, tailored to the known buying habits of individual customers, is now a practical proposition to many retailers as technology allows them to relate customers and transaction data. However, the legal framework surrounding this technological capacity remain unclear as legislators feel their way towards socially acceptable rules.

In some respects the consumers want things both ways. They demand privacy, yet also want to be treated as individuals. The database owner can provide this individuality by holding and using *more* information about customers, thus ensuring that customers are treated to information that is directly relevant. This should help the customers, whose supply of junk mail is reduced (mail is only 'junk' if it is irrelevant), and the suppliers, whose response economics are improved. There is little doubt that the legislative framework will settle in due course, but in the meantime the uncertainty that is creating disquiet throughout the direct marketing industry will continue. The only certain advice is that retailers considering steps towards direct marketing should seek current advice from industry specialists *before* embarking on long-term commitments to systems and capital investment.

Competitors

Thankfully you have access to plentiful information about your competitors. Indeed, retailers are particularly lucky business people. Your competitors set out their stall, literally, for all to see, and you are as free as your customers to assess the product, prices and services currently offered by each of your competitors. You need only make this assessment as objectively as your customers, yet this is the challenge that many retail companies fail to meet. Often retailers become so engrossed with their own traditions and beliefs about the 'best' way to trade that they fail to examine and analyse competitors' actions or their mutual customers' reactions. This can lead to surprise and dismay when customer dissatisfaction begins, often months or even years later, to show in the trading results.

The best way to avoid being taken by surprise is to set up a system to continually review competitor activity. Almost all the information you need is available in the public domain or through consumer market research. The only information you will not discover, directly, is your competitors' future intentions. Even so, you can make reasonable deductions from careful reading of annual reports, press articles and recruitment advertisements. You can also obtain stockbrokers' reviews, which are normally based on interviews with the heads of your competitors, and industry reports such as those published by Verdict, which also may include analysis of discussions with retailers' senior directors.

The steps you need to take to make sure that competitor information enters into your marketing strategy development are:

1 Collate and interpret industry information and market statistics.
2 Conduct consumer research that focuses as much on the usage of and attitudes to your *competitors* as it does on your own business.
3 Make sure that the information is collected and presented regularly.
4 Make sure that the information enters boardroom discussions.

Because there is so much information, the collection and analysis have to be systematic. Much of the information can be obtained in a form that is at least partially digested, in the form of selective press cuttings, industry reviews, stockbroker reports and sector market research. However, even with these benefits you may need to devote resources to bringing this diverse array of data together in a form that is fully understandable. I do not know of any external resource that provides this kind of service. Start by thinking about your aims. Your system should allow you to answer the following questions.

1 How have my competitors performed in the past, both in financial terms and in the marketplace?

2 How are they performing now, and are they getting better or worse?

3 What are their corporate and market strengths and weaknesses?

4 What exactly do consumers think of them? What do *their* customers think of *us*? What do *our* customers think of *them*?

5 If I were in my competitors' shoes, what would I do next?

6 What do my competitors *say* their plans are for the future?

7 How does this information affect my perception of my own company's opportunities, threats and competitive strategy?

Analysis of historical trends can be kept fairly simple, and indeed it is important to avoid getting inundated with excessive detail. Commercially available market information will give you market share trends. Be wary of looking at total market figures if either you or your competitors trade in a particular market segment (Figure 5.3). You might be misled by a falling share overall, which is hiding share growth in that retailer's target market.

Remember that attractive long-term trends, such as the example in Figure 5.3(b), may result as much from price inflation as from real growth. Broad trends also may mask more detailed changes that could be highly relevant to your business. Although this graph illustrates dramatic growth in the sales of clothing and footwear, major sub-sectors such as formal shoes actually have declined in sales value and volume in recent years. Important information can be hidden in summary data and graphics. For example the catch-all 'Others' shown in Figure 5.3(a) hides three of the fastest growing types of retail outlet: sports shops, market stalls and discount stores (Table 5.1).

It may seem a simple point to make, but many managers understand

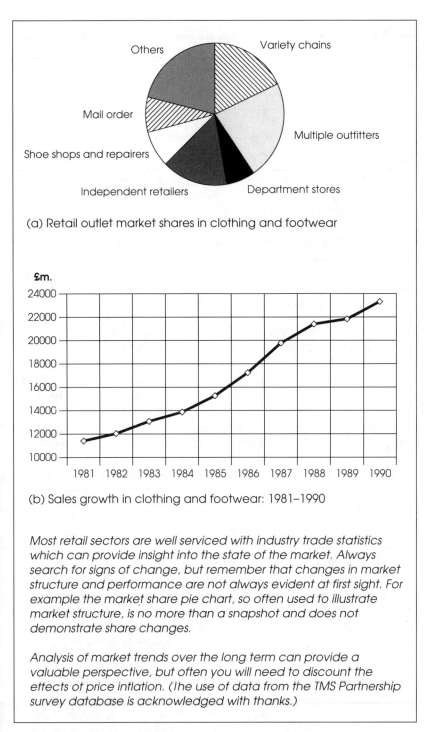

(a) Retail outlet market shares in clothing and footwear

(b) Sales growth in clothing and footwear: 1981–1990

Most retail sectors are well serviced with industry trade statistics which can provide insight into the state of the market. Always search for signs of change, but remember that changes in market structure and performance are not always evident at first sight. For example the market share pie chart, so often used to illustrate market structure, is no more than a snapshot and does not demonstrate share changes.

Analysis of market trends over the long term can provide a valuable perspective, but often you will need to discount the effects of price inflation. (The use of data from the TMS Partnership survey database is acknowledged with thanks.)

Figure 5.3 Analysing your retail sector
(*Source*: The TMS Partnership Clothing and Footwear Survey)

Table 5.1 Changes in outlet market share: clothing and footwear retailers (Indexed 1981 = 100)

Winners	1981	1990	Losers	1981	1990
Sports shops	100	309	Shoe shops	100	82
Multiples	100	136	Department stores	100	82
Market stalls	100	131	Independents	100	76
Discount stores	100	123	Coops	100	55

(*Source:* The TMS Partnership Clothing and Footwear Survey)

market statistics more readily if they are presented graphically. Presented as a table of figures, a rising sequence of market share figures may look promising. But they can hide a fall in the *rate of growth* that would be quite obvious from a graph. Also, look for a long history (see Figure 5.4). Two periods, say this year and last year, will tell you very little compared to a set of six-monthly statistics over five years. One period tells you nothing.

The major industry market research surveys can also provide competitive data on prices and product range, both of which can be useful in building up knowledge of the relative positioning of your competitors. The information also provides a useful benchmark from which to assess your own product mix and pricing structure. In at least two companies—one very large and one small—certain buyers were convinced their prices were in line with the market averages until this assumption was actually tested against market statistics. The prices *were* found to have been in line *three or four years ago*, but had drifted apart—little by little—to reach a point where the price structure had changed the retailer's entire market positioning.

Published financial statistics, available through annual reports or from Companies House, are notoriously unreliable guides to competitor performance. This is not because they are inaccurate, but because they show a very selective picture of trading performance. However, they are the only trading figures you can obtain openly and at least they provide a guide to your competitors' freedom of movement. Stock turn, asset utilization, margin and gearing ratios all provide useful indicators of the company's health. ICC's Business Ratio reports provide a useful source of normalized and comparable financial statistics.

After many years spent listening to consumers, I have learned never to underestimate either their intelligence or their perception. Take it from me, your customers know you, warts and all. Of course, they also know your competitors because they buy from them more frequently than you do, so who better to ask for information about

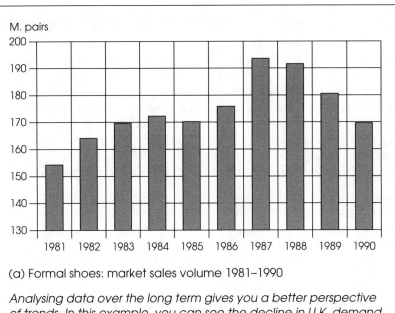

(a) Formal shoes: market sales volume 1981–1990

Analysing data over the long term gives you a better perspective of trends. In this example, you can see the decline in U.K. demand for traditional, 'leather-type' formal shoes. By 1990, unit sales had fallen back to 1983 levels.

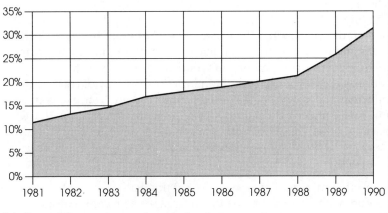

(b) Casual shoes: share of market value

The main reason for this decline is an upsurge in demand for trainers and other casual footwear. Not only have volumes increased, but average prices have risen from £7 to £21 as higher specifications and fashion trends have raised the prices customers are willing to pay. Thus casual footwear's share of market value has risen over ten years from 10% to over 30%.

Figure 5.4 Long-term market trends
(*Source*: The TMS Partnership Clothing and Footwear Survey)

competitors' strengths and weaknesses? Industry market research statistics are valuable because they show how consumers have 'voted with their feet'. However, they cannot alone tell you why customers used this or that retailer more or less regularly. By talking directly to customers you will obtain this less tangible information, which is so vital to a proper understanding of the competitive market in which you trade. Focus group discussions can provide the best method of obtaining this information. If you conduct a short series of groups *regularly*—at least twice each year—you will begin to build up a picture of changing consumer perceptions and preferences, and receive early warning of both competitive threats and opportunities.

You can use the same method as your customers to find out about your competitors: visiting their shops. You will never see shops through quite the same eyes as customers, but you will be able to observe things that customers may miss: changes in merchandise mix and the use of floor space, the arrival of concession operators or newly introduced EPoS systems. One exercise that is well worth while is to put yourself in the place of a customer. Write yourself a shopping list. Be specific and realistic—such as finding a washing machine to match your needs at home, or clothes for your son's holidays—and then try to buy those items. You will learn much about your, and your competitor's, ability to meet customer needs.

There is abundant information in the press about competitor activities. Most businesses see at least part of this information, but often it disappears into the waste bin at the end of the day. Fleeting ideas and impressions, which may have built up into a convincing picture of your competitors' movements, are easily lost. Press cuttings services provide a useful and long-established way of condensing this information. Now it is also possible to record and retrieve your own information using the latest Optical Character Recognition (OCR) packages that will work with a microcomputer. This way you can store any written information that looks as though it might be useful at a later date, and retrieve it almost instantly.

Collecting information is the essential first half of the battle. The second half is learning to *use* this information on competitors. The best way to ensure that this happens is to list competitive activity on the agenda of every general management meeting. An abundant volume of data will need to be digested into a short summary document, but as your management learns to expect a regular review

> *After many years spent listening to consumers, I have learned never to underestimate either their intelligence or their perception.*

of competitive action, you will start to consider competitive *reactions*. You may not always be in a position to do anything except take note, but this is so much better and safer than living in blissful ignorance!

Identifying threats and opportunities

Many managers are aware of the principal of SWOT analysis—the review of Strengths, Weaknesses, Threats and Opportunities. Those who have tried this technique have probably discovered the same problems that I encountered. Firstly, we often begin to discuss these matters without proper preparation, and as a result are casting round within a very few minutes for items to list under each heading. SWOT analysis ought to be a *continuing* process, allied to the environmental research programme, not just an agenda item when meeting to prepare next year's corporate plan. This process will give you, at least, a permanent and up-to-date list of external factors that are changing and may affect your corporate fortunes.

The second problem is that almost every threat can also be construed as an opportunity, and vice versa. Changing demographics may appear to affect the business in the short term, but highlight new opportunities in the future. Large competitors may look like a dominating competitive threat, but often they are the easiest source of new customers if you plan to differentiate. Thus you must introduce a degree of common sense into your analysis, and also take timing into account. Distinguish between short- and long-term threats and opportunities. Use timing issues to help find long-term goals and help focus on short-term commercial necessities.

You should also be careful to distinguish between strengths and opportunities, and threats and weaknesses. Threats and opportunities are derived from the environment in which your company is trading. Strengths and weaknesses represent assessments of your company's *internal* ability to meet *external* change.

Begin by listing all the environmental changes you can detect (see Checklist 5.1). There is no need to try to measure these very accurately. Now you should consider how these might affect your business. This is the stage at which I have found discussion and debate with business colleagues helpful. It also helps if you score each change, perhaps on a scale from –3 to +3, where negative scores are threatening, positive scores represent an opportunity, and zero is used where you think the change will have a neutral effect on your business. Your conclusions may be a little untidy, and opinions may differ, but you will find this is a very useful way of airing and focusing management opinion on the principal issues affecting direction.

Checklist ✓

5.1 OPPORTUNITIES AND THREATS IN THE ENVIRONMENT

Make a list of the changes you expect in the trading environment, similar to the one shown here, and consider how they are likely to affect your business.

Demographic
- Peaking birth rate
- Rising 5–14 age group
- Falling 15–34 age group
- Rising 35–54 age group

Social
- More households
- Smaller households
- Increasing affluence
- Inheritance of wealth
- Shift to service economy
- Less disposable time for many

Short-term economy
- Rising unemployment
- Cash poor middle classes
- Cost inflationary pressures

Consumer attitudes
- Trend to individualism
- Higher service expectations

- More knowledgeable customers
- More quality conscious

Retail competition
- Market specialization
- Focus on service
- Convenience shopping
- Extended trading hours
- Closer supplier links
- Industry concentration
- Cross border acquisitions

Technology
- Widespread EPoS implementation
- Management information in branches
- Database marketing feasible
- EDI supplier links
- Greater product reliability

If you operate in more than one market, you will need to adapt the analysis for each part of the business. It can also be very useful to review your competitors' position using the same analysis. You may well find that a changing environment will throw up new sources of competitive edge for one of the players in your particular field.

Of course, analysing threats and opportunities is only half the battle. The second challenge is to match these against your company's capability, for your profitability depends on your ability to adapt and fit into the outside world. This is the subject of the next part of this book.

Part III

Fitting the company with its environment

6

The company in context

There are two ways to analyse your market position. You can define the characteristics of your customers, and they can define yours, relative in each case to the competition.

'And what', enquired the head hunter, 'do you consider to be your particular strengths and weaknesses?'

This is one of the more predictable questions that recruitment consultants will ask, but preparing an answer never seems to get any easier. Do you second guess what they want you to say? Do you expose the honest answer, which you will probably have worked out for yourself many years ago? Or, for that matter, can you really provide an objective appraisal of someone you know as intimately as yourself?

Recognizing strengths and weaknesses

I use this personal illustration because the job of appraising your own company's strengths and weaknesses is equally difficult, and an essential first step in the process of matching your company to its trading environment. Once you understand what you are capable of doing, and any gaps in this capability that you need to close, you are well placed to determine your competitive stance and market position.

Whether you own the company or work for it, you have a close personal knowledge of the firm and the emotional capital involved, and this makes objective analysis of strengths and weaknesses very difficult. Most companies are also steeped in the received wisdom of generations of managers. Strengths are viewed in terms of the past rather than in terms of the current realities outside the company, while open discussion of weaknesses is often avoided since many managers fear it will be construed as criticism of their colleagues and their board.

Despite these difficulties, it is essential to reach an objective appraisal of both strengths and weaknesses, and compare these against the environmental opportunities and threats discussed in the previous chapter. When you try to define strengths and weaknesses you are attempting to put a value on your resources: your retail assets, brand values, financial circumstances, information technology expertise or your people. None of these resources necessarily has a value in its own right. Retail properties do not have a value unless someone is prepared to buy them. Managers do not have a value, however skilful they may be, unless someone is willing to pay for their time. Thus your company's resources are only valuable in the context of their use. I like the way this point is illustrated by two American business writers, Charles Hofer and Dan Schendel:

> ...resources have no value in and of themselves. They gain value only when one specifies the ways in which they are to be used. Thus one cannot tell whether it is a strength or weakness to be seven feet tall until one specifies what that individual is supposed to do. If he is to play basketball it is a great strength; if he is to ride a racehorse it would be a great weakness.

So the best way to assess the value of your resources is to place them in context (see Checklist 6.1). What marketing strategy do you want to adopt and how, in turn, does this fit with the market's threats and opportunities?

Let us assume, for example, that you run a successful chain of sportswear shops, selling the usual range of clothing and footwear associated with athletics and ball games. You have decided to diversify into winter sports and other outdoor pursuits through a new chain of stores. This market attracted you because you had noticed the rapid growth in skiing holidays that were being sold to an increasingly broad audience. Because skiing is inevitably a seasonal activity, you plan to sell clothing and equipment for walkers, campers and climbers during the summer.

The results of your market research have been positive. There is no doubt about the growth potential of the market. Outside the major cities you have found few specialist retailers. Among non-specialists only C&A seems to be offering serious competition in the ski wear field. A slowdown in retail spending and one or two warm winters both represent short-term threats, but you do not think that either problem represents a long-term threat to success. In addition to buying new units, you have decided to convert four of your existing shops, located mainly in provincial towns and cities.

Now you will need to examine your own resources, and determine whether these represent strengths or weaknesses. For example:

Checklist ✓

6.1 RESOURCE STRENGTHS AND WEAKNESSES

Review your company's strengths and weaknesses in relation to the market and its opportunities and threats. This needs to be examined in some detail, taking each of the following headings and adding detailed features relevant to your business.

	EDI supplier links	Management information in branches	Declining 15–34 age group	Service expectations	Quality conscious	Industry concentration
● Market information systems				?	?	
● Supply chain management and integration	?					
● Physical distribution and stock management	?					
● Value and suitability of retail property						
● Current merchandise range					?	
● Advertising, retail design and promotion skills		?				
● Availability and skills of sales staff		?	?	?		
● Information systems and technology	?	?				
● Management strength and depth						?
● Capacity to change and innovate						?
● Capacity to diversify			?			?
● Sources of sustainable competitive advantage	?				?	
● Sources of sustainable differential advantage				?		
● Financial strength and flexibility						?

Store locations   Are there enough customers in your local catchment areas? Despite increasing popularity, skiing is still a minority interest compared to many others. Your existing sites may be good for the current business, but you will need to consider whether they would be a strength or a weakness for such a specialist market.

Buying skills   Your buying team are highly experienced in sourcing sports clothing, but do they know enough about the skiing and outdoor pursuits market? There are new suppliers and new fashion trends to learn, and highly technical quality specifications to understand. Your present team may be a strength in your current market but a major weak link in the new project.

Selling skills   Do you have, or can you recruit, competent sales staff? Product knowledge and personal experience are demanded by customers in this field. 'Expert' customers will soon discover whether your staff know what they are talking about, and non-experts will be relying on your advice. Are you going to provide adequate training resources (which will probably be designed to teach selling skills to accomplished skiers and climbers)?

The object of this exercise, which you should apply to your own trading situation, is to identify resource gaps that will need to be closed in order to present a competitive offer to your market. You should always be looking for sources of *competitive advantage*: the chance to compete more effectively than other retailers through, for example:

- more efficient sourcing
- better stock turn
- higher quality staff
- more appropriate locations
- better information systems giving quicker response
- greater customer loyalty.

These are all comparative benefits. They are based on the relative success that you have in applying your corporate resources to the marketplace, compared with your competitors' ability to adjust and apply *their* resources. Marks & Spencer build competitive advantage through the very close relationships they build with suppliers, which feeds through to the marketplace in terms of quality and consistency. Boots the Chemists are reported to be making great strides in efficient stock management through state-of-the-art systems that allow more efficient use of retail space. Benefits feed through in terms of higher profitability and a better level of service for the customer. The booksellers, Waterstone, have an unusual retail strength: 93 per cent of their sales staff are graduates. This provides a widespread management resource, the ability to delegate management and buying responsibilities nearer the marketplace, and the differential benefit of informed advice for their customers.

Customers are not directly interested in these structural differences, but they are very interested in the way they feed through to each retailer's offer. They are looking for relative benefits: reasons why it would be better, for them, to use one retailer rather than another. Indeed every retailer should be aiming to create this *differentiation* in the customer's mind. If all shops were identical in every way, there would be no reason for customers to make a choice, and they would, I suppose, merely use shops at random. Thankfully life is not so boring. There are many differences in consumer needs and preferences, and many differences between retailers. However, you must not rely on chance or history to dictate how you, as a retailer, differ from others. Your differentiation should be based on understanding clearly how customers differ, and you should then design and implement an offer that matches those needs.

Market positioning

Market positioning is simply the process of planning and creating sustainable differences. Differentiation gives you security because it creates reasons for customers to use your shops rather than those of your competitors. But remember that your unique mix of benefits must be:

● wanted by and relevant to an adequate number of potential customers

● communicated to and recognized by those potential customers

● sustainable, as far as possible, so that other retailers cannot copy your offer.

The degree of differentiation you can achieve will depend in part on the type of products or services you are selling. For example, the basic service offered by High Street dry cleaners is difficult to differentiate. A dry cleaner who cannot clean clothes will not survive very long, and yet it is difficult to find a way of delivering *cleaner* clean clothes. Differentiation will have to be derived from other factors such as price, presentation, speed and the manner in which the service is promoted. Sainsbury successfully established a reputation for the quality of its fresh produce. While I am sure their buying and quality

> *Differentiation gives you security because it creates reasons for customers to use your shops rather than someone else's.*

control methods are first rate, there are many thousands of greengrocers who sell equally fresh vegetables. Sainsbury succeeded so well because they *communicated* freshness through their advertising, and created differentiation for themselves, extending probably far beyond the real, tangible product differences.

Clothing retailers can do much more to create differentiation through the product itself. They can offer different levels of fashion, specialize in particular types of garment such as knitwear, ties or suits, or particular end-users such as sportspeople, holiday-makers or business people. Each approach will appeal to a different customer profile.

There are, in fact, any number of dimensions that you can use to construct your own position in the market. A few examples will help to prompt your own thinking:

● Breadth of merchandise range

● Depth of range

● Price

● Quality

● Store location

● Customer lifestyle

● End-use of merchandise

● Degree of personal service, training and product knowledge

● Opening hours.

When you set out to establish a clear market position it is important to make sure that all the components of the retail offer are coherent. If you intend to sell high-fashion clothing, the shops must be located in appropriate centres where people expect to buy fashion and will be present in sufficient numbers. If the retail brand is already established it must have an existing reputation for fashion: you cannot expect people to transform long established opinions. The sales staff should be fashion conscious, and dressed appropriately, and the store design must fit with the same image.

Achieving this level of coherence is not too difficult for a new business, but it can be a very tricky problem for established retailers who are aiming to change their positioning, or apply existing resources to the development of a new retail offer. Often there is just too much temptation to apply existing systems and management values to the new business without considering whether the strengths that support the core business are appropriate elsewhere, or may even become major weaknesses in the move to a different market position.

Focusing on coherence makes good marketing. Firstly, it will make your proposition much easier to communicate. Advertising a clear proposition will be easier and more successful than trying to get across a confused message: if *you* are not quite sure why customers should prefer your offer, you should not expect customers to work this out for themselves. Secondly, customers like to know where they stand. A clear and coherent offer may not appeal to everyone, but for those who do find the offer enticing, there will be no doubt in their minds about the right choice of shop.

Measuring your position in the market

It is very difficult to decide where you would like to be positioned in the market if you do not know what your present position is. This may seem rather too obvious a point to make, but many retailers do not have a clear idea of the way in which they are seen by consumers. If pressed, they will recall the last advertising agency presentation and mutter indistinctly about C2D socio-economic groups or aspirational consumers. I have to admit that measuring market position *is* a mixture of art and science, and not always something that can be explained in one sentence, but it is a procedure you should undertake. Like a yachtsman plotting his position at sea, it tells you if you are in the right place and heading in the right direction.

There are two ways of tackling the problem. One is to look at the people who form your customer base. What are their characteristics and what do they have in common that helps you to define the type of people who choose to use your shops? The second and equally important approach is not to consider how *you* can define your customers, but how they (and others) choose to define *your* characteristics. What differences do they recognize between you and your competitors, and how do they rate the comparative benefits between you and your competition?

The first approach to the problem is the most common, if only because the data are usually available from syndicated market research surveys, or can be obtained through fairly straightforward customer surveys. You can generally define the customer base in terms of sex, age, social group, employment, purchase frequency and, perhaps, trade specific criteria such as the customers' interests in fashion. Each attribute gives you a different perspective, shedding a little more light on your customer profile. In addition to profiling

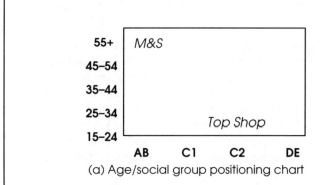

(a) Age/social group positioning chart

Market statistics can be used to help determine your market position, but if misused can be very misleading. The commonly used age/social group positioning chart to the right illustrates the problems. It accurately reflects the segments where M&S and the fashion retailer Top Shop achieve their highest market share, but it would be quite wrong to suggest that M&S sells only to up-market pensioners.

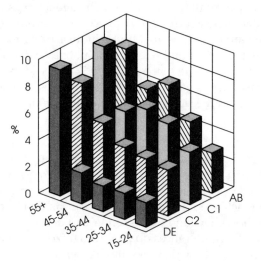

(b) M&S customer profile for women's clothing

In reality the customer profile is much more complex, with customers drawn from all parts of the market. This is illustrated in the chart to the left, which shows how M&S's customers are divided among both social groups and age groups.

Figure 6.1 Market positioning

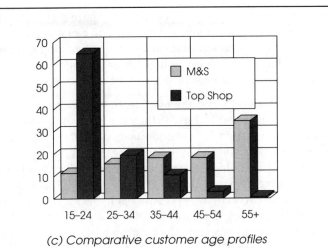

(c) Comparative customer age profiles

Nevertheless there is a marked difference in appeal between M&S and Top Shop, as a comparison of age profiles demonstrates. Note that Top Shop, which has one of the most focused offers on the High Street, still draws over 30% of its customers from outside its core market segment.

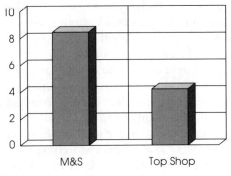

(d) Market shares, by value, for women's clothing

It is vital to look at market share as well as customer profile. Despite Top Shop's young appeal, the apparently 'old' M&S still sells almost twice as much as Top Shop to the 15-24 year old woman.

(*Source*: The TMS Partnership Clothing and Footwear Survey)

your own customers, you can of course compare this with the customer profiles of competing retailers. You can compare two characteristics, such as age and social group, on a single chart which gives you a basic map showing how several retailers are positioned in terms of differing customer profiles.

The danger of such charts, however, is that their apparent accuracy is fallacious (see Figure 6.1). Firstly, they can show only two characteristics when in fact positioning is often the sum of many different factors. Secondly, in order to create a meaningful map you have to define a retailer's 'typical' customer age (or social group). While one age group may predominate, you can be sure that there will be a wide spread of ages on either side of this core group. Nor can these charts recognize the scale of the customer base. Marks & Spencer, for example, have in their clothing business a clear bias towards older people. But it would be wrong to classify the customer base as 'old' when you acknowledge that they are also market leaders among 15–24 year olds in many product areas (see, for example, Figure 6.1(d)).

So you must treat all such analyses with some care. Each new piece of information will add to the jigsaw, but you should avoid jumping to unwarranted conclusions. You are trying to assess a very complex situation and you should not be tempted to distil your market positioning to a single snappy statement or a clever graphic.

While market statistics will give you a useful, rough guide to your position in the market, the consumer remains the best guide to lead you through this maze. Trade statistics will tell you how the money was spent, but only the consumer can tell you *why* one retailer was chosen in preference to another. You can use qualitative research projects to uncover this elusive information. Often you will discover that customers differentiate retailers in ways you had never thought about, and they will also point out to you areas which, in their view, lack differentiation. Be prepared for unpleasant news. You may find, as the UK shoe retailers have discovered to their cost, that the many attempts to differentiate retail brands have been totally lost on consumers. As far as shoppers are concerned, virtually all shoe shops look the same, stock the same products and offer the same undistinguished levels of service. The problem in this case, I suspect, is that the *retailer's* vision of differentiation—the brand on the front of the shop—bears no resemblance to the way *customers* expect to differentiate shoe shops. They expect to find differences in merchandise and, perhaps, the style and quality of service. Remember that retail brands form only a shorthand sign of all the other attributes that make up a distinctive market position.

Qualitative research can also be used to build *positioning maps* to help you assess visually how you and competitors are seen by consumers. The creation of these 'perceptual maps' is technically quite a complex business, and you should work closely with market research firms who are competent in this area. However, the process of gathering raw data from the consumer is not complicated, and neither is the assessment of the resulting maps. This form of research recognizes that many things are distilled into the customers' impressions of a retailer: history, merchandise, prices, location, advertising, quality expectations and many others. The back-room statisticians shake down customers' reactions to all these things and create a two-dimensional map that shows how each retailer relates to each other, how similar or different they are, and how closely they meet the customers' ideal.

It is not always necessary to apply this level of sophistication. Discussion group respondents can enjoy playing market positioning games that can be very revealing. One simple method that works well is to use cards marked with the names of your own and competitive retail brands. Respondents can provide you with useful insights by arranging the cards according to their perception of relative price, quality, service level, convenience and so on. Also, ask them to think of a car model that best fits their impressions of a retailer—an exercise that is both entertaining and revealing, quickly separating the pretentious retailers (usually personified as flash, underpowered sports cars) from the solid and reliable (Land Rovers), and the 'cheap and cheerful' (second-hand Escorts).

Market positioning strategy should aim to establish a close fit between your business and its trading environment. Through research and analysis, and a certain measure of honest introspection, you need to discover whether your retail offer is both distinctive and relevant, and that you have the internal resources to deliver it successfully. You need also to establish whether your existing position—as perceived by the customers—is tenable, and if not, what steps you must take to change both your positioning and the company infrastructure that supports it.

I hope you will uncover a very satisfactory position. But it is more probable that you will discover that something needs to change. It may be necessary to change your market position. You may have recognized that you have neither the right people nor the experience to sustain new developments in the business. You may have the right merchandise but the wrong systems. Whatever the cause, you are going to encounter the problem of managing *change* through the business.

7

Managing change

Change introduces a lot of inconvenience and most people will not bother unless they believe the consequences of doing nothing are even more distasteful.

Change is always present but its impact on the business is often never noticed until it is too late to adapt. We live at present in a very turbulent world and it is impossible for a business to remain static and unchanging if it wishes to survive. Elsewhere we have looked at some of the environmental changes that are affecting the retail industry. They *impose* change on retailers. Managing these changes productively is a very important part of retail marketing. In this crucial area the skills of managing people and managing assets come together. In the retail world people and assets can both put a brake on change. It is not easy to alter the location, appearance or stock of an entire chain of shops. Nor is it always easy to recognize when some adjustment is needed and push through sometimes fundamental decisions about the way the business is directed and managed.

Change is best accomplished when it is recognized as a way of life and constantly incorporated, little by little, into the day-to-day management of the business. It is better to adapt and improve the design of retail stores with each new opening than to wait until the existing style is demonstrably outdated, and then attempt a massive and hugely expensive refitting programme. It is better to monitor continuously the effectiveness of different types of retail location than to be forced later into a wholesale reorganization of the property portfolio, perhaps during a dull property market. It is better to improve information systems through regular review and intervention than to attempt a complete rewrite that may take three years to complete, often while existing systems are bereft of proper maintenance and are held together with string and sticking plaster.

Major changes have a high built-in risk factor, and in the retail world are often forced by years of inertia that have left the retailer, the assets and most importantly the market positioning out of touch with a changed market. Radical repositioning of the marketing offer is fraught with difficulty. Almost certainly you will lose the remnants of your existing customer base when they realize that the merchandise or character of 'their' shop has changed. But you are provided with no guarantees that the new market you hope to attract will become willing customers. Their only knowledge of your offer is likely to be a vague impression of what you *were*, and that—almost by definition—was not something with which they wished to associate themselves. You are likely to suffer a credibility gap: too many people simply will not believe in the relevance, to them, of the newly positioned retailer.

Repositioning within the market also often entails radical changes in the back office. You may lack appropriate buying skills. Computer systems that are adequate in one market may be totally inadequate in a new and perhaps faster-moving environment. Display and sales skills may differ. Retailers often forget this, recalling only their historical strengths and capabilities, and they fail to analyse whether these will be appropriate in a changed world. Acquisition—in effect another radical route into market repositioning—hides similar pitfalls. The skills that worked successfully in your core business may not be appropriate in the new environment; ask yourself whether the expensive present you are bringing to the party is really what is wanted or needed.

In this chapter we shall look at some of the reasons why change creates so many problems: as often as not, the *human* element of management is the cause of the problem. While systems, physical assets and merchandise may be out of date or inappropriate, this is the result of human action (or inaction): inanimate resources cannot be blamed for the company's problems. They may be inappropriate in the current environment, but they are *symptomatic* of a management problem rather than the *cause* of it.

Becoming sensitive to change

The first necessity is to recognize when change is affecting the business. 'That's obvious,' you may retort. 'When things are going badly my sales start falling.' Unfortunately this very real and tangible symptom of change usually appears too late. In order to react effectively and accurately we must be aware of the causes much earlier. Falling sales (or even a fall in the rate of growth) may be due to universal problems such as declining consumer expenditure, but

---

Repositioning within the market often entails radical changes in the back office as well.

equally they may be symptomatic of diminishing competitiveness—
for which there may be any number of subtle reasons.

You must make sure that your firm is *sensitive to change*. You need
both technical and human sensitivity. You can achieve technical
sensitivity through market and environmental research. The nuances
of change will be most evident if you monitor markets continuously.
By this action you will have a better chance of catching new trends as
they begin to emerge, rather than later when you are looking for
reasons to explain a sales disaster.

Continuous research will not just happen. There is a real budgetary
cost attached to some, if not all research, and this expenditure
requires a conscious decision and commitment. There is no need to be
profligate but you must be prepared to continue funding research
through good times and bad, and this requires a commitment
demonstrated from the top of the organization. If the budget battles
are left entirely to the market research manager or a lowly marketing
executive, the absence of support from the top will be taken as a clear
signal that research is 'fair game' for cost-cutting exercises.

Getting market and environmental research done regularly is one
thing; ensuring that the information is used is quite another. If top
management is committed to this research, the battle is largely won,
but more often this is not the case. You need to look at the reasons
why research systems are not already in place. Indeed, *you* may be
one of those reasons. Few people spend money on things they don't
really feel they need. And if, for example, you have spent the last 20
years building up a successful business, either as an owner or a
manager, I expect you consider you know the business and its
customers very well.

You can, however, get too close to a business. We have all done it. We
help to define and then re-absorb the culture of the place and start to
take for granted the unwritten rules and attitudes about 'the way we
do things around here'. You know the sort of thing: real decisions are
only made by the chairman (who is called 'Sir' or 'Madam' at board
meetings); our customers won't pay more for better quality (an
untested assumption—it's just always been that way); you can't trust
branch managers' advice on merchandise—they're trained to *sell* not
select merchandise; the marketing manager joined us from outside, so
can't really understand the business; advertising doesn't work (we
tried it in desperation during the '81 recession); those upstart
competitors will never make it (if we can't do better, why should
they?).

Attitudes like these get deeply embedded in the business, which can
easily become introverted. We tend to ignore external change because

it is not relevant to the way we do things. Alternatively, we sense and interpret change only in ways that fit our attitudes: those new competitors will not survive because they are not competing on price, which is the way we've always promoted the business.

If research *is* introduced, the results can be interpreted very selectively. Those findings that fit the prevailing viewpoint will be acknowledged, but will probably be used to confirm that the research project was never really necessary: 'It's nice to know we were right, but we've spent all that money learning what we already knew.' Those results that contradict widely held beliefs are likely to be discounted, often with considerable animosity. In his book *Strategic Change and the Management Process*, Professor Gerry Johnson records the occasion when retailers Foster Menswear saw the results of their first market research commissioned by a new marketing director:

> As a diagnostic statement the research was full, powerful and prescriptive. The immediate result of this analysis was that the report was rubbished by senior managers and directors. The analysis may have been perceived by its initiator as diagnostic, but it was received by its audience as a politically threatening statement.
>
> (*Source*: Johnson, G., *Strategic Change and the Management Process*, Basil Blackwell, 1987)

If you care to bury a research report, there is no shortage of well-established methods. Some of these methods are given below, drawn from a list compiled some years ago by Professor Andrew Pettigrew. They are included partly for your amusement, but also because they will alert you to the possibility that you, like the rest of us, may have been an offender. If you have adopted such methods, it may lead you to question whether you are as open to new information as you should be for the good of the business.

Ten ways to fend off a report that makes unpopular recommendations

1 Straight rejection: the researcher and his report are dismissed without further discussion. Needs lots of power and self-assurance.

2 'Bottom-drawer' it: the report is praised but nothing is done about it. The researcher, content with praise, may not press for action.

3 Mobilize political support: the line manager calls for support from colleagues who have similar positions to defend.

4 The nitty-gritty tactic: minor objections are raised to discredit and delay the full report (technical-sounding questions about the adequacy of sample sizes work well here!).

5 'But in the future...': the report is OK today but will not work in the future, so it's not worth implementing.

6 The emotional tactic: 'How can you do this to me?' or '...to my chaps?'

7 The invisible man tactic: the line manager is never available for discussion of the report.

8 'Further investigation is required': the report is sent back for more work. (If you keep this one up, you can later claim it is out of date.)

9 The scapegoat: someone else (e.g. head office) won't like it.

10 Deflection: the line manager directs attention to points where he has sufficient knowledge to contradict the researcher, and so discredit the whole report.

(*Source*: Pettigrew, A.,
Personnel Review, Warwick University, 1974)

You will have to do your own soul searching to determine whether your company is sufficiently open to change. If you think that change may not be totally welcomed by people in your firm, you can at least take heart from the knowledge that you are not alone. Most companies have problems maintaining an open attitude to new and not always sympathetic information. But if you can achieve this, you are much more likely to remain competitive.

Gaining commitment to change

If the first step is to achieve a 'listening' attitude, the second step is to achieve the flexibility and commitment to act on the information received. Sometimes this is easier said than done. Many management textbooks over the years have perpetrated the idea that companies react smoothly to changing conditions, adjusting organization structure and strategy to meet new competitive conditions. Things rarely seem to happen quite like that. In practice, little changes inside the company which bumps along in much the same direction, chiefly under the influence of its own momentum. In time the company, its practices and marketing drift away from the reality of the marketplace until the strains on the P&L account become unbearable. The crisis created by potential financial collapse, or the arrival of a take-over bid, finally provokes action. Usually it is the organization structure that changes first, as old hands depart and a new crew take over the helm, and the strategic direction of the firm is then hauled back on course.

Your organization's culture is often contributing to the hazards of managing change. Some retailers are more flexible than others. Many retailers have grown under the influence—often domination—of one person whose singular vision has carried the organization forward. The feature pages of the business magazines have been filled with the profiles of one-man (or one-woman) retailers: Sir Ralph Halpern at Burton's, Sophie Mirman at Sock Shop, Harry Goodman at Intersun, Sir Terrence Conran at Storehouse, Philip Birch of Ward White, and many more. It is noticeable that not all manage to survive or remain successful. Everything depends on the person at the centre of power. When he, or she, gets decisions right, the business often has the flexibility and enthusiasm to succeed. But when those decisions are wrong, disaster can be spectacular.

You will rarely find much in the way of strategic market research commissioned by this kind of firm. The vision of its leadership is the only research that will count in decision making. Politically astute marketing managers will know there is only one way to push through changes in marketing direction. They have to nobble the visionary leaders, drip feed them with the information and ideas they will later grasp and promote by their own hands. This is not the place for marketing managers who want to establish a reputation.

You may be interested to read what the business academic, Professor Charles Handy, says about this kind of culture. These words are not written about any individual firm or industry, but they strike me as a particularly apt profile of some well-known retail firms.

> These organizations are proud and strong. They have the ability to move quickly and can react well to threat or danger. Whether they do move or whether they move in the right direction will, however, depend on the person in the centre; for the quality of these individuals is of paramount importance and the succession issue is the key to such organizations' continued success. Individuals employed in them will prosper and be satisfied to the extent that they are power-oriented, politically minded, risk taking, and rate security as a minor element in their psychological contract.

> These cultures put a lot of faith in the individual, little in committees. They judge by results and are tolerant of means. Often seen as tough or abrasive, though successful, they may well suffer from low morale in the middle layers of management.

Charles Handy describes a contrasting culture—which he describes as

---

Many retailers have grown under the influence—often domination—of one person whose singular vision has carried the organization forward.

a role culture to avoid the pejorative overtones of the word
'bureaucracy'—that you will find in large and long-established
retailers, retail banks and mail order firms.

> The role organisation will be found where economies of scale are
> more important than flexibility or where technical expertise and
> depth of specialisation are more important than product innovation
> or product cost... The organisation will succeed as long as it can
> operate in a stable environment. When next year is like this year, so
> that this year's tested rules will work next year, then the outcome will
> be good.

> But role cultures are slow to perceive the need for change and slow
> to change even if the need is seen. If the market, the product
> needs or the competitive environment changes, the role culture is
> likely to continue to forge straight ahead, confident in its ability to
> shape the future in its own image. Then collapse, replacement of its
> top management or takeover is usually necessary.

> (*Source*: Extracts from Handy, C. B., *Understanding Organisations*, Penguin,
> 3rd ed., 1985. Copyright © Charles B. Handy, 1976, 1981, 1985. Reproduced
> by permission of Penguin Books Ltd)

Like me, you may recognize this description and smile a little. But if
you are working in firms with strong cultures, and seeking to change
them, you have a major problem on your hands. It is like trying to
push a supertanker off course. Only one person has the position and
tools to do that successfully: the captain in the wheelhouse. Even
then, you will recall, supertankers can take a very long time to answer
the helm.

In practice, major changes will need to be supported by, or at least
have the willing connivance of, the chief executive. If *that individual*
won't support a change, while doubtless giving reasons that may or
may not be right, there is very little chance that anything substantial
will happen. However, provided there is top management support
there are plenty of other people in the ranks of most firms who can
trigger or become involved in major changes of direction.

We have identified *crises* as important triggers for change. Sometimes
you don't have a convenient crisis at hand when it is still practicable
to introduce change in a managed fashion. Well, if you do not have a
crisis you could always invent one! This is a serious suggestion.
Change introduces a lot of inconvenience, and most people will not
change unless they believe that the consequences of doing nothing are
even more distasteful. It is not unusual for market research to be
commissioned for political reasons. If you have an unproved 'hunch'
that things are not going in the right direction, research will often
help you to make that hunch more tangible and give you reasoned

grounds for arguing the case for change. External market research may not even be necessary. I learned early in my career from a retail director who had a 'nose' for problems no one else had noticed. He was like a terrier following a fast dying trace of scent. For days, mounds of computer printout would grow on his desk until you all but lost sight of him. But eventually he would emerge triumphantly carrying his quarry—a page of calculations proving that there was, say, a fundamental flaw in the distribution system or uneconomic duplication in the merchandise range.

Whatever technique you choose, awareness and acceptance within the firm that all is not well is an essential prerequisite to change. It may take time and several disconcerting events to create the right level of concern. Foster's, the men's wear retailers quoted earlier in this chapter, provides a case in point. Here was a retail firm with a historical record of success. Indeed in the late 1970s it was one of the most successful multiple operations in the UK, with return on sales running at 14 per cent and a return on capital of 39 per cent. Who would want to change a success story like that? Nevertheless, Foster's management was already vaguely aware that changes in men's wear retailing were under way with fashion, never Foster's strong point, becoming ever more important to the customer. Recession and declining competitiveness took its toll on profitability, which all but vanished within two years. Yet the research programme of 1981, which underlined Foster's market inadequacies, was still rejected out of hand. Introspection and a basic belief in 'the way we do things' even survived a take-over by Sears in 1985, and the subsequent departure of many board members. The groundswell of opinion in middle management did not change until the company later embarked on a management development programme run by Manchester Business School. Introduced to strategic thinking for the first time, a whole stratus of management began to question both their own beliefs and the actions and direction of their more senior colleagues. For the first time, nearly ten years on, real uneasiness and discontent emerged as a desire for change. Most importantly, there was now a critical mass of people ready for, and wanting, change. Ten years earlier the then marketing director and his research report had been a lone voice calling in the wilderness.

Management education is recognized as one of the more successful triggers for change. Another approach is to set up temporary management structures to work on specific projects and new developments. Such arrangements provide an opportunity for established attitudes to be 'unfrozen' in a way that would be personally and politically difficult within the *status quo*. Some of the same managers at Foster's, who had so much trouble recognizing the need to change the marketing strategy of their own business, excelled when they were called to work part time on the development of a new, more up-market clothing business. Here there was no history or experience to fall back on. The value of market research was readily accepted, because it provided these managers with the information they lacked. Because there were no traditions or positions to defend, they were ready to plan the business from scratch, designing each component—merchandise range, retail locations, staff selection, training and store design—to fit the recognized needs of this new market sector. Perhaps most importantly, the managers' involvement in developing the fundamental strategy of the business created commitment for change, and 'ownership' of the business's future.

The power of project teams, not only to get things done but to change attitudes, can be gauged by two comments written at the time by outside observers—firstly, in relation to Foster's attitude to its own traditional business, and, secondly, a reaction to a presentation of the new business plan. Remember that both observers are talking about *the same managers*.

1 There is little evidence of systematic and comprehensive environmental scanning. Environmental sensing may take place but it does so personally, with little evidence of systematic analysis, and with a leap from personalized problem awareness to action.

but later

2 It was the most thorough and professional presentation I have heard for a long time, and I have been to many such presentations. Rather than starting out from what you have got, the study worked backwards from an identification of the marketing opportunity to a strategy for change. I believe there is a real window for Fosters here and your management convinced those of us there that they had the capabilities to undertake this task.

In some circumstances individual change agents can also trigger a change in management attitudes and objectives. This is often the chief executive, but others can perform this role providing they have professional or political influence. Sometimes they are newcomers, bringing in fresh attitudes or skills, and with those attributes the objectivity to 'see the wood for the trees'. However, they might be seen to fulfil another role: the boy who exclaimed 'the Emperor has no clothes!'. No one really enjoys being shown up, or having well-established beliefs stripped away. The shock can be effective in many firms but, equally, change agents rarely seem to live on with the company to enjoy the fruits of their labour. Change agents, in companies and countries alike, often succeed in losing their jobs. This is why consultancies are often valued as change agents. They are useful triggers for change, but the ground rules enable the company to continue regarding such outsiders as dispensable when their job is done.

Part IV
Key issues in managing retail markets

8

Marketing management

> *Marketing management is the process of mobilizing all the company's resources to exceed customers' expectations.*

Good marketing has to be managed through the organization . This vital process is not necessarily the function of a marketing manager. Every line and staff manager has responsibility for marketing. Let me take you back to Peter Drucker's definition of marketing: getting the company to have what the customer wants. (Contrast this with his definition of selling: getting the customer to *want* what the company *has*.) You need to determine what the customers want, and indeed what they expect. The process of getting this total product to the customers involves everyone. The buyers must identify and procure appropriate merchandise. Distribution and information systems departments need to make sure that the goods reach the customers when they are wanted. Retail operations, personnel and training functions must ensure that customers can find an appropriate physical and personal environment in the store.

I do not think any retail manager would dispute the logic of these statements. Meeting the customers' needs is the natural objective of retailers. Because we have common objectives, we should all be pulling in the same direction, and we should have a nation of satisfied customers. But we do not. We have millions of customers whose expectations are often unfulfilled and rarely exceeded. Inevitably the tight, customer-focused organization we aim to maintain is under constant stress, slowly pulled apart through confused objectives, operational failures, decisions and actions based on poor information and personal interpretations. Cracks and gaps appear, and the well-oiled machinery of the company we would have liked to run starts to creak and grind ominously.

Add a few external threats from inflation, recession or demographic changes and the company can founder.

Marketing management is concerned with closing those gaps and, as a result, refocusing the company's activities towards the customers.

Figure 8.1 shows you where to look for the gaps, and this chapter will give you some ideas to help you close them.

Your customers' perception of what you offer

The way your customers (or potential customers) perceive what you offer is absolutely central to your success as a retailer. Providing the products you sell are of some value, their *relative* value, as perceived by the customers, will determine how much you sell and ultimately your market share and profitability. If they believe you offer better value than your competitors, or represent a better way of spending their money, you will sell. This perception depends on the balance between your customers' expectations and your ability to meet them. When you exceed expectations you make money, your customers are happy, and their perceptions improve. When you fail to meet expectations, the results are reversed. The formula for success is simple:

Perceived value = Delivery/Expectations

Your job in marketing is to make this 'number' as big as possible. And the formula generates a new definition of marketing management for us: *Marketing management is the process of mobilizing all the company's resources to exceed customers' expectations.*

If we are to accomplish this successfully we must:

- understand, and as far as possible, manage customer expectations
- manage the successful implementation of the retail offer in all its manifestations.

The best way to do this is to break down the processes that, on one side, determine our customers' expectations, and, on the other, determine the quality of the company's implementation. This helps you to identify gaps in the system and find ways to close them. Figure 8.1 illustrates this process.

Do you know what the customers expect?

You do not have much chance of delivering the products and services that your customers expect if you do not *know* what they *do* expect. This may sound as though I am stating the obvious, but I fear it is the

> *You do not have much chance of delivering the products and services that your customers expect if you do not know what they do expect.*

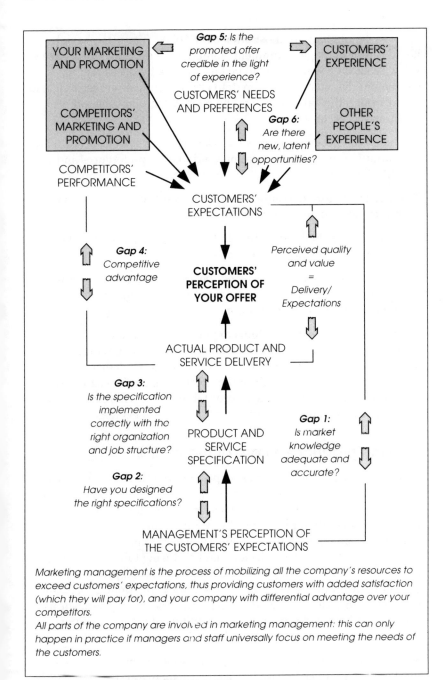

Figure 8.1 The global nature of marketing management

(*Source*: Adapted with permission of The Free Press, a division of Macmillan, Inc., from Zeithaml, V. A., A. Parasuraman and L. L. Berry, *Delivering Quality Service: Balancing Customer Perceptions and Expectations*, The Free Press, 1990. Copyright © 1990 by The Free Press)

obvious factors that are most often overlooked. Too often have I heard senior managers comment, somewhat scornfully, 'Of course we know what they want', only to be taken aback by the savage judgement that customers then deliver through market research, and later through the balance sheet. The most common problems encountered occur when:

1 There is an absence of formal market research systems to provide a continuing insight into customer and market preferences and attitudes.

2 There is a failure to communicate research and its operational implications to all corners of the organization.

3 There is an embedded culture in the firm, which dictates: 'We know what's best for the customer.'

4 Research gets 'bottom-drawered' because it is a threat to influential managers, it questions received wisdom or it suggests that previous decisions were wrong.

Getting market research systems in place is therefore your first priority. The chief executive must take the lead in encouraging access to this information and open discussion of its conclusions and implications. This might hurt in the short term, but it is certainly not as painful as the slow decline in profitability that will result if you let the company drift away from the customers' real needs.

Plan the product you are going to offer

If you know what the customers expect of you, there is a reasonable chance that you can deliver the merchandise, value and service they want. Be wary, though, of making assumptions. It is better to make your implementation plans specific. Manufacturers have at least some of this discipline forced upon them. They *have* to prepare and draw designs, specify materials, decide manufacturing tolerances, set up tools and quality control procedures before they can produce and deliver their products. Retailers should follow the same procedures, planning and writing down the product and service specifications. These must be based not on the assumptions of what consumers want, but in the knowledge of their needs and expectations.

Make these specifications specific. How else can you manage your marketing if there is no base line against which you can measure performance? If you find yourself thinking 'I'm not sure what they want...' too often, then you need to research your market. First, try to plan without reference to your existing custom and practice; then write down the things you actually do. This will tell you the gaps that you must close.

Your specification should start with a careful and explicit description of your target customers. This description should be as vivid and as realistic as possible: include details of your core customers' ages, sex, occupations, lifestyles, present shopping habits and preferences. Above all you should state the aspects of your retail offer that you think will appeal to the target customers, and then state why these will be more attractive than your competitors' offers. I know that in practice many of your customers—probably even a majority—will not fit exactly into your target profile, but the discipline of tailoring your offer to such a specific target will help to ensure a coherent design. Follow this with an explicit statement about each part of the retail offer: the product range breadth, depth and design philosophy, the location and design style of the stores, stock service levels, management style, recruitment policy, the approach of sales staff and customer care policies. Each of these statements of policy should also explain how they are related to the underlying marketing objectives of meeting and exceeding customers' expectations.

Distribute your specification widely and keep it with you at every meeting. Check every proposed decision and action against the specification. If it doesn't fit, don't do it.

Compare plans and performance

All retailers compare sales plans against performance. It is an essential control, but of course it tells you nothing of the reasons for any discrepancy. You will get this information by comparing your success in actually delivering your planned offer against the specification. You will get some of this information by going 'walk-about' inside the company and your stores. Some will come from internal management reporting of customer returns and stock shortage reports. Store managers and staff can relay valuable information that is not necessarily reported formally (remember reports tend to be designed only for *realized* problems). Set up a system to monitor customer complaints. Respond to every complaint that cannot be settled immediately in the store. This will do much to ensure that you exceed the customers' expectations, and you will turn a potentially lost customer into a dedicated supporter (see Ideas 8.1).

More formal market research methods can also come to your aid. 'Mystery shoppers' can assess stock availability, store appearance and staff treatment against a pre-planned specification. Exit interviews will give you immediate and factual reactions from customers who are just leaving the store.

Ideas

8.1 LOST CUSTOMERS

Lost customers are very expensive. Firstly, you will have to pay for finding a replacement,whose business may take months to build to a steady pattern as they put you on trial. Secondly, remember that you are not losing the value of a single sale, perhaps for only £10. You are losing a 'customer lifetime'. A customer of a clothing retailer could be spending £250 a year at the shop. Over ten years that's worth £2500. If your customer's disillusionment is passed on to three friends (and don't we all enjoy a good moan), that badly handled £10 sale could cost you £10 000.

When you find discrepancies between specification and delivery you will need to look for the underlying reasons. Some of these will be mechanical and easy to identify. Others may be subtle. The following list is not exhaustive but provides some examples.

1 Buyers may misinterpret or ignore the range specification.

2 Buyers are working to objectives that potentially conflict with the specification, such as a requirement to maximize input margin.

3 Lack of retail staff training or inappropriate training objectives.

4 Information systems that do not provide relevant data for managing customer satisfaction, for example by not including provision for monitoring and measuring returns.

5 Specification standards not reaching the staff at the 'sharp end', and who therefore make their own interpretation of standards.

6 Role conflicts arising from staff focusing on back-office demands rather than servicing the customers.

Customers' expectations

You do not have total control over customers' expectations. They are conditioned not only by what you do and say, but by the actions of your competitors, the background of your customers and the general trading environment. When 'Next' first hit the High Street, the new chain brought about a change in the customers' expectations of all clothing retailers, raising the norm for interior design and clothing style. Shops which previously appeared to meet market expectations quickly found that the goal posts had been moved and new minimum standards applied. I anticipate that the new breed of booksellers, typified by Dillons and Waterstone's, bringing vast ranges and a congenial atmosphere to the High Street, will have a similar effect on their trade. Tesco and Sainsbury have similarly altered the market for fresh produce, accustoming their customers, *who may also be yours*, to higher standards of presentation and choice.

Our expectations are also determined by others. We are all influenced by the opinions of friends and associates and listen to their experiences. Have you, for example, visited a restaurant for the first time on someone else's recommendation? Before you go there you will have established a clear level of expectation. Probably you will have invested emotional capital, banking not only on your own enjoyment but risking your reputation for good judgement with other friends or business contacts. When the restaurant fails to meet your expectations, as happens so often, you feel disappointment and a sense of injury. It does not matter whether your expectations were justified and accurate or not; the damage will have been done and you may never return. In managing the market, therefore, we have to try to manage expectations.

Establishing fair expectations

The first and fundamental step is to decide your market positioning. If you are not sure how you want to be seen, you can hardly expect your customers to have a clear idea. Lack of clarity will occur if you 'muddle along', reacting rather than planning, with an unclear and perhaps contradictory merchandise range, a mixture of price positions, and customer/staff relations that reflect a lack of human resource plans.

The worst outcome of this approach is not poor customer expectations but simply a situation in which customers do not know *what* to expect. They are too busy to sort out this problem for you, and will go to shops that lay out their stall more clearly.

If you are not sure how you should be positioned, or are not sure how you are currently positioned *vis-à-vis* your competitors, start on the market research *now* before you go any further.

The greater part of your positioning in the market is determined by what you do: the appearance of your shops, the selection of your merchandise, and the way you communicate with and service customers face to face. However, indirect communication is also important, because it will be principally your existing customers who have personal experience of your offer. Naturally it is also important to influence the expectations of other people, for many of them might become your customers in the future if they see you, think they understand what you offer, and like the ideas and products you put forward.

Advertising through conventional media, public relations, catalogues, etc., can be powerful tools in establishing potential customers' expectations. Because advertising can be powerful it can also be potentially dangerous. There is sound commercial logic in the ASA's requirement for 'legal, decent and honest' advertising. If you mislead somebody, whether intentionally or not, you will set up expectations you will not be able to meet in the store. This will result in a lower perception of your offer and you will lose customers. Of course you should advertise in a manner that makes your products and services attractive, but never fall to the temptation to over-sell.

An unfortunate drawback arises from any real improvements you make in product and service. You create another imbalance between expectation and reality, this time with the position reversed. Perceptions and expectations will lag behind your ability to deliver an improved product. This lag will be particularly acute if either you have made dramatic changes (as sometimes happens after a take-over), or your customers buy from you infrequently or irregularly. If the local supermarket changes, most people will know quite quickly, but if a dress hire shop changed its offer it might be years before the majority of its potential customers recognized this and began to alter their perceptions.

So there is a *prima facie* argument for an investment in advertising when you make a substantive change to your offer. The real need for this promotion, and the most appropriate media, will depend on your trading circumstances, but frequency of purchase should be an important criterion in deciding whether this will be money well spent.

Do not over-stretch people's credibility. If you have cause to change dramatically they may not believe you. The view that leopards do not change their spots is widely held, and often with justification. Indeed, I do not think it is practicable to carry out a major repositioning of a retailer without rebranding. It is difficult to discard a name that has a long history, may have family connections, and probably retains some positive characteristics. I have been involved in many long and hard discussions on this subject and indeed have been party to decisions to retain a name. However, experience tells me that this does not work. Do you remember Hepworth's? That rather dreary but upstanding multiple tailor where you or your father bought rather conventional suits? I cannot convince myself that young and fashion conscious customers would have found this a credible choice even if the merchandise changed completely. It would have stretched credibility too far. In fact Hepworth's did change. It became 'Next'.

Customers compare you with competitors

Customers will compare you with your trading competitors. We all do. As customers we compare the offerings of different retailers and decide the one we are going to use. Sometimes this is a very conscious decision—for example, when we want to buy a new car or a television. More often it is much less conscious, a feeling built up that this is 'my kind of shop'. Often there is little to choose between the products on offer. Indeed, with branded goods the products are often identical. Our decision is then based on a mixture of much less tangible opinions of price and service. We go to the retailer who, in our judgement, offers a total offer most nearly in line with our needs.

From the retailer's viewpoint there are two trading gaps that we can aim to adjust:

1 We need to close the gap between what we offer (and how this is perceived) and our market's perception of its needs.

2 We need to widen the gap between our own offer and that of our competitors.

If everyone in the market wanted the same thing, and all retailers understood what was wanted, these tasks would become contradictory. Every retailer would make an identical offer and the customers would simply flip a coin before deciding which retailer to visit. Luckily life is not so perfect. You can be fairly sure that your competitors do not have a perfect understanding of your market, and the variety brought about by geography, age, social, fashion and income differences ensure that markets can be segmented by the differences in needs.

Your marketing management objective is to capitalize on these differences and differentiate your offer, while at the same time meeting the requirements of an adequate number of potential customers. In accomplishing this objective your starting point is an accurate understanding of what your customers want—and we return yet again to the essential need for effective market research. You need to compare this with your ability to deliver a matching offer, and with your competitors' offers.

At the same time, make sure that your market's idea of what you offer is the same as your point of view. This needs some brutal honesty on your part. The things that you may take for granted as being important to customers may prove to be of little importance to them. Beware of the 'unique features' that your company has built up assiduously over the years. These are often so sacrosanct within the company that their relevance to the customer has never been questioned. Don't try to sell features when your customers want to buy benefits.

Your first step in analysing the opportunities for useful differentiation is to find out those things that are important in you customers' buying decisions (Figure 8.2). Don't do this solely by relying on your judgement. Although experience is very important, and its value should never be underestimated, in this case your judgement will be

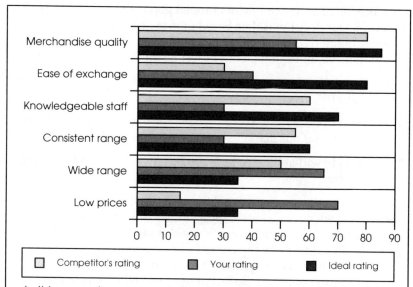

In this example, your reputation for low prices is well understood, but this is a relatively unimportant factor for the customer, though your competitor is seen to be almost out of court on price. Quality is seen to be most important, but you lag behind competitors. Similarly you are seen to be more difficult when handling exchanges, and to have less knowledgeable staff. Your range is seen to be wider than necessary, but even so does not fulfil the more important requirement for consistency. By trading more quality for price, and making goods exchange visibly easier you could greatly strengthen your position vis-à-vis your competitor.

Figure 8.2 Compare customer preferences and perceptions

The things that you may take for granted as being important to the customers may turn out to be of little importance to them.

coloured by history. Independent market research will yield the objective assessment you require. Use research also to discover how your customers rate your ability to satisfy their criteria, and how they rate your competitors (Figure 8.3). Now write down the things you actually do and deliver. Where are the gaps? Where do you fail to deliver the things that are really wanted? Are there cases where you over-deliver, creating costs for yourself but no material benefit for the customers?

The comparative performance of you and your competitors

The two parameters that determine your ability to compete are the levels of your differential advantage and your competitive advantage.

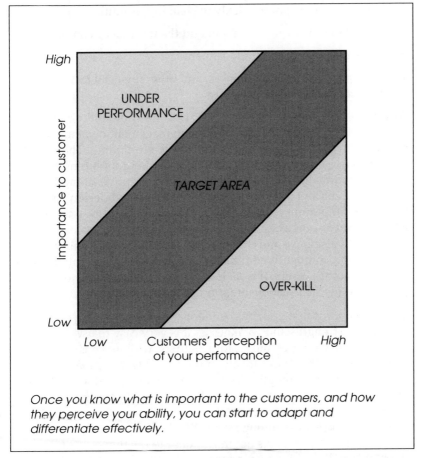

Once you know what is important to the customers, and how they perceive your ability, you can start to adapt and differentiate effectively.

Figure 8.3 Match competence and relevance
(*Source*: Christopher, Martin and Richard Yallop, 'Audit your customer service quality', *Focus*, June/July 1990)

We talked about differential advantage in the preceding section. This is concerned with the consumers' perception of the beneficial differences between you and your competitors. Competitive advantage is concerned with the way in which your company is structured and managed, allowing it to trade more efficiently and effectively than your competitors. These could include:

- the number, size and location of retail outlets

- the physical distribution system

- your stock, sales and financial information systems

- the skill and experience of your design and merchandise buying teams

- the degree of integration back through the supply line

- your ability to respond quickly to changing conditions

- the quality of your management and the training of your staff

- your access to capital for investment

- the degree of your indebtedness, and other financial factors that could affect your responsiveness.

Any of these factors could enhance or restrain your ability to compete. Their relevance to marketing management depends on their relevance to the consumer and your market positioning. Their relative importance to you depends also on your competitors' strengths. You should certainly list the areas of potential competitive strength. For example, if you sell own-branded merchandise, and design has become an important element of your product offer, this is a potential strength and a source of competitive edge. But if your major competitors also have and utilize equivalent design capability, this ceases to be a competitive *advantage*, and becomes an essential key to *survival*. In other words, it is no less important, but it will not serve to provide you with a sustainable competitive advantage.

This is a concept that you must understand. In reviewing your own company's strengths and weaknesses it is very easy to list acknowledged abilities and historical 'firsts' without considering objectively whether these are any more valuable in the market than your competitors' strengths. Consider which of your assets, whether tangible or intangible, really add value to your offer in the eyes of your customers. Take, for example, your retail staff training. Many companies focus their training on selling techniques and administration, as often as not in response to the things most likely to 'hurt' internally—sales performance against budget and the trials of sorting out inaccurate administrative documents. Your market research would probably reveal that such matters were far from the minds of the customers. They might be more concerned about dealing with sales assistants who understood the products being sold and could provide accurate and detailed advice on the features and benefits of each brand. In this case you will add more value by focusing your training programme on product knowledge.

Looking for latent opportunities

What did we all do before Sony invented the Walkman, Xerox developed plain paper copiers, and 3M introduced Post-it note pads? We got by without them. We listened to tapes and records at home; we circulated office reports and talked to colleagues rather than just copying documents to them; and we recycled the back of envelopes for notes and reminders. But even so we fell over ourselves in the rush to adopt these new products because they provided a better solution to our needs—sometimes to needs we had never really considered before, because we didn't really *expect* a solution.

This is the final gap in the marketing chain: the gap between customers' needs and preferences and their expectations. As customers we decide what we can expect of a shop, or indeed of a whole retail sector. Sometimes we do not place much hope in finding a shop that will meet our best expectations. Occasionally we are pleasantly surprised, perhaps by a shop that stocks a wide size range, or remains open until late in the evening. These innovations can release a previously unfulfilled demand, perhaps unrecognized by any competitors and sometimes unacknowledged by customers as well.

I doubt whether my neighbours in a sleepy, domestic suburb would have put much money on the chances of a local convenience store trading successfully. Most of them would have reckoned that they did all the necessary shopping during the other six days. Yet now the store is there, opening every day of the year, and usually to 10.00 pm, the place positively humming, even on a wet Sunday afternoon.

New opportunities in retailing lie buried deep in the market, and you need insight to uncover them. You have to prospect for them in the same way that you would search for oil. You need good research and a willingness to search and search again. Above all when you do find an opportunity you need the courage to 'pick up the ball and run with it'. There is a big difference between being courageous and foolhardy. More retailers have been foolhardy than have shown commercial courage. Even the biggest have blundered into acquisitions and overseas development without a shred of research to justify the millions of pounds of shareholders' funds they commit to their adventures. But if you analyse your market carefully and objectively you will find opportunities and the arguments for investment. But there will always be many more convincing reasons put forward against innovation than are put forward in its favour. Be on your guard against these; a few of the more common reasons to avoid change are shown in Checklist 8.1 opposite.

Checklist ✓

8.1 TWELVE REASONS WHY RETAIL MANAGERS DON'T INNOVATE

- *'Nobody else has done it, so it can't be a real opportunity.'* Well, they wouldn't, would they, if this is a genuine opportunity to innovate? But beware, the 'gap in the market' may be there because it is uneconomic for the industry to fill it successfully. You would have to tackle the more difficult task of changing the industry economics.

- *'We tried something like that in 1964 and it didn't work then.'* Corporate memories can be very long, but remember as well that the original attempt may have been misdirected and circumstances may have changed.

- *'There is an element of risk.'* Of course there is. A company's job is to identify and manage risk.

- *'The MD wouldn't like it so I won't suggest it.'* What is the MD doing if not positively encouraging innovation? If you are the chief executive, are you doing, saying or implying anything that might discourage people from bringing forward ideas?

- *'The MD will take all the credit and glory, so why bother?'* Read the comment above.

- *'Group HQ wouldn't like it.'* If you're the Group MD, read the comment above. It applies to you too.

- *'We don't have time.'* You are probably right. The biggest risk attached to most innovation programmes is that inadequate resources are provided. If you have the confidence to back the idea, you must back it adequately and not just give lip service to innovation so that you can make the right noises in the annual report.

- *'We haven't any money for investment.'* If this is a fair comment, put the effort into the core business so that it can generate investment funds.

- *'We can't accept start-up losses.'* Few innovations make an immediate return. So, is this an excuse for inactivity or a symptom of deeper problems that need to be sorted out first?

- *'We haven't got the experience.'* Probably you do need fresh experience. It is much less risky to recruit the talent you need rather than try to bluff your way into new areas.

- *'It's a nice idea, but can we make it more like we are doing already?'* Organizations do not like change, and they will try to redraft new ideas into a form that is not really new at all. You may convince yourselves, but you will not convince the buying public.

- *'Let's think about it again next year.'* Why are you *really* putting it in the bottom drawer?

9

Quality

The art of successful retailing can be succinctly put as: 'Selling goods that won't come back to customers who will.'

I cannot think of any area of retailing where a continuing relationship between the shopkeeper and his customers is not important. Customers *will* return if they believe they are obtaining value for money, and the quality of the product and service you provide will determine each customer's perception of your value. Customers' perceptions of *product* quality will be founded as much in their impressions of the overall *service* provided as in the absolute quality of the merchandise. In retailing, product and service quality are inextricably linked.

The art of successful retailing has been summed up with a rather neat definition: *Selling goods that won't come back to customers who will*. This brings the issue of quality neatly into focus.

Every business needs to remain competitive. Some are lucky enough to market a unique product or service that cannot be obtained or substituted elsewhere. This ensures that customers are left with only two options: to buy or not to buy. If your heart is set on owning a Rolls Royce, there is only one manufacturer who can make one.

Generally speaking, High Street retailers are not so lucky. Like most businesses in any trade you must try harder to remain competitive, gaining and keeping the custom of people who have plenty of alternative sources of supply. In the end nearly all your marketing decisions are concerned with maintaining competitive advantage, using whatever levers and tools you have available. You can change your prices, modify your range, redesign your shop, move to better locations or launch an advertising campaign. All these actions may increase your sales and profitability if they are done for the right reasons, but they all invite the competition to match you step for step. 'Next' launched a radically new approach to clothes retailing and spawned a whole generation of 'me too' retail formats. Olympus did the same for sports shops.

Quality is another tool that can lever more competitive advantage out of the marketplace. Surprisingly few retailers have capitalized on the benefits it can bestow on the bottom line. I suspect the reason for this is that quality depends more than most attributes on *people*, whose behaviour can take a long time to change and much hard work to maintain at above average levels. Also, retailers have not paid enough attention to discovering what their customers really want, and have not discovered the high value and priority that customers will put on above-average quality.

Whatever the reasons, the evidence of the High Street shows the strength of good quality in maintaining a competitive position. The classic example must be Marks & Spencer, whose concept and standards of quality are embedded in the minds of staff, suppliers and customers alike. Quality delivers security to both M&S and to its customers. Think what happens when their quality falls down and the sleeve comes adrift from your new shirt. Do you complain to all your friends, and vow never to set foot inside the store again? No, you don't, even though this might well have been your reaction to a more nondescript fashion chain. In practice you take it back, knowing it will be exchanged without an argument, and feeling almost apologetic for finding a chink in their armour.

Likewise, think what happens when the service quality of M&S falls down, and you cannot find the colour or size you wanted from their smart new coordinated designer range. Do you blame their crass inefficiency, their computer, or their idle staff, as you would be tempted to do elsewhere? No, you blame *yourself* for failing to arrive early enough in the day or week, when other more organized shoppers might have been more lucky.

The moral of these little tales is that an assured and consistent level of product and service quality will sustain you through the bad times as well as the good. People accept that accidents happen. But if your reputation is more marginal, just one unfortunate episode can be enough to tip the balance, ensuring that one customer, and perhaps several of that customer's friends, never set foot in your store again.

I remember a classic example of this when I was working for a children's wear chain, now a major and successful national company with a high reputation for quality. But at the time product quality was undistinguished and service was uneven. If a product failed to perform satisfactorily the most usual customer reaction was a resigned shrug of the shoulders, and little else. Customers hardly felt

> *An assured and consistent level of quality will see you through the bad times as well as the good.*

it worth returning the goods to the shop because the next garment
would be no better, they thought, and there was bound to be an
upsetting argument with the manager. So the fading, threadbare
garment would stay in the wardrobe, providing a constant reminder
of the customer's misfortune every time the door was opened. This
was no way to build a business. You cannot afford to lose five or ten
years of regular custom for the price of a kid's shirt and a more
positive attitude to quality within the business.

Quality affects perceptions

Undoubtedly, therefore, quality has a strong effect on customers'
perceptions of a store. Quality does not have to be in the 'Rolls Royce'
class, but it does need to be in step with the way customers perceive
the shop's overall offer. If the retailer trades under a style called, say
'Everything Must Go!', with a pile-it-high, sell-it-cheap philosophy
and permanent red Sale banners, quality expectations will be tuned to
that level of trade. Customers will be delighted if the product and
service quality is better than they expected, but their initial
expectations will not have been very high.

By contrast, if you put creased merchandise, with threads hanging
free, into a sophisticated, polished wood and carpet environment,
their overall perceptions of the store will be quickly damaged. This
will happen even if the very same people would happily buy the
same merchandise at the same price at the local market.

People also like consistency in quality as in other features of your
offer. If service or product quality is inconsistent, even if at times it is
better than the most optimistic expectations, you will create
discomfort. Customers hate discomfort. 'I just want to know where I
am', or 'I wish they wouldn't keep on chopping and changing' are
two of the commonest complaints levelled at shopkeepers.

The trouble with quality is that it is a very intangible selling point that
defies measurement. This may come as a surprise to your quality
controller, who is used to measuring products against sample
specifications. The controller deals with *actual* quality, which can be
measured. The customers do not have access to the sophisticated
measuring and testing equipment of the quality controller and more
often has to rely on judgement: they establish a *perception* of quality.
Some of these perceptions will be based on experience, but their
judgement will also be based on looks, staff, and other people's
opinions.

Only the customer can judge quality

Because the judgement of quality, like beauty, lies in the eye of the
beholder, there is no fixed reference point for judging quality.
Customers' perceptions of your quality can change for many reasons,
and not all of these are within your control.

- *Perceptions may change if you change what you are doing*: new
  products, new specifications or new suppliers. However,
  remember that there will be a time lag between actual and
  perceived changes. Sometimes it can take years for improvements
  in quality to seep through into your market's consciousness, unless
  you take steps to signal the change through, say, store design
  changes or relevant advertising and promotional campaigns.

- *The customers' own needs and expectations can change.* Individual
  requirements may change, for example as customers grows older
  or changes lifestyle. Market segment attitudes can also change over
  time, with the needs or expectations of an entire group modified by
  social, demographic or economic shifts.

- *Your competitors may change what they are doing*, thus altering the
  standards by which customers judge quality. The major food
  retailers have done this during the past few years, creating norms
  for variety and product quality that make other supermarkets look
  tired and unimaginative. 'Next' achieved a similar sea change in
  the perceptions of mail order, particularly among consumers with
  no experience but often vivid perceptions of traditional mail order
  catalogues and their service offer. Conditioned by years of direct
  response advertisements in the Sunday supplements, which
  always quoted 'delivery within 28 days', customers were amazed
  to find the Next Directory promising 48-hour delivery. (However,
  for the major catalogue companies this did not represent a
  technical problem—they established 2–3 day deliveries years ago,
  but simply *omitted to tell anyone* outside their traditional markets.

The effect of quality on profitability

All sources of competitive advantage are worth while only if they
enable you to maintain or improve profitability relative to your
competitors. In any market, the more uniform the offer in terms of
price, product and service, the greater the uniformity of profit levels.
An offer that is truly differentiated, or a business process that is better
or cheaper than that of competitors, will yield above-average
profitability. This is the sure test of competitive edge, and one that
quality passes confidently on the available evidence.

A lot of investigative work has been done by the Strategic Research Institute, which maintains a huge and detailed database of company financial and trading information. Among their conclusions is the confirmation that quality does have a real and very significant effect on profitability. Firms delivering high quality in their products and services achieve returns on investment more than twice those of otherwise viable firms at the other end of the quality spectrum. I can think of few other policy changes you could make that could have such a significant effect.

The Institute's PIMS study (Profit Impact of Market Strategy) measures quality *as perceived by the company's customers,* and *relative to the competition,* the two key components discussed earlier. There is no attempt to measure absolute quality, partly because this would be difficult to measure consistently across different trades, but most importantly because it is not directly relevant. Why does higher relative perceived quality result in higher profitability? (See Figure 9.1.) The benefits demonstrated by the PIMS research programme are far reaching and credible in the light of practical experience:

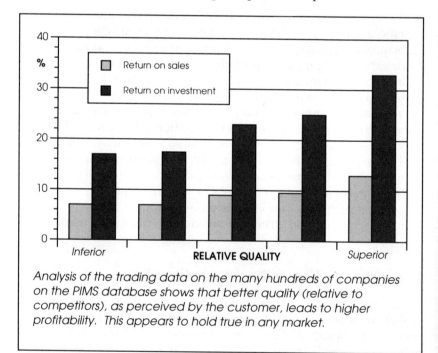

Analysis of the trading data on the many hundreds of companies on the PIMS database shows that better quality (relative to competitors), as perceived by the customer, leads to higher profitability. This appears to hold true in any market.

Figure 9.1 Quality and profit
(*Source*: Reprinted with permission of The Free Press, a division of Macmillan, Inc., from Buzzell, R. D. and B. T. Gale, *The PIMS Principles: Linking Strategy to Performance*, The Free Press, 1987. Copyright ©1987 by The Free Press)

1 Stronger customer loyalty.

2 More repeat purchases.

3 Less vulnerability to price wars.

4 Ability to command higher relative prices without affecting market share.

5 Lower marketing costs.

6 Improvements in market share.

Marks & Spencer provides a graphic example of how every one of these benefits can be incorporated into a retail business. Mail order companies will also recognize the reality of these benefits because they, more than other types of retailer, are able to measure the cost and profitability of individual customers. New customers are expensive to acquire. In a conventional retail environment you may not notice this, because the costs are hidden. You do not know how many new customers arrive through recommendation, and you do not know the direct impact of advertising and promotion. But in direct marketing these costs can be calculated. A new customer can cost £30 to £40 to obtain. You may require each new customer to spend £300 before you have recovered your acquisition costs, and if your trade depends on repeat purchases your aim must be to maximize the time over which the customer trades with you. If you lose too many customers too soon, you will lose money and go out of business.

By contrast, satisfied customers create a virtuous circle. They continue to trade with you, yielding new gross margins without adding to overhead costs. While you may advertise to bring in new customers, you do not have to replace dissatisfied customers who have dropped you from their shopping repertoire. Satisfied customers are less likely to risk dissatisfaction by going to your competitors. They are also more likely to recommend you to their friends, who become new customers without you incurring additional advertising costs. And if that satisfaction depends on features other than price, you will be less susceptible to competitors who challenge your position with lower prices. Indeed, price is often used by consumers as a measure of quality. If the price is too low, they question the adequacy of your quality.

The vital importance of quality to customers

Quality would not be so much of an issue if it were not so important in the customers' eyes. The decision to use a store results from the subjective assessment of a whole range of potential benefits. These include:

- *Location* Is the shop conveniently located, near the other shops I use, close to parking or the bus stop?

- *Opening hours* Is the shop open when I need it?

- *Range* Does the shop stock a wide enough range in the sizes or colours or brands I want?

- *Staff* How do the staff treat me, and do they know what they are talking about? Do they look down on me or take me seriously?

- *Price* Are they competitive—if there is a close alternative store—and can I afford the overall price levels of the shop?

- *Quality* Is the quality good enough to do the job, and is it fair in relation to the price I am prepared to pay?

- *Image* Does this seem to be a shop catering for people like me?

Rarely do we find a shop that gives us a tailor-made profile that fits exactly with our own perception of our needs. In reality, consciously or not, we make compromises and trade off one benefit or drawback against others. My research in several retail markets yields an interesting conclusion: quality is the one factor that customers are least prepared to trade for another. In the final analysis they will opt for quality and sacrifice other benefits. They will literally go out of their way to get better quality.

You can use, as I did, market research to evaluate how your market trades off the different components of your offer, using a statistical technique called, not surprisingly, trade-off analysis. In the markets I have examined quality leads all other benefits by a wide margin, and is becoming more important over time. Quality also becomes a more significant factor as the customers grow older, resulting both from the necessity to buy wisely when family incomes are strained by the expense of growing children, and the discretion that arrives with greater maturity. Even so, the young and fashion conscious, unencumbered, 18–24 year olds still rate quality above other factors.

Perceptions and expectations

I have highlighted the importance of customers' perceptions. For them (and you, because you are also a customer) perceptions *are* reality. I have no doubt that there are some shops that you never enter, because you do not think—for reasons of image, price or quality—that they are your kind of shop. How do you know, if you've never visited them? You are making a judgement based upon your perceptions, and these can be very strongly held without the need for explicit evidence. Similarly, your actions (or in this case inaction) are based on your perceptions. There was a long forgotten advertisement for Guinness stout, which featured a girl saying, 'I've never tried Guinness because I don't like it'. Think about it. Her expectations were determined by her perceptions rather than her experience, to the obvious frustration of the Guinness marketing team.

How many potential customers do you have lurking out there in the High Street, ignoring your shops because they are acting on the evidence of their perceptions? Do they *think* that your quality is inadequate? Are they right?

If you did persuade or cajole them into your shop, how would they react? What happens when perceptions meet reality? Would they say 'That's just what I expected', or would they be surprised? Rightly or wrongly, we all take a view about the product or service quality we expect from a supplier. Our perceptions lead to an expectation of a certain level of quality. If the actual quality encountered *exceeds* our expectations we are delighted. If it does not meet our expectations, we are not only disappointed, we feel we have been 'done' and our confidence is seriously undermined.

When our expectations are exceeded we feel very pleased with ourselves. We are much more likely to use the shop again, and we shall probably tell our family or friends. Our general level of confidence in the shop rises. This, for the shopkeeper, is a case of nothing succeeding like success, and the shopkeeper's only problem, though this is one I can live with, is that the customers' expectations will be re-aligned to the new and higher level of service, making it more challenging over time to continue exceeding expectations.

When our minimum expectations are met, we are satisfied. This is the neutral state in which most business in a stable relationship is conducted between customer and retailer.

It is much more serious when the shopkeeper fails to meet customers' expectations. The relationship can quickly turn sour. An isolated incident in an otherwise successful record is not necessarily damaging, but a succession of problems afflicting a regular customer, or a single occurrence for a less established one, will be enough to lose that customer for life.

Because expectations are based on perceptions they are, yet again, based on relative rather than absolute criteria. Your expectations might be very low. If your British Rail sandwich turns out to be fresh, crisp and tasty instead of the tired cardboard you expected, you are likely to be quite unreasonably pleased, and convinced that BR is finally on the mend. However, in contrast, if a supplier promised a delivery on Friday afternoon, and it actually arrived the following Monday morning, you might feel very disappointed and frustrated even if the delay had no detrimental effect on your business.

Ideas

9.1 A USEFUL FORMULA TO REMEMBER

$$\text{PERCEIVED QUALITY} = \frac{\text{DELIVERY}}{\text{EXPECTATIONS}}$$

Although there was no real problem, the supplier created one by raising expectations that it could not fulfil (see Ideas 9.1).

So one of your important objectives in managing quality is to manage customers' expectations of quality. Too high a level of expectation can be as damaging as too low a quality product or service. Over-zealous advertising or an over-sophisticated store design can raise quality expectations to a level you cannot meet consistently. Your advertising and store design may indeed be the right direction for you to go, but you must ensure that the products and services you offer are in concert with these other signals, which consumers will use to form a judgement about the quality levels they should expect.

Improving quality

This book does not set out to prescribe detailed quality specifications. These will naturally vary from trade to trade, and each sector of the industry has its own experts able to advise on specific product quality issues and standards. My concern is primarily with the management of quality and its use as a marketing tool (see Checklist 9.1). As we have seen, quality can help to secure your competitive position and allow you to develop a more stable business that is more immune to price competition and to the commercial risks of occasional, accidental lapses in quality standards.

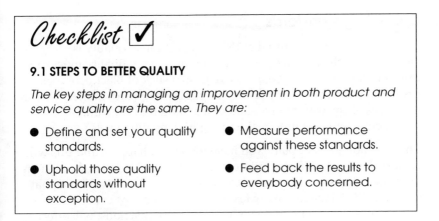

Checklist ☑

9.1 STEPS TO BETTER QUALITY

The key steps in managing an improvement in both product and service quality are the same. They are:

- Define and set your quality standards.

- Uphold those quality standards without exception.

- Measure performance against these standards.

- Feed back the results to everybody concerned.

Defining standards

You must define the standards of service and the standards of product quality that you intend to maintain. If you do not do this, you will confuse your suppliers, the people working in your business, and your customers.

Defining standards is different from assuming, expecting or demanding standards. Do not assume that your suppliers know the standards you require. They may believe their own standards are appropriate to your business, and they may well be, but does each of your suppliers conform to the *same* standards? Ask your partner to try on different clothes of the same size, in the same shop, and you will discover that standards usually vary considerably.

Similarly, you must not assume that your own employees share the same standards if these are not spelled out. Most people will adopt standards of work and behaviour that they *believe* will be right for their market, but without universal standards there is a risk that some people's assumed standards will be quite inappropriate. This does not imply that they will be lax; indeed, they may be over-zealous in applying their perception of company rules, and lose valuable long-term custom in the process.

You need standards because customers *want* standards. Above all, customers like consistency of service, product quality and market positioning. You have little chance of achieving consistency if you do not set standards to which everyone connected with the business can try to adhere.

> *You need standards because customers want standards. Above all, customers like consistency of service, product quality and market positioning.*

Upholding standards

Your objective is to ensure that the right attitude to quality is embedded in the organization. The commitment to quality must run through the company, like the message in a stick of Blackpool rock. Break open the firm at any point—on the switchboard, in the office, in the shops or the warehouse—and you should find the same, consistent commitment to maintaining high quality levels.

This will not 'just happen'. You have to make it happen, and this will require demonstrable commitment from the top. Unscrew the sign on your door that says 'Managing Director' and replace it with one that says 'Quality Manager'. Now leave the door open. At every opportunity, ask yourself how your actions, or inactions, will affect quality either directly or by inference. Is it really saving money to leave that planned maintenance scheme on the shelf for another year? Is your insistence on proof of purchase before a customer can exchange something really saving you money or losing you future trade? Should you really accept that delivery of popular, high margin stock when you know some of the seams are faulty?

To begin with you will probably be accused of being pedantic, perhaps even of being ruthless. But in the end, if you persevere with the quality issue, you will win. You will succeed because your staff are also customers. They may not be *your* customers, but they are certainly someone's customers and they have the same respect and need for quality services and products. Once they recognize that they are free, and indeed encouraged, to maintain the same standards at work that they would wish to receive as customers, they will become your best advocates.

Measuring and feeding back performance

When you set off on a cross-country journey you keep an eye on the road signs, the map and the time. You use this information to keep track of your progress. If you do not do this you can easily get lost and find yourself either delayed or straying from your intended route. Constant feedback helps you to stay on track, and you need this as much with quality management as you do for more mundane tasks such as getting to an appointment on time.

You will need to set up systems to get feedback on quality management (see Checklist 9.2). You may already have these systems in place for measuring the quality of the merchandise you sell. You certainly need to check samples against your technical specifications, and to check incoming deliveries against your samples. But do you have any method of checking how merchandise performs in use? This

Checklist ☑

9.2 FEEDBACK ON QUALITY PERFORMANCE

- Use the merchandise you sell in your own home.

- Encourage other head office managers to do the same.

- Encourage shop staff to talk with known customers who appear to be coming in less often. Is there a quality problem?

- Collect and collate information on returned goods.

- React to this information— don't just file it.

- Tell suppliers what customers think of their goods.

- Commission market research to find out how *your* customers assess quality.

- Circulate the research report to every employee.

- Try to measure all the factors which affect quality perceptions: you can't easily improve things you do not measure.

does not have to be elaborate. If you sell clothes, for example, are you or your family or staff wearing some of the clothes you sell? Do you do the washing and ironing? You will find out soon enough whether your quality measures up to the day-to-day needs of your customers.

Do you encourage your retail staff to talk to your customers and find out what they think of the goods they have bought from you in the past? Do you collate information on returned goods? Much more importantly, find out what happens to this information. If you are not sure, you have a problem. Summary reports should be on your desk and you should react to them. This will ensure that everyone starts taking more notice of returns.

You can also use market research to find out about quality standards and consistency. A few focus groups held with customers will give you a very accurate guide to their view of both your service and product quality, and will also show you how this compares with your competitors' performances. Quantitative research techniques can give you even more specific information, by providing you with a measure of customers' attitudes to quality. This may be more expensive, and it may not be essential, but if you need conclusive proof to demonstrate the scale of a problem to other managers in your company, well-conducted quantitative research data are not easy to refute!

Product quality

You are dependent on your suppliers to deliver improved product quality, but their performance depends on your attitude to quality. The first step is to make sure that your suppliers understand your commitment to quality. At the start of your quality campaign you may have to depend on some convincing preaching, but as time goes on quality become much more demonstrable and measurable. When you have the data to show how rising sales or improving customer perceptions match quality improvements, share this with your suppliers. When your staff are as committed to quality as you are, they will start preaching as well. Make sure that your suppliers meet your staff, and they will get the message too. In time suppliers' commitment to quality will develop because they will recognize an opportunity to build business with you.

By all means negotiate prices with enthusiasm, but remember that you get what you pay for. If you beat suppliers into the ground they will start looking for ways to economize. To begin with this can be very healthy, because they may uncover new ways to manufacture more efficiently. In the long run, however, they may start cutting corners and substituting poorer materials or cutting back on quality control procedures.

There is a well-documented trend towards closer supplier relationships, often with a reduced list of preferred suppliers, and this can yield real dividends in quality management. You both become more interdependent, and more information is shared between you. The result of this improved and more consistent communication is a quicker and more accurate reaction to the market, and deliveries that arrive on time and on specification.

However, such relationships take time to build and depend on mutual trust and commitment. You will not have this at the beginning. You will need to impose your standards of discipline, and sooner or later you are going to reject deliveries that fail to meet your specification. There is very little chance that this will happen on a line you didn't really want anyway. It will be one that is immensely popular, carries the best margins of the season, and links with other products in your range. The temptation to accept delivery will be enormous, but you must resist it. Send it back. With luck you will only have to do this once with any supplier. And if it happens with annoying frequency, do you really want to continue the relationship?

Service quality

Service quality can be much more difficult to manage than product quality. It is more difficult to measure. Service is also intangible: you cannot keep reserve stocks of service and send them out to branches who appear to be running short. Service is created and delivered in an instant, yet memories of service can be long. The customers' judgement about service is the only valid measurement, and is likely to affect their usage and attitudes of the service provider for a long time.

Despite the transient and intangible nature of service, it is a fundamental part of the product you sell. Customers do not make an artificial separation of product and service quality. If service is poor they will happily ignore a first-rate product. Yet despite its vital importance service has a poor reputation in this country.

Look closely at your training programmes. Is there a focus to this activity? There probably is, and it is likely to include selling techniques, administration and product knowledge. But do you teach people about service? Do you really understand what service is, and do they understand its importance as part of the total product? If you do not know which elements of service are important to your customers, or how well you succeed in meeting them, you are inviting disaster. You must do whatever market research the size and budget of your company allows to get answers, and then share this information with all your staff.

You also must ensure that you are not asking them to resolve a conflict of responsibility created by your own rules. For example, one of the key criteria by which customers judge children's wear shops is their perceived willingness to exchange or refund purchases. This is not because mothers are unable to make up their minds. It is because they are often unaccompanied by their children (or if they are, the kids are fretful and tired) and cannot be sure that the clothes will either fit or be liked by the children. If your rules make it difficult for mothers to return items, or they have to fill in forms and wait for counter-signatures from the manager, you will be failing to deliver a core component of the product and you will lose custom to more enlightened competitors.

So what exactly is service? Set out in Table 9.1 is a list of the dimensions of service established by an American academic research team. It provides a very explicit and encompassing guide. The relative importance of the various dimensions will vary according to your business. However, the table provides a very good framework for judging the areas on which you should focus attention. It can also be used as the basis for market research to discover how your market ranks each component, and how well your business succeeds in meeting their service needs.

Table 9.1 Dimensions of retail quality

Quality dimension	Description	Questions customers ask
Tangibles	Appearance of the store, its merchandise and displays and staff	• Am I at ease and comfortable in the shop? • Does the merchandise look good? • Can I find what I want? • Do the staff look helpful, competent and approachable?
Reliability	Ability to perform the promised service dependably and accurately, and supply goods of dependable quality	• Are the goods I want in stock? • Am I sold things that perform as I wanted and expected? • Does the store do everything it promised me it would do? • Do staff show a sincere interest in solving my problems?
Responsiveness	Willingness to help customers and provide prompt service	• Are staff available when I want service? • Am I kept waiting? • Are staff willing to help me?
Competence	Possession of the required skills and knowledge	• Do they know about the products they are trying to sell? • Will they give me reliable advice? • Do they help me in an efficient way?
Courtesy	Politeness, respect, consideration and friendliness of staff	• Do staff interfere when I just want to browse? • Do they seem to look down on me? • Am I made to feel important or uncomfortable?

Credibility	Perceived trustworthiness, believability and honesty of the retail company and its staff	• Am I getting honest advice? • Am I being sold something I don't really want? • Can I trust these people?
Security	Freedom from doubt, danger or risk	• Could I bring something back without an argument? • Would they handle a complaint courteously? • Do they sell safe and reliable merchandise? • Am I being pressurized?
Access	Physical access to the store and its merchandise; ease of contact with staff and the personal approachability	• Is there good physical access to and around the store? • Is the store open at convenient times? • Are staff available and approachable?
Communication	The retailer's ability to keep customers informed, and ability to listen to them	• Can I find my way around the store? • Are they interested in my point of view and my needs? • Do they provide useful information? • Do they keep in touch, helpfully, by ads, catalogues, etc?
Understanding the customer	Customers recognize that the retailer makes an effort to know them and their needs	• Is the style and quality of merchandise consistent? • Does the store seem to understand my needs? • Do staff ever address me by name, or recognize me?

(*Source*: Adapted with permission of The Free Press, a division of Macmillan, Inc., from Zeithaml, V. A., A. Parasuraman and L. L. Berry, *Delivering Quality Service: Balancing Customer Perceptions and Expectations*. The Free Press, 1990. Copyright ©1990 by The Free Press)

10

Retail location strategy

> *Your first priority is to make sure that you understand the way people in your market choose where to shop.*

There is no such thing as a national retail market. This may seem an unlikely assertion to make in a country in which the retail trade is dominated by national retailing chains. Many companies certainly have nationally distributed outlets, and often they are household names, promoted and advertised with uniformity across the country. You can measure their share of national markets and compare consumer perceptions, usage and awareness. But in real, day-to-day trading terms retailers compete in local markets. Each shopping centre represents a different market where resident retailers compete for their share of local expenditure. Indeed, not only do retailers compete with each other in a shopping centre, but shopping centres also compete with their neighbours.

Thus local influences such as the physical size, number and position of retailers, the trading tone of the shopping centre, the presence of competing centres, and the demographics of the local population all combine to influence the performance of an individual trader. In the case of multiple retailers, their overall national performance is neither more nor less than the sum of many local, individual branch performances. This means that the competitive environment at the local level can be critically important to the multiple retailer's overall success. If the branch portfolio is not well planned and maintained the proportion of local stores trading in inappropriate locations can rise to the point where the overall fortunes of the group are put in jeopardy. This could happen even if the store brand is both attractive to consumers and well received by them. To this extent the success of local trading is independent of the national marketing and market positioning strategy.

If the overall value of a retailer's offer is poor it is likely to fail almost everywhere. It is unlikely that it will be redeemed in particular locations. But, in contrast, an attractive offer cannot be guaranteed to have market or financial success in every location. Financial success can be compromised by unusually high rent and rate overheads or poorly managed variable costs such as labour or stock losses. And an inappropriate location that does not match the market positioning of the retail brand can wreak havoc also.

For the retailer, therefore, it is just as important to manage local markets as it is to manage national markets. Retailers have always managed branches, often with great efficiency in the implementation of promotions and the management of costs. But you must take a wider view of local markets, recognizing the external factors that affect trade—particularly the suitability of the local shopping centre and the sources of competition in the local environment.

Fitting location decisions with marketing strategy

It is essential not to underestimate the importance of achieving coherence between your overall marketing strategy and the location of individual branches. Most shoppers leave home with a reasonably clear idea of what they wish to buy. This will influence their choice among available shopping centres, which of course differs markedly in character. Small suburban centres are ideal for everyday food shopping and are particularly useful for people who can spare little time away from home or cannot travel easily. City centres deliver much greater variety, often more choice of merchandise and more 'entertainment value'. They are attractive to people who have the time, money and transport to enjoy them but are positively unpleasant for a mother shepherding young children through the crowds and bus queues. Thus a young, free-spending office girl will see little joy in visiting her neighbourhood shopping parade to find this season's fashions, while her mother is unlikely to travel 25 miles into the city centre for the weekend's food supplies.

Recognize differing shopping habits

Shopping habits will therefore be determined by customers' personal circumstances, and the match between their perceived requirements and the available shopping centres (see Figure 10.1). For each centre they will develop a personal shopping repertoire: a short list of retailers in each merchandise category which perception and experience suggests may be suited to their needs (Figure 10.2). The size of this repertoire varies. The young will visit more shops than the old. Generally women want to visit more shops than men. Shops outside this repertoire languish almost unnoticed. Sometimes they are

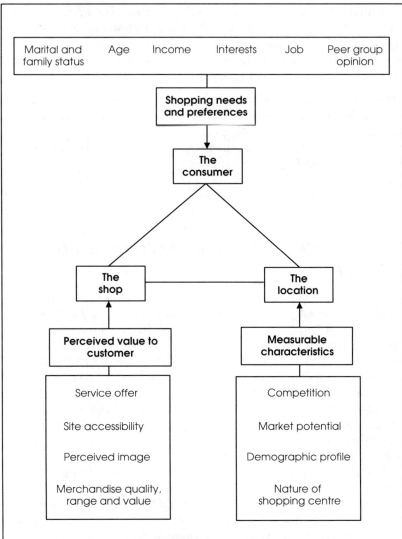

The objective of local market strategy is to achieve a fit between consumers' needs, the market positioning of your stores, and their location. Any mismatch will reduce the efficiency of your stores and the effectiveness of the basic marketing offer.

Figure 10.1 Location strategy objective

clearly and understandably irrelevant. A young, unmarried adult is unlikely to notice children's clothes shops. But, equally, shops will be discarded from the list because they, or their merchandise range, appear out of place in the context of that particular shopping centre. Imagine what it would be like to discover a branch of Asprey's in the less pretentious areas of Handsworth or Neasden, or a suburban

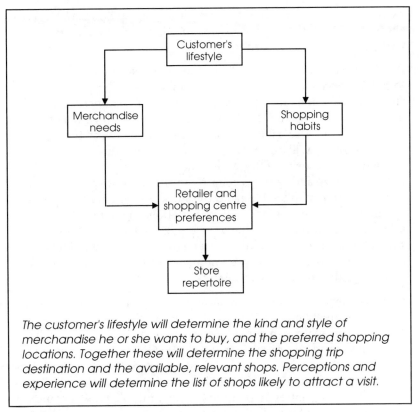

The customer's lifestyle will determine the kind and style of merchandise he or she wants to buy, and the preferred shopping locations. Together these will determine the shopping trip destination and the available, relevant shops. Perceptions and experience will determine the list of shops likely to attract a visit.

Figure 10.2 The customer's site selection process

butcher trading in the upmarket Burlington Arcade. Of course the lack of fit between retailer and shopping location is usually more subtle. More often you will find that ranges stocked are too small or too fashionable, or of inappropriate price and quality. Unfortunately such subtleties can be sufficient to tip the economic balance of the outlet towards unprofitability.

The need to adjust to local conditions can be a particular problem for multiple retailers who stock a nationally distributed range and aim for a uniform brand position in all their outlets. If they are to succeed efficiently, this uniformity must be matched by a constant and appropriate shop location policy, which can be difficult to maintain in the shifting sands of shopping centre development. It certainly requires a thorough understanding of the retailer's customer market needs and shopping habits, combined with excellent information on the many thousands of shopping centres in this country. Equipped with both knowledge and single mindedness, however, the retailer *can* build a chain of aptly located branches. But you must avoid the temptation to open branches for attractive but irrelevant reasons: for example, the development of a new, all singing and dancing shopping centre, the perceived need for 'flagship' branches or the rush to build up an 'economic' network.

An alternative approach is to tailor the range and image of the store to fit local needs. There are practical limitations to this strategy. If one shop style and one range is inappropriate for 500 shops, it is equally inappropriate to try to run 500 separate entities, each with a unique style and stock. A sensible solution usually lies between these extremes. Much will depend on the capability of your stock management systems. If the system monitors and controls stock by range, line, size and perhaps colour you should be able to detect local variations in demand and amend the stock package accordingly. You are already probably aware of local variations in the merchandise sales mix. The important thing to recognize is that while these are sometimes caused by central or branch management decisions, or local space restrictions, the predominant cause is local competition and local shopping needs and habits.

In the UK there is a substantial variety of shopping centre 'characters' and the relatively minor changes in emphasis that modified stock packages can achieve may not be enough to ensure a close match between your retail proposition and the needs of the local shopping population. My own research has demonstrated that there are at least two dozen significantly different kinds of shopping location among the 1000 largest centres, and I doubt if any multiple retailer could operate efficiently in each of these centre types.

Living with history

I expect you have heard the tale of the apocryphal country yokel who, on being asked for directions, studied the horizon and stated helpfully, 'Well, if I were you, I wouldn't have started from here.' So it is with most multiple retail businesses. Their retail property portfolio reflects many years of history, changing needs and objectives and the debris of past take-overs and mergers. If you were starting from scratch, you probably would not select many of the branch locations in which you are trading with one retail format or another. Wholesale closure or re-allocation of branches can be an expensive business and is not always practical in a depressed property market or poor trading period. But in the end it will be

> *You are probably aware of local variations in the merchandise sales mix: the predominant cause is local competition and local shopping needs and habits.*

necessary, otherwise your long-term financial performance will be constrained and dictated by long-forgotten property decisions.

Most large retailers will find that they have a significant proportion of their outlets sited in centres that are inappropriate and restrict their overall profit potential. You will need to grasp this particular nettle because, as I discuss later in this chapter, location strategy has greater leverage on profitability than almost any other management action. In the end there are only two choices. Either you dis-invest from the locations that do not fit, or you run a portfolio of businesses, allocating the most appropriate sites to each of several retail brands that meet different customer needs. If your company already maintains more than one retail chain, this can provide an excellent opportunity to improve the return on your property assets, simply by redistributing retail branches to be used by more appropriate retail businesses.

Finding the right fit

There are a number of techniques that can help you to evaluate the most appropriate types of location for your retail business. These methods do not identify specific locations, an important step that is covered later and for which there are now several technical aids to help decision making.

Your first priority is to make sure that you understand the way people in your market choose where to shop. There are two senses to the word 'where' and they are both appropriate in this context. Firstly, there is the geographic sense. People will make decisions about the town or shopping centre they will visit, and this decision will depend on their personal circumstances and on the type of goods they want to buy. Secondly, they will choose where to shop in the sense of 'which shops do I want to visit?' Indeed, this question will often determine the shopping centre that is most appropriate for a particular trip. Table 10.1 provides some examples to demonstrate how people in different situations and with differing needs and preferences may make this decision.

It should be no surprise to find that shopping habits and preferences depend very much on individual lifestyles and family circumstances. This can be very important in branch location planning, because it is vital to position branches in the shopping centres frequented by the retailer's target customers, and where they go and expect to find different categories of merchandise. We all vary the frequency, value and destination of our shopping trips according to our needs and preferences. You can use common sense and personal experience to predict these patterns, and market research can (and usually should)

Table 10.1 Lifestyle and shopping habits

Shoppers	Lifestyle	Shopping needs	Shopping habits
Tracey	A single girl aged 20 and living at home with her parents. Works as a 'temp' in offices mainly in the centre of Wolverhampton. Has a 'steady' boyfriend and goes out to pubs and clubs with him twice a week. Occasional nights out with the girls from work.	Likes clothes and likes buying them. Buying things for the flat she hopes to get this year with her boyfriend. Mum buys the food and household goods.	Enjoys browsing at lunchtime. Goes into Birmingham every fortnight or so on a Saturday. Visits 8–10 fashion shops and buys from three. Doesn't use local shops except places like Boots for cosmetics.
Richard and Gill	Married, two children aged 2 and 4. Living on an undistinguished Barratts estate in Harrow. He is a contract programmer working in Central London at the moment. Gill used to teach but is staying at home until the kids are at school. They haven't got the money or time to go out more than once a month: usually to friends or an occasional Chinese meal.	Mainly household shopping. Time, money and toddler combine to restrict both shopping and its enjoyment. Richard enjoys going to B&Q and browsing in Dixons but little else. Gill buys most of his clothes including suits from M&S. Takes them back if they don't fit. Gets her clothes from C&A and sometimes from Next or Richards.	Gill only has a couple of hours to shop and sort out the house when one child is at nursery school. Occasionally has the car but usually pushes a 'buggy' to the local shops. Goes to Brent Cross about once a month, the supermarket on a Friday night and rare Saturday visits, when Richard can babysit, to West End for her own clothes.

**Harry
and Pat**

In their late 40s and living in Bridgwater, Somerset. Kids have left home. Harry's unemployed since the plant closed last year, but he has a Forces pension and good redundancy money. Pat works part time as a cashier in the local supermarket.

Luckily the mortgage is paid up, but they don't want to buy much anyway. Slowly replacing worn out white goods: they go to the big stores near Bristol. But for everyday shopping, Bridgwater has most of the shops they need.

Pat buys the food each day from the shop where she works. Likes to buy clothes occasionally from M&S and a small private shop in Taunton. About three times a year they go to Exeter for a day out and a browse in the shops.

Albert

In his 70s and a widower. Used to be a toolmaker at Jaguar but now lives in Kenilworth. Lives on his own but likes visiting his children and grandchildren for Sunday lunch. Still a regular at the bowling club.

Doesn't reckon he needs to buy much now. Replaced the toaster last week and plans to buy a new TV eventually. Still using a car coat bought from Burton's in 1975—his daughter can't get him out of it. Most of his clothes are bought for him at Christmas. Has a drawer full of unused thick, woolly socks.

Walks into town every day to buy food from the Coop and Kwik Save. Usually finds time for a drink at his favourite pub while he's there. Hasn't been into Coventry (4 miles way) for three years. Reckons he'll get lost because they've changed it again. Never been to London but still likes his week in Bournemouth every June.

be used to identify these without the risk of introducing personal prejudices. Using a guide, such as Table 10.1, you can establish how, when and where your market does its shopping and plan your location strategy accordingly.

You may recognize your own customer types in Table 10.1. Certainly it provides a useful framework to think about the likely train of thought in your customers' minds. But you would be wise also to carry out research to confirm this important information. A few focus groups will provide this. Your research objectives are to identify:

● your customers' lifestyles, needs and preferences both for the products you sell and the type of shopping environment they prefer (if any!)

● their shopping patterns—location, frequency, reasons and transport methods—and the ways these are linked to their lifestyles

● the reasons why they choose to shop with you and the other relevant retailers in the area.

It is important to conduct this research across a selection of representative geographic areas. For example, if you have shops sited in city centres, suburbs and small towns you should carry out interviews with people living in all three areas because you will find quite different habits and attitudes. Similarly, you should cover the age and lifestyle breadth of your customers.

When you have done this research (and I suspect even as you start to plan it) you can compare the customers' views of 'site' selection with your own. Almost certainly you will identify stores that do not fit the customers' needs or expectations, simply because they are sited in the wrong centre.

A second approach that often yields valuable insight is to categorize your branches according to their merchandise sales mix. It would be unusual to find a chain of shops which demonstrated a common pattern of sales by product group across all branches. Usually there are significant and sometimes surprisingly large variations, with product types that are important sales contributors in some locations yet hardly register elsewhere. There may be internal reasons for this, such as lack of display space or even a reflection of sales staff preferences. But usually the reason will lie in the store's location.

The process of establishing these categories may need to be quite sophisticated since the mass of low-level sales data that will need evaluation may be too complex for manual analysis. A statistical process known as 'cluster analysis' can be used to help with this work. The process seeks to identify groups, or clusters, of branches that exhibit similar sales patterns across the range of products you sell. Because there may be many hundreds of products involved, and perhaps hundreds of branches, computers are a practical necessity for the number crunching. However, in skilled hands the output is simple and revealing. When you look at this do not be surprised to find that you can identify common themes emerging from among each cluster of branches. You will see, perhaps, that some are city centre branches, others may be associated with industrial areas or even particular industries, and others comprise mainly domestic suburbs, inner city areas, cathedral towns or ports.

In comparing these locations with the profile of the merchandise being sold—and also through your research into customer shopping habits—you will begin to discover some very interesting and actionable information about why your branches succeed or fail. Indeed, this brings us to the next topic in local retail marketing: the analysis of branch performance.

Analysing branch performance

Naturally you are already carrying out branch performance analyses. But if this is limited to reviewing comparative costs and P&L accounts you will be missing a fund of valuable information. Unfortunately, while financial accounting systems report facts and effects well enough, they often provide little insight into causes. Indeed, financial data taken in isolation can be downright misleading. When you identify a branch that is delivering average or above average profitability, it is easy to discount this from further analysis and focus your attention on loss makers. But while the branch may be returning a *satisfactory* profit, do you know *why* it is performing adequately, and do you know whether this profitability is *optimized*? By taking a broader and deeper view of performance analysis I have found loss-making branches that are actually performing better than any reasonable manager should expect, and previously ignored profit makers that came to be identified as gross under-performers.

There can be many reasons for variations in performance. Some will be internal and manageable factors such as management calibre, energy efficiency in heating and lighting, poorly regulated staff costs or high levels of stock losses. Conventional management accounting systems normally will identify such factors where they afflict particular branches. There will be many external factors, though, that accounting systems will report symptomatically in the sales line but cannot identify. These can include the effects of shop location within the centre, the degree of shopping centre fit with your retail offer, inappropriate stock ranges, direct competition with your store and the effects of indirect competition from neighbouring shopping centres.

While retail managers have always recognized that all these factors will affect performance, it is only recently that proper analysis has become practical for the working manager equipped with a desktop computer. The most commonly used tool is a statistical method called multiple linear regression. Behind the complicated name lies a simple approach. Regression analysis assumes that one factor—which is unknown but you would like to predict, such as sales volume or market share—is determined by a number of other factors that *can* be measured. These might include share of sales area, the size of the local market, and the presence of certain competing retailers. Before you carry out regression analysis you presume that such factors could be influencing performance. This analytical method is valuable because it tells you which factors *are* important, and *how* they help to predict, say, market share (see Figure 10.3).

The result of regression analysis is expressed as an equation. This can appear somewhat daunting when there are a number of variables affecting performance. Thankfully, though, it can be applied very simply and you will need little more than a pocket calculator to determine the potential market share for a particular location.

A regression equation may look something like the one shown below, but it could include up to a dozen or more variables. Many ordinary spreadsheet programs are capable of calculating regression equations, but although the tools for such arithmetic are now easily accessible, you should recognize that there are many potential pitfalls in misusing and misinterpreting data. The analysis should be carried out by someone who is thoroughly familiar with both statistics and retailing, otherwise you may start leaning too heavily on simple but misleading formulae.

Sales (in £000s) = [8.26 × Market rent per sq. ft]

+ [0.21 × Share of competitive sales area]

+ [16.5 × Pitch quality rating]

+ [22.2 × No. of variety stores in centre]

+ [8.41 × Catchment population (in 000s) aged 18–24]

− [2.83 × Catchment population (in 000s) aged 50+]

You will notice that the nature of the data can be wide ranging, and while basically straightforward it will require effort, even dedication, to elicit figures for every town and branch in your portfolio. You will

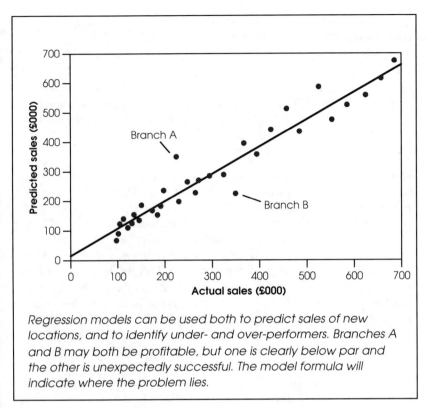

Regression models can be used both to predict sales of new locations, and to identify under- and over-performers. Branches A and B may both be profitable, but one is clearly below par and the other is unexpectedly successful. The model formula will indicate where the problem lies.

Figure 10.3 Sales prediction models

also need data for prospective new branches and their town or shopping centre. In the above (imaginary) 'sales' example you see only those variables that proved to be useful predictors. You may need to consider three or four times this number initially because you do not know at the start which information is going to be most relevant.

So, is all the effort worth while? In making property decisions that commit many hundreds of thousands of pounds to long-term investment, *any* methods that reduce the risk of error are worthy of close examination. No statistical system will come with cast iron guarantees of success, but with effort and some good luck you should be able to develop a model that can predict sales performance to within an accuracy of ±10 per cent. And although you may develop the model to predict sales for *prospective* branch locations, the greatest value can lie in retrospective analysis of your *existing* stock of branches.

The model will yield an estimate of expected sales for any location, including those in which you trade already. You can then compare actual and predicted sales to identify those branches whose performance differs significantly from expectations. This can be a valuable way of appraising branch potential, and you will also identify the reasons why these branches are so good or bad by looking at the equation variables that contribute to the discrepancy. You may discover, for example, that the selling area of the branch is too small, and this will lead you to consider whether an alternative and larger site can be identified in the shopping centre that will maximize the potential profit yield.

Once you have built up a database of comparative information on each branch you can carry out other analyses, and these need not require any special knowledge of statistics. For example you should try splitting branches into groups based on data such as their share of competitive selling space, or market share, and calculating the average profitability of each group. You may be as surprised as I was to discover how such factors can drive profitability. Elsewhere I have mentioned the work carried out on the PIMS database which relates market dominance to profitability and this seems to be no less true for local shopping markets than it is for national and international markets. The two charts shown here (Figure 10.4 and 10.5) provide graphic examples of the differences in profitability that can result from different types of store location. The actions that you need to take to improve the overall efficiency of your property portfolio can suddenly become abundantly clear.

Measuring local markets

Effective branch performance analysis presumes the ability to quantify and describe local markets (see Ideas 10.1). Until a few years ago this presented a major stumbling block because there were few practical ways of gathering meaningful information. This has now changed with the arrival of several organizations supplying quite accurate data on small areas, together with the expertise to manipulate it. Technology has also helped bring local market analysis on to the desk top. Five years ago you would have depended on massive, one-off analysis exercises using specialized mainframe programs. Now you can buy complete packages of data and programs that can be installed on ordinary personal computers.

The essential question you want to answer is simple. 'What is the size, extent and nature of the market surrounding my branches and, importantly for future planning, other locations where I might wish to trade?' (see Checklist 10.1).

One problem in providing a satisfactory answer is clear immediately. You cannot break up the country into a number of mutually exclusive

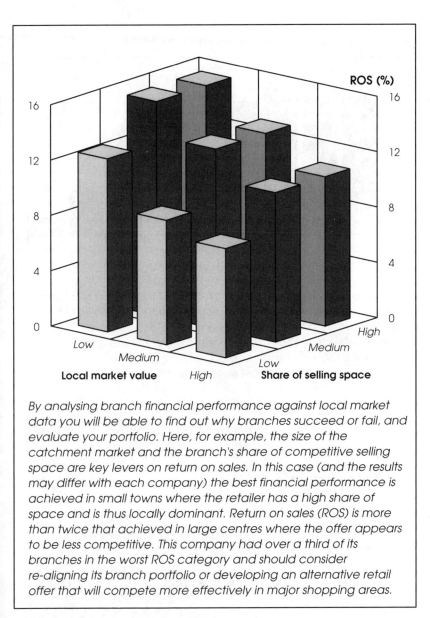

ROS (%)

Local market value   High   **Share of selling space**

*By analysing branch financial performance against local market
data you will be able to find out why branches succeed or fail, and
evaluate your portfolio. Here, for example, the size of the
catchment market and the branch's share of competitive selling
space are key levers on return on sales. In this case (and the results
may differ with each company) the best financial performance is
achieved in small towns where the retailer has a high share of
space and is thus locally dominant. Return on sales (ROS) is more
than twice that achieved in large centres where the offer appears
to be less competitive. This company had over a third of its
branches in the worst ROS category and should consider
re-aligning its branch portfolio or developing an alternative retail
offer that will compete more effectively in major shopping areas.*

Figure 10.4 Which factors drive branch profitability?

blocks surrounding each town; nor can you assume that, say, a 10-
mile circle around the town centre will indicate the potential
catchment area. People simply do not shop this way. We visit
different centres for different purposes. We may be willing to travel
50 miles to buy furniture from an IKEA store, or 20 miles to look for
clothes in a city centre that we believe will offer wide choice. But

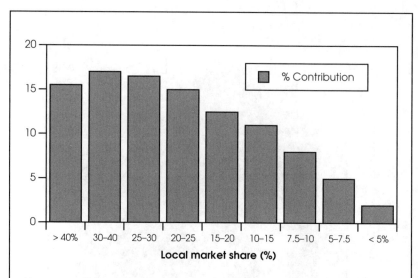

You may discover some unexpected facts, such as this relationship between local market share and contribution, which mirrors the results obtained at a national level on the PIMS database. The higher the market share, the greater the level of profitability achieved. Use your branch database to find out the circumstances that are most likely to yield high local market shares.

Figure 10.5 Local market share can drive profitability

Checklist ☑

10.1 LOCAL MARKET RESEARCH

These are the essential questions you need to ask when assessing a new location, before you consider the site itself.

- Are there relevant potential customers living or working in the area?

- Do they use this shopping centre?

- How much will they spend there in total?

- What is the nature and strength of the local competition?

- What market share can I reasonably expect?

- Is this enough to give me a viable business?

Ideas

10.1 LOCAL DATABASE APPLICATIONS

This list gives you an indication of the varied applications for local market and branch performance databases once these have been established.

- Assessment of prospective new locations.

- Development of location 'hit lists' for future expansion.

- Catchment area mapping.

- Estimates of market expenditure and share.

- Assessment of true level of national coverage.

- Branch performance analysis.

- Sales prediction for new branches.

- Assessing the impact of changes (such as increased selling area) to existing branches.

equally we may travel just a mile or two to buy bread, meat or vegetables. The factors involved can include:

- the importance of the purchases we have in mind

- the time we have available

- the time, expense and ease of travelling

- the availability of shopping centres

- the relative attractiveness of different shopping centres in the area for the kind of shopping we want to do

- our own personal preferences for shops and shopping.

The possible permutations are limitless, and in practice you have to make some assumptions in categorizing both customers and shopping opportunities. For example, the local High Street below my office is dominated by convenience shopping: food, CTN, banks and building societies. During the week shoppers are predominantly retired people or young mothers shopping with their children. Both groups have immediate needs to buy ordinary household provisions and limited ability to travel far from home. In contrast, my local city centres are bustling with office workers at lunchtime and young people shopping for entertainment as well as need each Saturday. Their habits reflect both shopping needs and interests, and the nature of the shops and stores in these very different locations.

There are two ways in which you can evaluate where your shoppers are coming from (to describe the catchment area) and the amount they are spending with you and your competitors (to determine the value of your local market and your share). One is to survey shoppers using a simple market research questionnaire. If carefully planned this can be very accurate but it is also very expensive if you need to replicate the exercise in many different centres. Most High Street multiples with less than 100 branches would need to survey every location to build up a reliable picture that could be applied to new locations. Also you would need to interview some 500 shoppers in each location to provide reliable data on each branch.

Catchment area modelling

Thankfully there are now alternative methods that will yield sufficiently accurate data at less prohibitive cost (see Ideas 10.2). Several proprietary systems are now available which model catchment areas on the relative attractiveness of different shopping centres. The data used to describe each centre is based on the number and type of stores present, parking facilities, etc., and is combined with an estimate of the time it would take shoppers to travel from different points surrounding the shopping centre. When combined

Ideas

10.2 CALCULATING CATCHMENT AREA MARKET VALUES

There are many possible ways of calculating the local catchment market values. The best choice will depend on the data to which you have access. Here is one method that can be applied if you have shopping population data from one of the geo-demographic databases and some national per capita spending estimates.

The catchment population for each age group is multiplied by the per capita spend (drawn from market research surveys) to deliver annual spending estimates for each age group, and a total for the catchment area—in this example amounting to some £5m. Not very sophisticated, but this has proved to deliver sufficient accuracy for many location planning decisions.

Age group	Catchment popl'n	Per capita spend	Market value
15–19	2432	£528	£1 284 096
20–24	2578	£501	£1 291 578
25–34	5613	£393	£2 205 909
Total			**£4 781 583**

with local population data, the systems allow you to estimate the 'shopping population' and analyse its profile, yielding figures which often differ dramatically from the resident population and local authority boundaries.

Once you know the profile of the catchment population this can be allied with national or regional expenditure data from other market research surveys to estimate local expenditure. While these are still nothing more than estimates, they can be refined by adjusting and calibrating the model using more specific company data sources. For example, if you run a store credit card or collect customer addresses for other reasons, you can match customers' home addresses against the model's predictions and build in correction factors to apply in unknown territories.

While none of this arithmetic is perfect, experience tells me that the results can be both credible and usable, and for many High Street retailers can be applied even without corporate data to tailor general market and catchment area estimates.

The information has immediate use in helping you to evaluate branch performance. But it is also useful in identifying areas where new branches would be successful, by searching for locations that match both your own shopper profile and the catchment profile of successful branches. The proprietary systems available can be tailored to search quickly for potential sites, establishing a 'hit list' of locations for property agents. This can be much more refined than relying on a list of the largest or busiest shopping centres, and may—in tandem with your target marketing strategy—lead you towards less obvious but more profitable and appropriate locations. Indeed, I have had personal experience and success in identifying and targeting community shopping centres for one retailer, and this enabled us to obtain many highly suitable if unfashionable sites that were not in demand among other retailers.

This illustrates an important concept in location planning. We all hear much talk about 'prime sites'. If you can clearly establish the kind of location that is of most value to the customers, you may find opportunities to build business that is not only successful in sales terms, but is highly profitable because you are circumventing the headlong rush by retailers for currently fashionable locations.

There are other less obvious benefits to be gained through a thorough understanding of catchment areas. One of these is the elimination of competing branches. In larger and well-established multiples it is quite likely that there are neighbouring branches that compete with each other. Local analysis systems can help you to identify these problems and to measure the degree of interference.

*Ï*deas

10.3 WHAT IS YOUR *REAL* MARKET SHARE?

*When you compare national market share figures you can obtain
a misleading impression of your competitive strength. This is
because two competing retailers may have different numbers of
branches and trade in different catchment areas. It can be very
illuminating to compare your share of total served catchment
expenditure with that of your competitors. The following example
illustrates this point:*

UK market value £5000m	Retailer A	Retailer B
Sales	£400m	£250m
National market share	8 per cent	5 per cent
Served market value	£3000m	£1250m
Share of served market	13 per cent	20 per cent

*Thus although Retailer A has a higher share of the national
market, Retailer B competes locally with greater success. Retailer
B may be choosing more appropriate shopping centres, but in
head to head competition in the same shopping centres Retailer
A is likely to lose business to Retailer B.*

*Calculating this comparative information for your own business is
a painstaking but clearly worthwhile exercise which can be
accomplished using modern geo-demographic databases.*

● Locate your own and other major competitors' branches, assigning each to the most appropriate shopping centre on the database.

● Sum the number of people in your various catchment populations. Do this by age group for greater accuracy. (Comparison with national figures will tell you also the national penetration level.)

● Do the same for each competitor.

● Use national per capita spending data to calculate the value of the geographic markets you serve, and separately, do the same for each of your competitors.

● Use turnover figures (or industry market research data for greater compatibility) to calculate each retailer's share of the served markets.

A few words of warning

Branch performance analysis relies on statistical methods that can greatly help direct your decisions but, nevertheless, they remain estimates and mathematical compromises. This arithmetic can be misused very easily, and you need to be careful to avoid putting political interpretation on the data to support or subjugate old internal arguments.

Most of the methods I have outlined also need data on quite a number of branches to provide useful information. In general you will need at least 70 branches to develop a meaningful performance analysis.

You will need to develop databases for both geo-demographic data and branch operating and performance data (see Checklist 10.2). Take care to ensure that these are as closely compatible as possible and can be properly cross referenced. Your internal data will probably be drawn from several sources, and you should be aware of the risks of mixing data that are potentially incompatible, especially when you are going to apply statistical analysis. Your information systems manager will be happy, no doubt, to explain the risks of failing to achieve data integrity. Current geo-demographic systems are very helpful in identifying the towns and shopping centres that are most appropriate, but there are still practical limitations. Particular problems I have identified include:

1 Newly established, out-of-town shopping centres that may have no (or an atypical) resident population in the immediate surrounding area. Systems based on travel time models tend to give too much weight to this neighbourhood population.

2 Centres in which non-resident populations from distant areas form an important part of the local retail economy. Central London is the prime example of this (though workplace population data can alleviate this to some degree). Major holiday and tourist centres can also cause problems.

3 Central London has many small shopping areas and streets that are in close proximity but have very different 'characters'. To date, data systems can take some account of the different store profiles, but do not allow adequate distinction between the different customer profiles found frequenting these centres. For example, active shoppers in Bond Street and South Molton Street can be very different from those using Oxford Street just around the corner.

4 These models cannot determine the best site within a shopping centre. Pitch quality is of very real importance but can be strongly affected by apparently minor factors such as pavement width,

Checklist ✓

10.2 PLANNING LOCAL DATABASES

Think through these questions before approaching one of the geo-demographic data specialists such as CACI, Pinpoint, CCN Systems, SAMI or Super Profiles.

- *How large is each chain?* You will need a minimum of 60–70 branches to use statistical techniques for branch performance analysis and turnover prediction.

- *Do you operate more than one chain of shops?* If so, you should be able to improve long-term profitability by more active management of the portfolio, switching property into the most appropriate chain for the location.

- *Is the chain expanding?* If so, you can use geo-demographic databases to identify prospective locations that will suit your business.

- *Do you need to make property acquisition decisions quickly?* If so, you need a database system in-house that will cut response times to an hour or two. Otherwise you may be able to rely on bureau facilities.

- *Do you have many outlets sited within conurbations rather than city centres or 'stand alone' towns?* This type of location stretches the capability of current geo-demographic location planning systems. Ask suppliers pointed questions about how their systems will handle this situation.

- *How much can you afford to spend on setting up a location planning system?* Use of a bureau service minimizes outlay (£500–£1000 per site) but is expensive if you have regular demand for data. A national system run from your desk top could cost £40 000–£50 000 initially, but is cheap to use and maintain.

- *Are you prepared to collect your own data on site quality, local competitors, etc?* This is slow and time consuming but will improve your ability to create efficient branch performance models.

- *What is the cost of a poor location decision?* Estimate this opportunity cost before discounting planning systems because they are 'too expensive'.

- *Do you want mapping facilities?* At relatively low cost you can map catchment areas, your own and competitive outlets. This can be helpful in assessing the extent of your geo-demographic coverage and the likelihood of branches competing with one another.

neighbouring shops, traffic flow and entrances to car parks. There is still no substitute in these cases for on-the-ground inspection and the analysis of pedestrian flow counts.

In spite of these reservations, geo-demographic systems work well in the majority of the 2500 shopping centres likely to be interesting to most multiple operations, and can greatly reduce the risk of store location errors.

Local market analysis and management can be a detailed, intensive and time-consuming activity—both for the planners and analysts at head office and for the managers in the field. It is easy to forget the strategic relevance of location policy in the mass of data and decisions needed to manage the portfolio. The fundamentals, though, remain very simple:

1   You can't turn a sow's ear into a silk purse! However skilful your local market analysis may become it will not compensate for the lack of an appropriate market position that recognizes and delivers value to your target customers.

2   However, you will reduce the risk of nullifying a good strategy through trying to implement in places that are inappropriate to the target consumers' needs and habits.

3   In establishing good local marketing expertise you will learn a great deal more about your customers' shopping habits and preferences, and this will help you to refine and improve the quality of the fundamental offer.

4   You will discover that, other than establishing a credible and valued market position, there is no management decision that will have greater leverage on profitability than site location. I anticipate that at least 85 per cent of your branch profit performance will be determined not by internal management control, but by local and external factors. You *have* to understand and work around such factors as local competition, demographics and market size if you are to maximize the profit potential of your basic retail offer.

11

Advertising

> *There is no doubt that a shop is its own advertisement, and prominent exposure on the High Street can reduce the need for other forms of advertising.*

Advertising causes a lot of heartache for retailers. Some managers advocate the benefits of advertising, assuming that a*ny* publicity is bound to result in extra business, while others take a more jaundiced view, assuming that no advertising is *ever* going to recover its investment let alone contribute additional profits. I am always intrigued by the unconditional commitment with which each side maintains its point of view. Rarely does there seem to be rational argument—merely a conviction that those on the other side are wrong.

Advocates both for and against advertising can be right, of course. It depends on the circumstances of the business. Every retailer needs to communicate with customers and potential customers. I do not think there can be any argument against that. Indeed, you should be communicating continually. However, the question of what you need to communicate, and to *whom* and *how*, will depend on the trading situation of the retailer, and above all upon your future objectives.

Advertising will work effectively only if it is tied into the company's overall objectives and business strategy. If this does not happen, your advertising budget will at best be wasted and at worst can be totally counter-productive. Advertising activity should flow naturally from the larger issues of objectives and strategy, in the manner shown in Figure 11.1.

In this figure I have used the word 'communications' rather than 'advertising' to remind ourselves that we need not be restricted to the normal notion of advertising: i.e. bought space in magazines and newspapers, posters or broadcasting media. Your own shops, staff and public relations activities are equally valid advertising media which, in some circumstances, may be much more cost-effective.

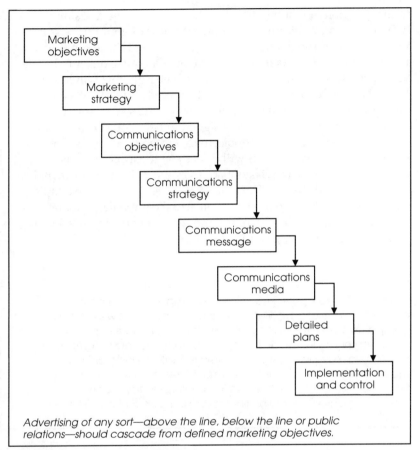

Advertising of any sort—above the line, below the line or public relations—should cascade from defined marketing objectives.

Figure 11.1 Advertising and business strategy

Never be tempted to start advertising unless you have defined the marketing objectives you aim to achieve through this exercise. If you do this you will greatly increase the risk of failure. You may find media salespeople and even some agencies pushing you towards media decisions as the first step in the chain rather than one of the last. It is not unusual for magazines to make you 'unrepeatable offers' over the phone, which if you accept, you will probably regret later as the costs of originating the advertisement soar past any feasible return in additional sales. Similarly, avoid the temptation to start internal discussions with comments such as 'I think we ought to be on television now that we're bigger/our competitors are doing it.'

Advertising decisions

Should you advertise? Well, it depends… There are no easy answers to the question of whether you should advertise. The decision depends on your objectives, the current status of your business in the marketplace, the available advertising media and the amount of money you have available for investment. Of course this number of variables produces many permutations. The right mix will lead to helpful and valuable advertising, but choose to advertise in the wrong way and you will waste your money, however laudable your motives may be. Figure 11.2 is designed to help you sort out your current business status, your objectives and your priorities. Together with the notes that follow, it will direct you towards a positive decision and reduce the risk of bad investment. Fill in your own line before reading the notes. The following three contrasting examples (see Figures 11.3(a)–(c)) are based on actual companies, but are not completed with any inside information—merely the application of general trade knowledge and some common sense.

Examples

EXAMPLE 1 (see Figure 11.3(a)). This example shows a large, well-established national retailer of children's clothes. However, its strong competitive position is being eroded by variety stores and up-coming specialist multiples. This has happened partly because competitive retailers have improved their skills in this market, and partly because this retailer appears, in the consumer's eyes, to have lost its way. Because the chain is represented in most large town centres, advertising on a national scale is feasible, but is unlikely to be very

Branch network	National	Local
Length of time in business	Mature	New
Working capital	Plentiful	Restricted
Store locations	Prime	Secondary
Competitive position	Market leader (top 3)	Follower (the rest)
Customers' purchase frequency	Frequent	Occasional
Transaction value	High	Low
Purchase	Willing	Distress
Shopper lifestyle	Promiscuous shopper	Conservative shopper
Consumer awareness level	High	Low
Positioning strength	Clearly perceived	Dimly perceived
Positioning quality	Well perceived	Poorly perceived
Positioning strategy	Established	Repositioning

This checklist will help you to decide whether advertising will help your business. Check your current status against the following headings before reading further. Figure 11.3 shows this checklist completed for three contrasting examples.

Figure 11.2 Advertising decisions

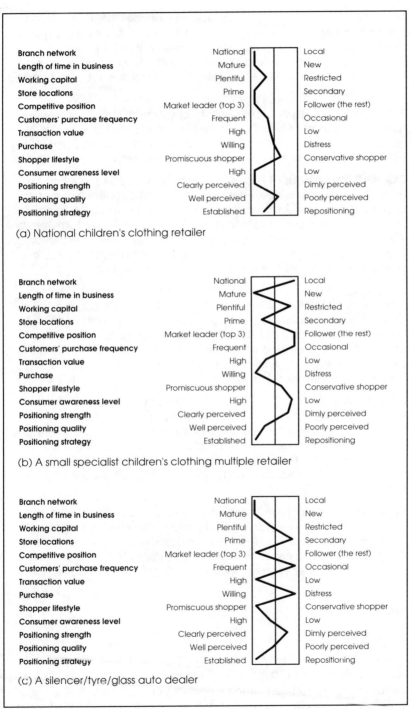

(a) National children's clothing retailer

(b) A small specialist children's clothing multiple retailer

(c) A silencer/tyre/glass auto dealer

Figure 11.3 Contrasting examples of advertising decision contexts

useful if it becomes merely a flag-waving exercise. Awareness levels are already very high, the stores are easily accessible, and mothers make frequent shopping trips. While blessed with a relatively conservative shopper who does not have much time to shop around or the money to take risks, the retailer's main problem is a deteriorating positioning quality.

Prescription: The essential precursor to any advertising is to solve any tangible problems of merchandise range and service quality. Then national advertising will be practical, and should be aimed at re-establishing the retailer's previous quality positioning.

EXAMPLE 2 (see Figure 11.3(b)). By contrast the second retailer has some 20 branches distributed liberally around the southern half of the country. It is an up-market, niche operator with its own singular design style. Historically it has attracted a small but loyal band of followers, but even these tend to use the company's outlets for 'special occasion' clothes and so buy infrequently. A large part of its target market, even at local market levels, has little awareness of the retailer.

Prescription: The company needs to achieve a high profile within its niche market, but is heavily restricted in its choice of feasible media. PR could make an important contribution in gathering fashion editorial coverage in the national and local press. Direct mail, if carefully targeted, could well be cost-effective and the company should find ways of enlisting its existing customers to introduce friends through a 'member get member' campaign.

EXAMPLE 3 (see Figure 11.3(c)). The third example typifies any of the established tyre, silencer and auto glass replacement multiple chains. Here the pattern is quite different from the other two retailers. Tyre and silencer dealers are very important to us when we need them, but never at any other time. We resent paying them substantial amounts of money, and often shop around for the best prices. They are often sited in out of the way locations.

Prescription: Advertising is a prerequisite for success, because these retailers cannot rely on passing trade and live with low awareness. A company that advertises not only its availability but its service quality (and supports this in practice) has an opportunity to use advertising to differentiate its offer in an otherwise undistinguished business.

Notes

Branch network

The spread of your operations is clearly relevant to media choice. A national chain has the full range of media from which to choose, including television and national newspapers and magazines. Large retailers' markets are at once national and local, and local media can still be a sound choice even for the largest companies. There are large national networks of tyre and exhaust dealers, for example, but they usually advertise in the local press, recognizing that this is the key marketplace where potential customers look for supplier information. However, the cost of using, say, 150 local newspapers can be much higher than utilizing a small range of national media. It is also a more complex management operation, since there are many more media owners to deal with and a multiplicity of copy and space variations.

Regional and local retailers may be more restricted in their choice of medium, and may be able to choose only from one or two local newspapers. However, national media can hide one or two secrets under their all-encompassing appearance. A number of magazines print regional sections within the body of the publication, allowing you the potentially beneficial association with national titles, while restricting distribution (and cost) to relevant areas. Regional newspapers, cinema advertising, local radio and poster sites are also possible contenders.

Length of time in business

A long-established business should have entered the public consciousness, with any formal market research you conduct showing a high level of consumer awareness (though of course this will only be apparent in areas in which you are represented). If you are already well known it will be very difficult to increase sales simply by mounting an awareness campaign. Your advertising will need more specific and achievable objectives: to get existing customers to spend more, or switch competitors' customers to your cause. You will need to demonstrate credible reasons before they will change their habits. Just shouting 'Me too, me too, I'm over here!' is unlikely to be very successful.

Newer businesses have a different problem. People will readily accept that they have not heard of you, and will happily give you an encouraging hearing, providing you have something useful to say. Your advertising will need to focus on explaining the differential benefits of your offer, and provide people with a tangible or emotional incentive to visit your store. To succeed you need to be very clear about why you are better. Most potential customers will want to know this because—unless you are very lucky—they will have been shopping with a competitor, somewhere, long before they ever heard of you. I hope you will have sorted out this issue of differentiation before you start to plan any advertising, which is quite incapable of making a durable silk purse out of a pig's ear.

Working capital

Advertising may be cost-effective, but it is never cheap. Any form of advertising is going to require a cash investment and in purely practical terms this cannot be allowed to make too large a hole in your working capital. Certain forms of advertising consume much larger amounts of money than others, and the payback period will also be dependent upon your advertising objectives. The cost of entry into local newspaper advertising is quite low in theory—you should be able to buy a useful amount of space in one edition for a few hundred pounds. At the other end of the spectrum television advertising has a very high up-front cost. Unless you are able to make sensible use of rostrum camera origination (essentially a series of still images, and difficult to lift above the 'cheap and nasty' look) you could well be spending at least £100 000 to produce a 30-second advertising film. At that stage, of course, no one has seen your masterpiece and a further investment of £150 000 will be needed to achieve any sensible level of exposure. Even this will buy you into only one or two provincial regions.

Some advertising can be sufficiently topical to succeed with only a few insertions (for example, to promote a forthcoming Sale), but mostly you will need repeated exposure over several weeks for your message to seep into the consciousness of your prospective customers. So what may have seemed like a low-cost option can still require considerable resources to have any chance of being effective.

The speed with which you can hope to recover your investment can also vary. 'Off the page' direct marketers benefit from an immediate revenue stream, usually flowing before the media bills become payable. You may obtain the same benefits from topical retail advertising, where time-limited offers should produce (if they are going to work at all) a flow of paying customers straight after publication. However, there are also fully justifiable advertising objectives that will produce no measurable cash returns in the early stages. For example, if customers' purchase frequency is low, it could take several months for all those who can be persuaded to switch to your outlet find a need to pay a visit. You cannot rely on people's memories of a short, swift campaign. You must advertise regularly over an extended period, catching a small part of your market each time when they are needing or contemplating a new purchase.

Store locations

There is no doubt that a shop is its own advertisement, and proffers the continuous advertising support discussed in the previous note. It can be a very powerful advertising medium because it reaches all the senses—sight, sound, touch, and smell (as bakers know well!)—and is under your total control. Because of this, shops have the ability to both reinforce and destroy your intended marketing strategy. Be careful not to over-promise through one medium, such as television, and under-deliver in the store. The conflict of images and impressions will damage customer perceptions. There is nothing worse than having your hopes raised and then dashed when reality strikes home as you walk into the shop.

But nevertheless, prominent exposure on the High Street should reduce the need for other forms of advertising, and many very successful retailers have grown up without any other form of external communication. However, if you do not have a good flow of potential users walking past the front door, you will need to use other methods to achieve recognition. New outlets, sited either in secondary positions or out-of-town locations are a particular case in point. Here, you cannot rely on passing traffic to find you and quite long-term advertising will be necessary. You will not be able to combine long-term advertising with low-turnover businesses. The media investment may be small in relation to a large furniture, camera or hi-fi store (and minimal for a large food store) but off-site clothing shops with no established trade would have difficulty clambering out of the publicity tank trap that their chosen location will have created.

Competitive position

Retailers with a high market share have less to gain than those with smaller shares from advertising focusing on a 'Try me' theme. By definition, a large part of the market has already found that retailer's performance satisfactory. Negotiated discounts apart, both large- and small-share businesses are going to pay the same advertising rates, but the high share retailer has a smaller pool of potential customers from which to fish. In this context you should think of your market share in local rather than national terms. Few retail brands outside the major food retailers and Marks & Spencer could honestly consider themselves to have a substantial national share relative to competitors. Single figure shares are common even among nationally recognized brands. Therefore, you should focus on local market shares. There are various geo-demographic systems that will help you to calculate these, but in the absence of any other information, estimate your share on the basis of your share of selling space. If you have an established business in a good location, and more than 20 per cent of selling space, I suspect that you will find advertising an uneconomic way of introducing new customers.

Customers' purchase frequency

If your goods are bought frequently (such as food or drugs store goods) advertising has a different role to play compared to infrequently purchased items. People are likely to be well aware of potential suppliers of these day-to-day goods, and know about the relative qualities of different merchandise brands. They do not need to discover whether they should buy toothpaste, or what to do with it, or where to buy it. They will be much more interested in price advantages between different retailers. They can find out about this either through advertising or through store displays. Advertising can be very important in this situation, because once customers have elected to visit one shop, it is much less likely that they will take the time to visit other competitive outlets on the same shopping trip for routine purchases. It is even more critical for out-of-town stores. While you might visit the shop next door for one item, which seemed particularly expensive, you are much less likely to drive to the other end of town. Shoppers decide which out-of-town store to use before they set out, and this decision will be based on habit and experience, and can be modified only by advertising (or occasionally by disillusionment with another retailer).

There are many things that we buy infrequently: cameras, hi-fi, jewellery, a new car, or perhaps a new tap for the bathroom. We have little experience of each retailer, and may not even be clearly aware of those who sell the products we want. Equally, retailers do not know when we will want a new tap (though there may be seasonal patterns) but need to make sure that we can find their names when this potential demand suddenly turns into reality. So, somewhat perversely, infrequently purchased goods need to be advertised frequently, and often continuously. Advertising may also need to be more explanatory if we know little about the product or the service offered by the retailer. This form of advertising does not have to be expensive—*Yellow Pages* might well meet the need precisely, but in some markets continuous advertising may be necessary.

Transaction value

This is closely and often inversely linked to purchase frequency. We think much more carefully about where to buy a new CD player than a bar of chocolate. The CD player costs much more and the results of our decision stay with us for a long time. Advertising, therefore, needs to be both informative and reassuring. Often product advertising may be funded by manufacturers and distributors, but as a retailer you need to recognize that customers are also buying your advice and service, which they see as an integral part of the product. Advertising can help to establish these perceptions in the potential customers' minds before they make the key decision about where to look.

Purchase

Tyres and silencers provide prime examples of distress purchases. We don't really want to buy these at all, and the need is generally forced upon us unexpectedly. When the silencer suddenly blows, perhaps our first experience in years, most of us have no clear idea of where to go for a replacement. Neither can we drive noisily around the county in search of a dealer. What most of us do is look in *Yellow Pages* or the local paper, half remembering that suppliers advertise there each and every week. Our decision will then be based on price, availability and perhaps brand images established through more penetrative television advertising.

We also tend to be rather resentful of such purchases, which are forced on us unwillingly. The supplier can do much to minimize this resentment, and establish brand loyalty for that distant repurchase by the way the transaction is handled. Recently I had a broken side window on my car and took it to an auto glazing centre the following day—a Sunday morning. I did not relish parting with money to solve a problem I did not cause, but the helpful reception, comfortable lounge, television and free coffee did much to ensure that I would return to the same centre at some uncertain but almost inevitable date in the future.

Shopper lifestyle

This is an important issue that has nothing to do with consumers' moral or political predilections! Some shoppers—predominantly young adults—find virtue in choice. They positively prefer to shop around, visiting a wide variety of shops at frequent intervals. For this group, which I have labelled 'promiscuous shoppers', shopping is interesting and fun. They build up a detailed, first-hand knowledge of retailers, and although they buy frequently they spread their favours around many different retailers whose basic image fits their preferences. This means they are also more likely to travel in search of choice, filling up the city centre shopping areas every Saturday.

Because they are so knowledgeable there is less need for advertising to create awareness. Your advertising investment is likely to be wasted in telling people things they already know, and can be better used to help support your market positioning. This is a fashion conscious group of people, and if you can use advertising to create a style of your own you can get yourself onto the 'must be seen there' list of shops. But you will also create an imperative need to deliver your promises, because it will not take many days for customers to discover whether the promises you hold out are supported in the reality of your store and merchandise. The advertising medium that you use is very important, because every medium has its own imagery, and this must be consonant with the image you are trying to create.

Conservative shoppers are much more difficult to shift. They like to know where they stand and what to expect. In my retail experience, older men (over 25 year olds!) tend to be the most incorrigible conservatives. They are both a challenge and an opportunity, because it can prove difficult to persuade them to change, but, if satisfied, they will become your most loyal customers. They can be responsive to advertising if you offer a genuine improvement in the shopping experience. Their idea of improvement is probably to avoid shopping altogether, but they will settle for a reduction in the hassle involved. Again you need to make sure that the advertising promise (which you might consider making through carefully targeted direct mail) is fulfilled in the store, particularly in the vital area of service.

Consumer awareness level

You must examine awareness levels in relation to your target market. Very focused retailers may have very low levels of general public awareness, but well known to their customers who may travel long distances to visit the shop. I used to be involved in competitive target archery, and like all *afficionados* past and present I can tell you exactly where to find the handful of retailers specializing in this field.

These two retailers have very high levels of market awareness—probably close to 100 per cent—and have little need to advertise beyond catalogues sent to existing and personally introduced customers. But if you have low awareness within your market, you must advertise in order to raise this level (see Figure 11.4). People who do not know you cannot try you. As I have discussed in more detail elsewhere, awareness must be translated into visiting, and this must be translated in turn into purchasing. Advertising needs to do more than mark your stores on the map. It must offer convincing arguments to move potential customers to action, and bring them into your store. Once there, the way you operate the business will determine whether or not they leave with bags in their hands.

Positioning strength

Often there is a gap between the product and service mix that you offer and potential customers' perceptions of your offer. As far as your potential market is concerned, it is their impressions that count, and if those impressions are unfavourable it is most unlikely that they will take the trouble to visit your shops. You can use advertising to alter these impressions and bring them into line with reality. However, you must be totally objective in your assessment of your own offer. It is easy to blame consumers for being too stupid to understand the quality and relevance of your stores.

If you are convinced that there is a real gap between perception and fact, advertising may work. However, you should remember that this

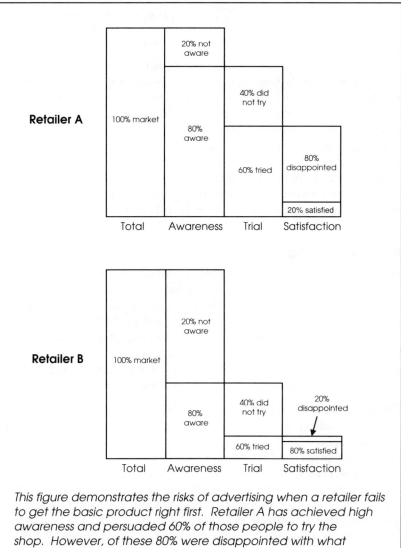

This figure demonstrates the risks of advertising when a retailer fails to get the basic product right first. Retailer A has achieved high awareness and persuaded 60% of those people to try the shop. However, of these 80% were disappointed with what they found. Retailer B has lower awareness, fewer of those who were aware of the stores tried them, but 80% of these (numerically more than Retailer A) were satisfied. Retailer A oversold the proposition and needs to improve the offer, especially since most of the disappointed trialists will not risk another purchase. Retailer B can gain real dividends by increasing advertising because the offer is welcomed by consumers.

Figure 11.4 The hazards of over-selling through advertising

(*Source*: Reprinted with permission of Prentice Hall, Englewood Cliffs, New Jersey, from Kotler, P., *Marketing Management: Analysis, Planning, Implementation & Control*, Prentice Hall, 7th ed., p.591, 1991. Copyright © 1991 Prentice Hall)

option will be slow and expensive because attitudes can be very difficult to change, especially if you are well known and well established.

You will have more chance of success if your perceived position in the market is merely fuzzy rather than substantially different from reality. Here advertising can be very effective because you are using a communication tool to relieve a communication problem. Think of it as wiping the condensation off a camera lens. You do not have to do anything to the subject, but just make it more clearly visible to the viewer. But before you tackle any problem that you put down to consumer perceptions and attitudes, make sure that those concepts are really understood. Commission the market research that will be needed to give you this information. It costs you money, but much less than the amount you will risk on any form of advertising.

Positioning strategy

Whether or not you bless your past actions and future intentions with the term 'strategy', your business will have a position in the marketplace relative to your competitors. Advertising can help to reinforce this—for better or worse. So do make sure that you know how your offer is positioned and where you intend to take the business in the future before launching into any form of advertising. If you advertise simply because you think it would be 'a good thing' you may be making trouble for yourself in the future.

Changing the positioning of an established retail business can be a very slow and expensive task. Advertising can help you, but not until you have altered the fundamentals of your business, and this may include new merchandise, new attitudes, new systems and new shops. It has taken many years for Tesco to change from its 'pile it high, sell it cheap' position in the 1960s to its present status as a quality food retailer rivalling Sainsbury's. Only quite recently have Tesco introduced national advertising to support this position. To have attempted this much earlier would have been counter-productive, because too few new customers would have found the standards of store interior and merchandise range in place which Tesco's new positioning strategy promised.

Choosing and using an advertising agency

The job of finding the right agency is a mixture of methodical analysis and more subjective considerations. By following a few rules of thumb you should be able to short list agencies that are suited to your business and your advertising needs, but in the end a satisfactory working relationship depends on individuals. At its best the agency/client partnership is very close and it will work well only if there is mutual trust and the personalities 'click'. The following guidelines will help you to plan your selection. You will have to make some assumptions about the type and scale of advertising you are likely to require, and if you have worked through the previous sections of this chapter you should have a realistic view on these matters.

Size of agency

Agencies range in size from huge multi-nationals to small businesses run by one person. Size need not affect the quality of work that an advertising agency can deliver, but it may affect the treatment you receive. I am not at all confident that small-scale advertisers will receive the necessary level of service from large agencies, where the new business represents no more than a pimple on their sales graph. Conversely, a large account awarded to a small agency will certainly receive attention but you may stretch their resources to a dangerous degree. Aim to be a reasonably large fish in the pond, where your budget will represent somewhere between 5 and 20 per cent of the agency's business. Many of the larger agencies are broken into smaller groups, split either by geography or specialization. Your size criteria can be based on the subsidiary business.

Type of work undertaken

You can find lists of agencies in larger public libraries or, from time to time, in magazines such as *Campaign* and *Marketing Week*. These listings, often shown as a league table, usually indicate both the size of the business and the way billings are split between television, radio, press and other media. You will see that a number of the larger London agencies are dominated by television. If you think you will need TV advertising, that's fine, but for many retailers press advertising will be much more relevant.

The agency's organization and financial structure and the focus of their skills will be geared to their existing business. Press work is very labour intensive, particularly where many local media are involved, and demands a lot of detailed artwork, progress chasing and administration in relation to the level of billings involved. Firms dominated by television work may not be set up to handle this, and often the many staff involved will be sitting on some very expensive real estate in central London. These overheads may not be significant in a multi-million pound TV campaign, where the majority of costs are invested in air time, but will make a serious impact on press campaigns. Agencies in the provinces and less fashionable parts of London may not be so glamorous, but they may be able to deliver better value for money.

If your plans lead you towards direct marketing campaigns—mail shots, door-to-door distribution or any form of direct response advertising—you should head for specialist direct marketing agencies. They tend to be down-to-earth, hard-headed individuals because they know they can be judged on results. You know exactly how many coupons are returned, or how many items are sold. These agencies have a calculating and critical approach to campaign planning that generalists often lack, and they are therefore in a position to save you a great deal of money that might have been spent wastefully by less practised agencies.

Location

It is very easy to become overawed by the glamour of working with fashionable West End agencies. They have talent without doubt, but give some thought to the costs involved not only in their overheads, but yours as well. Someone in your firm is going to need frequent contact with the agency, and travel and time costs can soon add up to a significant amount. Whether it is your staff or the agency's who do the travelling, you will wind up with the bill sooner or later. 'Incidental' costs for couriers, Red Star and taxi services can also swell rapidly, and these are rarely taken into account when agency and client first begin to work together. They serve simply to sour the relationship later if they have not been considered and estimated at the start. So my advice is: Do not ignore local agencies simply because they are local and lack public awareness.

The selection process

Identify no more than six agencies that seem to fit your needs based on the comments that have been made above. In the next stage you are aiming to reduce this number to a short list of three or four at most. Arrange to see them on their own territory. I find this works better than receiving a deputation at your office, since you can pick up a feel of the place, which is difficult to quantify but very important. Your main aim is to get to know the people who run the business, let them get to know you, and pick up information about their business in general. I think it is also wise to take with you the staff who will be in day-to-day contact with the agency. They should be involved throughout the selection process, and will not thank you for 'foisting' on them an agency they do not trust.

Checklist ✓

11.1 THE FIRST MEETING WITH THE AGENCY

When you first visit a prospective agency you should go prepared with a checklist of questions in your mind. Not all of those that follow require a specific answer from the agency, but they will serve to help you review your overall impressions.

- How long does it take you to travel from your office to the agency; how much does it cost?

- Is your reception at the agency efficient and courteous? How well is the receptionist handling other arrivals and telephone calls?

- Planning, creative and media input will be needed if the agency is asked to prepare a formal pitch. Are these functions represented at the original meeting so that they can meet and listen to you face to face?

- Has the agency completed any basic research into your company, its trading performance and your market?

- What are the agency's billings (the amount spent by its clients on media)?

- How are these split between different media? Does the agency have sufficient experience of the media you are likely to use?

- Roughly what proportion of their total business would your account represent?

- Does the agency have experience in your market and trade?

- Who are the agency's current, active clients?

- Are there any potential conflicts of interest with their existing clients?

- Is the agency asking probing questions?

- Are the agency people challenging—constructively—your assumptions?

- Do you find their comments interesting or thought provoking?

- Do you find yourself liking and/or respecting the agency people you meet?

- Do they show you round and allow you to talk to other staff in the agency? (If they don't offer you should ask—this is a useful way to pick up the atmosphere.)

- Is the agency asking for more information from you before preparing a full pitch? Are these requests specific and relevant?

Use Checklist 11.1 as a basis for your agenda. Give the agencies some basic information about your business, though it is always useful to see how well they have done their own homework prior to your visit. Don't expect complete, and free, market analysis and strategy proposals. There is no reason why the agency should invest considerable amounts of money in speculative research at this stage. However, you should discover whether they have a grasp of the issues involved in retail marketing and communication.

The elimination process is very subjective. If you do not feel comfortable with a firm, that is a perfectly good reason to reject them even if you cannot put your finger on the precise reason. Such feelings do not augur well for a long-term relationship. Look at the practical issues as well. Some of these are listed here.

1 Where is the agency located?

2 What costs are involved in travelling to and from the agency?

3 Does the agency have retail advertising experience?

4 Is there any potential conflict of interest between yourself and other clients?

5 Will they need to recruit staff to manage your business?

6 Have you met and do you respect the person who will be in charge of your account?

Once you have identified a short list of three agencies you can move to the final selection procedure. While it can be tempting to ask for more detailed work from more than three companies, you are likely to dilute the level of effort invested by each agency if they believe they are entering a lottery rather than competing for the account. There are two common approaches to briefing short-listed agencies. One is to give them a specific project, and ask them to develop detailed proposals including artwork, media plans and costings. The alternative is rather more general, requesting an analysis and recommendations for your communications strategy at a higher but less detailed level.

The advantage of the specific brief is that you see and can compare the creative approaches of the three companies. However, you do restrict the agency's ability to review your overall communications objectives; this is an exercise that they should undertake before getting down to the detailed level, and they may have second thoughts about execution of the brief if subsequently you appoint them and they start considering the wider issues. The other risk is that agencies may be reticent to invest quite substantial amounts of time and money in speculative creative work within an artificial relationship. They may argue, in some cases on the basis of bitter experience, that the potential client will simply hijack the best ideas to implement themselves or pass to a competitive agency.

If you want your short-listed agencies to produce specific and detailed proposals—perhaps for a special promotion, for new branch openings or the launch of a new design image—agree the rules of the game beforehand. This will save later misunderstandings and recriminations. Your agreement should cover ownership and use of copyright to specific creative devices, and the costs of developing detailed proposals. If you are to obtain a valid appreciation of each agency's abilities you must be prepared to spend adequate time with their personnel during the development of their proposal. Make sure that they know you are prepared to do this, and provide any reasonable information about the company and its trading, market and financial data. However, wait for them to take the initiative in asking for this information. The questions they ask (or lack of them) can be one of the most revealing parts of the exercise.

As an alternative to a specific, project-based brief you can set wider guidelines for short-listed agencies. Ask each agency to review your communications strategy, and the part they believe they should play in planning and implementing this strategy. I favour this approach because it reveals the extent to which the agency really understand your business and markets. You will see less direct evidence of their creative output, but you can still see the quality and character of the work they have produced for other clients. I knew one retail marketing director—an ex-managing director of an advertising agency—whose brief was always simple and concise: 'Tell me why we should have an advertising budget at all, and why your agency should manage it?' Most agencies seemed to be distinctly uncomfortable with such a wide brief, but I find it attractive because it gets to the core of the problem.

When the time comes for final presentations, make sure that everyone in your company who will be working with the agency is involved and party to the subsequent discussions and decisions. You do not want the agency to be managed by someone who retains deep reservations about the choice of agency. Even if you cannot reach a consensus decision, at least everyone will have had a chance to express a point of view. While subjective assessments will remain important criteria, agree beforehand a list of considerations that can be scored and compared for each agency. It is important to put your views on paper at the time, since memories can become very imprecise over the course of several meetings. A typical list is shown in Checklist 11.2.

Checklist ☑

11.2 REVIEWING THE AGENCY PITCH

There are many judgements you will need to make in comparing the presentations of your short-listed agencies. Often this is made more difficult by the variation in style and content of each presentation which makes direct comparisons hard to make. This checklist is a useful 'score sheet' to help you analyse each agency's input in a methodical manner.

● Has the agency understood your business? (But take care not to confuse any constructive criticism of past actions with a lack of understanding.)

● Do they understand the market in which you operate?

● Have they asked for relevant information and used this sensibly?

● Are they simply playing back your own knowledge without adding a new perspective?

● Where they are making sensible use of your own market and company data, are they still accurate or have they been misused or misinterpreted? (Though you should allow for a different interpretation if supported by sound argument.)

● Have they proposed a creative brief or execution that fits the commercial analysis? (Sometimes you will see clever creative solutions that bear no relationship to the marketing solutions previously proposed.)

● Is there a media plan?

● Is this plan justified by the commercial objectives? Does it look as though the media planners have been involved in the project from the start, or brought in two days before the presentation?

● Is the media plan properly costed?

● Has the agency proposed

specific criteria to analyse the success of their activities?

● Have they detailed the arrangement for managing your business? Will they provide contact reports so that there is no argument about decisions and actions agreed in meetings and telephone calls?

● Have they detailed arrangements for invoicing costs and fees? Which overheads will be carried by the agency, and which will be passed on to you?

● Will the costs of production and artwork be included in any fee or charge separately? Does the agency propose to mark up these costs, and by how much?

● Will you have direct access to creative and media departments working on your business? (Some agencies try to channel everything through an account manager. I believe that their key players must have face-to-face contact with the client.)

● Who will be working on your business? Can you work with *them*? Will they need to recruit new staff and in what capacity?

● Can they provide references from other clients?

● Can they communicate their ideas to you clearly? (If not, what chance have your customers?)

Fees, costs and commissions

You must agree specific arrangements. In the excitement of the moment, with glossy solutions to all your marketing problems displayed before you, it is easy to dismiss these arrangements with a casual remark: 'Of course, we shall deal under the usual terms and conditions.'

The traditional arrangements provide for an agency to earn a 15 per cent commission from media owners from all media placings on your behalf, and a mark-up of 17.65 per cent on bought-in production such as photography and print. In practice the mark-up often can be higher if there is no specific agreement. I dislike these 'standard' arrangements simply because they *are* standard, while few clients have standard problems and needs. I prefer to pay an agency for the work *they do*, rather than a commission based on the work performed by a subcontractor. If the agency produces a brochure, for example, which requires a reprint, I find it difficult to justify a substantial mark-up on the printing costs simply for making one phone call to the printer.

Therefore I think you should consider negotiating a fee with the agency for their time and skill. In the short term this could cost you more, because the most intensive effort is likely to go into developing the first campaign. But in the long term you pay for what you get, and this also makes the agency more directly answerable for its work and standards. You can see where your money goes.

There has to be a high degree of mutual trust between agency and client. As a client you will need to treat the agency as an extension of your company and be prepared to share any relevant information. They have a specialist job to do, and you must give them the freedom to use their specialist creative, media-buying and administrative skills. This does not mean that you should be uncritical. You should expect them to impose self-discipline on administration and shout loudly if there is any evidence of poor record keeping, liberal expenses or inaccurate invoicing. Creative departments will respond also to a searching examination of their ideas. Ask questions constantly and you will get better and more cost-effective creative solutions.

The agency must also trust you. Despite their title, advertising agencies are not your agents in legal terms. When they buy outside services or media they do so as principals and are liable for those charges. Quite a few agencies have gone out of business when clients have defaulted on payments.

Make sure that you have regular personal contact, and set aside times for review meetings. This will ensure that problems are caught early and either solved or used to demonstrate that there are irreconcilable differences. Your agency contact should also include creative and media staff. If you rely purely on account managers to transmit your views there is a risk that some nuance will be lost in the transmission. Creative people need to get a personal feel for your ideas, your company and the market if they are to deliver the most appropriate work.

It is equally important to communicate internally, especially within a large company. Other operating managers need to understand and contribute to the communications strategy and its implementation, otherwise there is a danger that the internal advertising or marketing managers will be seen to become isolated from the business, with their outlook directed towards advertising agencies rather than the company.

I believe that the client and agency should form a team, producing output that is greater than the sum of the parts. You will not achieve this easily; at times this requires plenty of lively argument. Don't be afraid, therefore, to argue your corner as strongly as the agency should be prepared to express their point of view. This is particularly true when considering their creative output. The agency should have tried and discarded many different creative approaches before settling on one or two to discuss with you. You are under no obligation to settle on their proffered alternatives without discussion. If you do not think they have the right solution, be prepared to fight back. Providing you put up a constructive case, your viewpoint can be the catalyst necessary to turn competent creativity into something very special.

12

Press and public relations

There are many groups of people who are interested in your business. The more they understand, the more understanding they will be.

I can think of few topics that cause more discomfort at budget time, when accountants seem particularly to relish their gamekeeper role.

The trouble with PR expenditure is that it is extraordinarily difficult to justify in any normal calculations of cost-effectiveness. The easy solution to the problem is to decide that what cannot be measured is not needed, and scrap the entire budget item. But you may be left with a niggling suspicion that it might have *some* value, especially when you meet the next predatory journalist with the helpful demeanour of an African vulture.

You usually resolve the problem with a compromise. Your PR manager or consultant pleads and threatens you with column centimetres, competitions and local radio interviews, and your new finance director, whose photograph has just appeared in the appointments column of the local newspaper, grudgingly accepts there might be something in it. 'But *next year*, give me the *facts*, please.' In the end you agree to maintain last year's budget (which was actually exceeded) plus an inflation factor (which for this particular budget is wildly optimistic).

So is PR really worth having? In principal the answer has to be 'yes'. You need to manage and exploit every opportunity to communicate with your market and any other influential audience. PR is one of the tools at your disposal, but do not be tempted to pigeon hole PR. Like other communication skills, it has developed its own battery of techniques, but all communication are a form of PR and need to be integrated in their objectives. Every contact between one of your staff and the public is in fact an exercise in public relations, and there are far more contacts of this sort than will ever emanate from a PR department or consultant. Your customers are not your only PR targets; here is a list of your principal audiences:

- Customers
- Potential customers
- Local government officials
- Commercial estate agencies
- Local journalists
- Local residents affected by your business
- Competitors
- National trade and professional journalists
- National consumer journalists
- Financial and City analysts
- Decision makers in regulatory bodies
- Politicians and civil servants
- Trade associations
- Financial journalists
- Bankers
- Investors
- Suppliers
- Employees.

Not all of these categories will be relevant to every retail business, but remember that customers can be influenced by friends, relations and newspapers. Badly handled PR can have an invidious effect on your trade. It is said that one bad experience by an individual will be retold to ten people, while good experiences are, on average, only related to three. Journalists have the capability to alter this ratio out of all proportion.

Your objective is to try to get as many people as possible to think, read and talk positive things about your business, and to minimize the number of damaging incidents. You want to do this because, in the end, people's perceptions of your company will influence their buying behaviour. The only unknown, and it is one that will never be accurately quantified, is the degree to which customers will spend more, or less. Since most PR requires an investment in forethought rather than substantial amounts of cash, the question of cost-effectiveness is perhaps not as significant as you first thought.

We can consider the practical issues of PR management under the following headings:

- Product and service promotion
- Corporate and financial PR
- Stakeholder interests
- Managing the PR effort.

Product and service promotion

All retailers aim to get their products in front of the buying public as frequently as possible, and have them shown in the most attractive light. That's why you have shops, and why you spend considerable amounts of money on shop design and display materials. Unfortunately not all those who might be your customers visit your shops, and even established customers may only be occasional visitors. Financial journalists and bankers may not visit your shops regularly either, and press coverage raises your visibility to these people, who read magazines and newspapers just like the rest of us.

Since most people do read magazines and newspapers, this provides your chance to display your goods in different surroundings. There are two ways of achieving this: you can buy advertising space, over which you have almost total control, or you can try to persuade the journal to feature your goods and your name in editorial coverage. But remember that you have virtually no control over how this merchandise will be used.

To achieve this, both you and the publisher must have coincident objectives. You want to sell more goods, either directly by featuring merchandise for sale in you shops, or indirectly by establishing an attractive, symbiotic relationship between your brand image and that of the magazine.

The publisher wants to sell more magazines. Every day, week or month space is to be filled with material that will interest and excite the readers. If you have an image with which the publisher would like to be associated, he or she will want to feature your name. If you just sell appealing merchandise, the publisher might want to feature this (but probably not exclusively) in theme articles on fashion, food, drink, holidays or whatever.

It would be nice to think that a product PR campaign could be planned, targeting your merchandise at the most appropriate feature writers, and seeing the results beautifully presented and captioned with prices and branch addresses. Sadly, things never seem to work that way. In practice fashion retailers, for example, might find their sophisticated new creation 'coordinated' with the most extraordinary garments, which will be 'layered' on yours (that is, covering them), and your credit will be printed in a mass of tiny type at the bottom of the following page, sandwiched between two advertisements for house insurance.

Never mind, the coverage was at least free. At least it was after you paid for the photographic samples (now cut up the back to fit the model), several motor bike courier runs, faxes, and the PR consultant's time and lunch.

You may be gaining the impression that product PR is a very random affair. And so it is, mainly because you depend on other people whose objectives are not always the same as yours. That is not a reason to dismiss the help that the press can give you. It just means that you must recognize their needs in your dealings with the press. Bear in mind the following guidelines about journalists.

1 Their prime objective is to produce and sell periodicals and, indirectly, sell the resulting readership to advertisers.

2 Your job is to convince them that the attractions of your merchandise will help them to interest and retain their readers.

3 In principal, they plan and produce the editorial a long way ahead. For a monthly magazine, the content will be agreed at least three months ahead of the cover date. This means, for example, that an Autumn fashion feature in the September issue will be planned in June. You would need to have 'sold in' your merchandise in April or May, long before you see bulk deliveries of your new ranges.

4 In practice, although these lead times are long, final product selections, photography and writing will be rushed and left to the last possible moment before the printer's copy deadlines.

5 Feature writers prefer newsworthy, colourful, unusual, slightly OTT product. This is usually the category of stock that lies gathering dust on your shelves and rails, but the coverage just might help you sell the ordinary, boring stock that most people actually buy. Nevertheless, you might be able to sell the idea of a 'back to the classics' theme from time to time.

6 Most journalists have neither the time nor the inclination to seek you out. You must find them.

7 National media journalists live and work in London. If you do not trade in London, assume they have never heard of you. If you need PR support, consider opening a shop in central London.

8 Writers worry about promoting shops and products that are not widely available—it prompts a lot of 'Where can I get...?' phone calls they would prefer not to receive. If your distribution is limited, it helps if you can offer a mail order service. However, this general rule does not seem to apply if you have a single shop in Covent Garden. *Everybody, darling,* shops in Covent Garden, don't they?

9 Features editors like competitions, especially when there are big value prizes. They want *you* to provide the prizes. But you will then get more control over the content of the feature—you will probably get solus coverage, and probably be allotted more space—so the exercise can be worth while. If you have any capacity for database marketing, competitions can be a very good idea, because they generate many thousands of names and addresses. For example, if you distribute a catalogue for either retail or mail order promotion, this can be a very effective way of creating mailing lists.

Local *v* national media

Most of my comments relate to national magazines and newspapers. Local media can be equally useful to you, and possibly the only real choice if you run a smaller regional operation. Local newspapers do not have the budgets and resources available to nationals. They work mainly in black and white, publish on newsprint, and only infrequently arrange their own photographic sessions. They also have many pages to fill each week.

Here you have an opportunity to take greater control, and circulate press packs that include photographs, captions and a short article written in an interesting journalistic style. If your material is used there is a fair chance it will go through the system relatively untouched. However, do not expect local papers to publish everything you send them. Your material still needs to be topical, it will be competing with dozens of other press packs, and the journal has to be seen to be reasonably even handed. If your material is published by a particular paper twice in a year, you will be doing well.

Corporate and financial PR

Apart from the buying public there are many other people you need to influence to create awareness, good impressions and positive views. These are people with a direct or indirect stake, or interest, in your business. They include employees, suppliers, financial institutions and shareholders. The next section deals with each of these groups, but first there are a few important points about 'corporate' PR in general.

The first principle is to keep people informed. You never know when you might need help, and any individuals or institutions who may be able to assist will be more inclined to provide help if they know you and your business. Financial markets in particular do not like surprises, especially unpleasant ones, so I believe that you need to be reasonably open with your information. (However, if you are a publicly quoted company you do need to be aware of the Stock Exchange rules on providing potentially price sensitive information.)

Disaster planning

Secondly, disaster planning is just as important in this area of business management as it is in establishing plans for dealing with computer failures, fires and thefts. Public relations disasters can and will happen, usually when you are least prepared. Among the incidents I can recall, have been:

- the tragic death of a baby suffocated in a sleeping bag designed and made by a retailer's supplier

- a suspended lighting system collapsing on customers in a shop

- sex discrimination lawsuits brought by employees

- a postal strike which, at least in the press's view, threatened the viability of a mail order company

- discovery by a fashion journalist of an 'own brand' product that looked remarkably like a 'designer label' creation she had just seen in Paris.

While these are all quite isolated incidents they can easily run out of control and bring into question your ability to manage public responsibilities and your financial security. Do remember also that incidents reported in your local paper may be picked up by journalists in more influential positions, and before long you can discover national media knocking at your door. You may not be in any way responsible for what has happened, but if you do nothing responsibility may be attributed to you in any case.

The most common, and worst reaction is to run for cover, failing to return 'phone calls or issuing ambiguous 'no comment' responses. While you may not be ready to say anything substantive, a plain 'no comment' response may be translated on the lines of: 'Despite repeated approaches the company refused to be interviewed or to answer any of our questions.' You will be damned as guilty and you will have missed an opportunity to calm the situation before it gets out of hand. At the very least you should thank the journalist for making you aware of the problem, get as much detail from them as you can, and say that you will investigate before returning their call. Find out when their copy deadline occurs. If there is a real and embarrassing problem you may be able to delay any statement until after the deadline. It may not be so newsworthy next week. But if you promise to get in touch by a certain time you must do so, even if it's only to issue a holding statement, which should be credible.

Your best protection is to make sure that a system is in place to deal with unexpected problems. Above all, make sure that people in the company know how to contact you. A receptionist reporting that all your directors are tied up in meetings may be accurate, but too few journalists will believe her.

Keep in touch...

You can minimize PR risks and maximize opportunities by keeping in touch. Whenever possible, make a point of getting to know journalists who may write about you, your business and your markets.

On the positive side, they are more likely to approach you for information or comment if you are personally acquainted, or at least known to be a reliable entry in the journalist's contact book. When a potentially damaging story breaks, you are more likely to influence someone you know, especially if a trusting relationship has already been established.

How do you get to know these journalists? Certainly there are too many possible candidates to meet individually, but in most trades you will find a small number of faces that appear regularly at conferences and exhibitions. Have a chat with them, and make sure they have your business card. From time to time people will also ring 'out of the blue'. Avoid the temptation to ignore the call. Once a company is recognized as uncommunicative the calls will stop, and so will the coverage. And if you've ever wondered why some people in your trade appear to get constant coverage and quotes while you do not, look objectively at the way you talk to the press. This, of course, is also why some back-bench MPs get more media coverage than their front-bench colleagues—they never refuse an interview, and are therefore recognized as a reliable source of views.

> *Once a company is recognized as uncommunicative the journalist's calls will stop, and so will the coverage you want.*

Stakeholder interests

There are many groups of people who are interested in your business. These include your employees, suppliers, financiers and shareholders. Generally speaking, the more they understand, the more understanding they will be. Therefore, it is in your interests to keep them informed and to be as open with your information as the law and commercial common sense dictates. While some matters are commercially and competitor sensitive, I suspect we all tend to over-rate both the value of this information to competitors, and the likelihood of them reacting in any concrete way. Better awareness among employees and suppliers is, I believe, going to have a more positive impact on your business than the possible negative impact of competitors knowing more about your company.

Employees

Of course your staff know what's going on... don't they? It is easy to take your employees for granted, and to assume that they know as much as you. But you must not forget that you are in a privileged position, not only because as a manager people tell you things (though they may be things people think you would *like* to hear), but also because you are at the centre of the network.

In contrast, put yourself in the place of a part-time sales assistant in a branch in Truro. You might be hundreds of miles from head office, you've never seen the place and probably never will. But does that make you any less interested in the business? When you bear in mind the critical impact your staff have on the total service that customers buy, employees become an important PR target.

Take your staff seriously and they will take you seriously. Keep them informed of the company's progress—good or bad, tell them about new products, stock availability and quality problems. Tell them about the company's development plans. One of the most successful companies I know brings all its staff to annual conferences and new merchandise shows and explains its corporate plans in the kind of detail that investment analysts can only dream about. It enjoys an unparalleled level of staff commitment which not only carries it through the bad patches but ensures a level of enthusiasm and self-respect that is clearly communicated to customers.

Suppliers

Suppliers are no less important to you. The old adversarial relationship begins to change when both parties begin to recognize that they are mutually dependent. Even in sectors in which the retail buyers are highly concentrated and wield tremendous power, they are still dependent on successful supplier relationships since few retailers would now consider manufacturing their own merchandise. For smaller retailers, their suppliers can have the upper hand, viewing their smaller customers as expendable in the face of more demanding key accounts. Doubtful quality and late, split deliveries can result.

There is no easy solution to this problem, but again you can apply persuasive PR tactics. Make sure that suppliers see your shops, and understand your plans for expansion and their potential part in this. If product quality is a fundamental part of your offer, ensure that suppliers know this. Prepare a brochure that sets down your requirements, your track record and your goals in black and white. Invite suppliers to your retail conferences. Make sure that they can listen to your staff. Give them relevant extracts from your market research reports, especially any verbatim customer comments relating to the sort of merchandise they supply.

You will also have to make some hard PR decisions. If merchandise deliveries are late, or do not meet your specifications, refuse to accept the delivery. This can be difficult when you know you could sell at least some of it. But if product and service quality are important to you, any other action will degrade consumer perceptions and tempt suppliers to treat you as a 'soft touch'.

For a multiple retailer, estate agents and developers are also suppliers. Keep them informed of your business developments and show them, either directly or through an illustrated brochure, what your shops look like. Tell them about your target market and the type of shopping and catchment area you seek. There are many hundreds of multiple shop companies—too many for developers to picture individually when they are looking for tenants. Put 'a face to a name' and you are more likely to be offered more and better sites.

Financiers and shareholders

You may have one or both depending on the size of your business. Most of us get a little nervous when dealing with financial institutions, whether this be the friendly local bank manager or a major corporate investor or financier. Much of the essential contact will be outside the realms of conventional public relations. However, it is always worth remembering that even the biggest institutions are made up of, and managed by, real people with their own perceptions and prejudices, and who are shoppers themselves—exposed to the joys and perils of the High Street.

They will be getting their own personal messages from your shops, your staff, and from the PR coverage you obtain through the media. This is bound to influence them, directly or subconsciously, when considering decisions that will affect your business. Certainly if you run a regional operation it is likely that London-based City people will have no personal knowledge or experience of your business. That is when you need to consider other forms of communication. The annual report is clearly one vehicle, with a legal responsibility to report to shareholders giving you a superb opportunity to communicate your message to a key target audience. I wonder why so many companies fail to make full use of this, pushing out Chairman's Statements which range from the downright boring to scarcely credible pipe-dreams.

There are other opportunities to inform. You can produce your own brochures and newsletters aimed at interested corporate readers rather than customers. If you do produce these, however, they need to be accurate, consistent and regular. If you do launch the proverbial 'greatest thing since sliced bread' you must be prepared to comment on its progress—a long and hollow silence may raise one or two questions about its subsequent success.

Managing the PR effort

The key question to decide is whether you need your own PR department or an external PR consultancy (or possibly a combination of both facilities). I recommend the use of an external service, backing this with an internal department only when the economic sense of doing this is becoming clear cut.

You may need to separate product PR and corporate PR services. The two elements of your PR programme address different audiences, each large enough to merit contact lists too long and different in nature for one individual to manage. Product specialists build up their own contacts in, for example, fashion and home magazines and the fashion and feature writers of daily newspapers. They will rarely come into contact with financial and business journalists.

Most product PR consultancies are small operations, often individuals working on their own account. Small size is not a disadvantage, providing the consultant has efficient ways of keeping in contact with his or her office base. Essentially you are buying the services of someone with good personal contacts: a stylish office and large back-up staff are not necessary. However, the individual must run a very efficient operation that can be relied upon by both clients and journalists to follow up messages, keep appointments and handle merchandise samples effectively and promptly.

Your search for a consultant can start with the people who know them best—the journalists writing for the magazines and newspapers your customers read. It is worth taking the time to make a few telephone calls and make some informal requests for advice and names. The quality of individual PR consultants can vary considerably, and working journalists soon discover the people who can deliver a reliable service.

Effective working relationships depend on personalities as always, and you should meet three or four candidate consultancies. A good relationship is going to require trust and mutual respect, and the initial sifting and briefing process is going to give you both an opportunity to assess one another. Ask to see evidence of previous work and follow up references from existing and past clients. You should give all consultants the same brief to which to respond with a proposal. The brief should give background information on the company and outline the business objectives you believe that PR can help you to fulfil. Leave the PR consultants to recommend the methods for reaching these objectives: this is their area of skill rather than yours, and their interpretation of your aims will help you to assess their suitability. Ask for cost estimates that separate fees, projected expenses and the costs of running any specific events (such as press shows) that they may recommend in the proposal. Watch out for hidden costs such as the provision of sample ranges, which may eventually reach a significant amount.

Do not tie yourself into a long contractual relationship, but equally you should ensure that the projected contract period allows time for the consultancy to run up to speed. They will need two or three months to introduce their new client to their contacts, and there will be a three or four month lead time after a successful introduction before anything appears in the press. Therefore, I would suggest an initial twelve-month contract in respect of agreed fees, but you would both be wise to build in a one-month notice period (on either side) throughout that first year. If the relationship proves unworkable there is no point in souring this further by tying each other to unproductive contracts.

Look very carefully at costly proposals for sponsorship, major events and competitions. In the early stages you may both get a little too enthusiastic, and if you are not careful you may only start thinking about cost justification when the bills start dropping onto your desk. When dealing with a small consultancy business you would be wise to contract directly with any third party supplier involved in costly

PR events. They are likely to put a heavy cash flow strain on the consultancy where it acts as an intermediate contractor. You want the firm to be worrying about the PR effort rather than taking unnecessary risks with their bank loan.

Once a PR consultancy is in place you must be prepared to support their work. It is no use complaining about the absence of press coverage if you never supply samples or prices when requested. Unfortunately PR people are at the mercy of the short-term outlook of many editors and writers, and often you will get requests for help, products and information at short notice and at inconvenient times. You will have to live with this, but do keep a weather eye on the consultancy to make sure this is not evidence of slipshod planning by them.

Plan to have regular review meetings to follow up past actions and future plans. The consultancy should be able to demonstrate how time has been spent, and that they are aware of impending opportunities. Talk openly about your disappointments *and* your successes. Most of these relationships seem to fail because neither party has understood both the problems encountered and the realistic opportunities. Often the client had over-optimistic ambitions that the consultancy had failed to argue against or tone down in the excitement of gaining new business.

If you wish to maintain good relations with the City and other corporate institutions you will need to use a specialist consultancy. These are usually larger firms with retainer fees to match. The large PR firms will certainly offer to look after all your PR interests, and may indeed be equipped to do this. However, you should subject them to the same level of investigation as the small operation, and pay more attention to what they say and what they have done than to the glossy brochures. In product PR, firms do not need to be big to be effective.

Internal PR departments create a more or less permanent overhead and you need to think carefully about cost justification. As with so many other areas of business, you now need to think carefully about the nature of the job. Is it a core skill that is continually required and fundamentally important to the business, or can the skill be rented by the hour or day? Even though I have employed PR departments while a manager in multiple retailing, I have still not convinced myself that a full-time PR staff is essential or cost-effective.

This is especially true if your head office is located outside London. In the PR business you must be close to your market, and journalism is London based. The only way to resolve this is to establish a London PR office. But this means that your PR manager will not be in close enough touch either with his own staff (if he is based at head office) or with the board (if he is based in London).

Of one policy I am convinced. There must be a PR 'product champion' in the company. Public and press relations must be on the agenda of every board meeting. A company's relationships with its stakeholders are too important to be left unmanaged, and almost every policy decision is likely to have a positive or negative effect on one interested group or another. That product champion may be the chairperson or managing director, but other senior and influential managers can ensure that these matters are under review. It may be the personnel director, for example, or the marketing director, or a non-executive director. Or the responsibility may simply be implanted within the culture of the board, ensuring always that someone will ask, 'Yes, but how is this going to affect the attitudes of our stakeholders?'

13

Direct marketing

The most fundamental advice on mail order systems is simple: don't try to re-invent the wheel. Somebody, somewhere has met all the problems you will encounter, and many more besides.

In the days before big corporate retailing Mr Smith, the shopkeeper, used to sell his goods to Mrs Jones. There was an identifiable and usually continuing relationship between two people who knew each other by name. Mrs Jones knew what Mr Smith kept in stock and knew, for example, that his smoked bacon was particularly good. Mr Smith had a clear idea of Mrs Jones's preferences, knew that she visited his shop every Friday and had a pretty shrewd idea of what she would want to buy, and how much she would spend. In time he was able to adjust his stock to meet her requirements, optimizing the profit he could make from her business.

Today retailing is very different. Mrs Jones has become an unidentifiable part of the retailer's 'target market'. Retailers sell their merchandise and services to customers rather than named individuals. They record branch and company sales rather than sales to individual customers, and the sales pattern of ranges rather than the purchasing habits of individuals.

Direct marketers approach their business from a different and earlier perspective, which Mr Smith and Mrs Jones would have been happy to recognize. Direct marketers aim to establish a trading relationship with named individuals, monitoring and reacting to the purchasing patterns of each separate customer, recognizing that their corporate sales and profit performance is no more than the sum of each of these individual relationships. The two approaches can lead to a different perspective of the retail management process. Both types of business manage the things they can *measure*. Retailers manage merchandise and other assets at corporate and usually branch level. Direct marketers do this too, but they also aim to manage *customers* and *customer relationships*. They can do this because direct marketers have much more specific information available on each of their customers.

With a properly planned and managed customer database they know not only each customer's name and address but also record each customer's buying pattern: what each has bought, how much was spent, and when and how frequently these purchases have been made. They know how much it has cost to acquire each customer, an expense every retailer incurs but few outside direct marketing can measure. They have a further important advantage over conventional retailers: they know which customers have *not* bought. This may be either because the customer (or more accurately prospective customer) has requested, say, a catalogue but bought nothing from it, or because goods that were ordered were subsequently returned. With an accurate measure of the cost and source of lost sales, direct marketers can act to reduce this important but previously intangible expense.

Armed with this information the direct marketer can measure the costs and profits appropriate to individual customers, tailoring both customer recruitment and ongoing promotion costs to match and often enhance the profit potential of each customer.

Lesson retailers can learn from direct marketing

The direct marketing business develops three management disciplines that are not always well practiced in High Street retailing. They:

1 focus on customers and customer profitability

2 constantly measure the effects of their management decisions

3 test ideas, and keep testing.

Retailers need to develop these habits if they are to succeed in introducing any direct marketing disciplines within the framework of a conventional retail business.

Customer information

The customer database is the lifeblood of the direct marketing company. Clearly no mail order firm could conduct business without keeping a record of customers' names and addresses. But the customer database is more than this: it is a record of the firm's entire

> *The customer database is a record of the firm's entire relationship with the customers from the time they first made contact.*

relationship with each customer from the time he or she first made contact. It is the equivalent of a retail manager's memory and experience of all regular customers, which equips the manager with a knowledge of customers' preferences and buying habits. A good retailer can use this knowledge to build sales by guiding customers to appropriate merchandise and introducing new ideas and offers that will appeal. The retailer can also establish a personal customer relationship that is ongoing and induces each customer's loyalty.

The direct marketer's database may exist on computer disks rather than in human memory, but it can achieve exactly the same objectives. It can contain any information that sheds useful light on the firm's relationship with its customers, but practical experience across the world has identified quite a short list of items that describe customer behaviour. They describe past transactions and predict future transactions—for better or worse we all tend to be creatures of habit—and they are:

- **Frequency** How often does the customer buy something?

- **Recency** When did the customer last buy something?

- **Amount** How much does the customer usually spend on each transaction?

- **Category** What sort of merchandise does the customer usually buy?

Any High Street retailer will recognize these indicators to be relevant in normal personal shopping, though they will be able to make particular judgements only for customers they know well. This makes it difficult to exploit the information in sales development policy unless you are able to record the transaction history of individual customers. Technological change is beginning to make this a practical proposition for the retailer, and we shall return to this topic later.

Gathering these data should not present a problem to the direct selling firm. In order to complete a transaction they must have the constituent data, which includes the name and address of the customer (or prospect), the date of each transaction, the order value and a record of the goods sold on each occasion. Armed with these basic data, a picture can be built up, over time, which describes the continuing relationship and can be used to calculate the descriptive indicators embodied in the 'FRAC' acronym.

In fact many mail order companies still do not have a true customer database. While they must have the customer's name and address coupled to financial data to track transactions, this is not always linked to records of recruitment and promotional history, or to details of the products bought by each customer. Like retailers, these companies have maintained separate records of these business transactions because information technology was not sufficiently advanced to allow fully integrated customer records to be maintained. However, this is now possible, even with quite modest computer hardware and software packages, and the benefits of a full customer database are substantial.

Can the retailer benefit from the disciplines of maintaining a customer database? Potentially there are major advantages. You can re-establish a personal relationship with customers, providing them with *relevant* information about special offers and new merchandise because you *know* which products interest them, and where and when they are most likely to buy. You learn also which groups of customers offer the greatest profit potential. You can use this information to target these customers, and to frame promotional plans to find customers of a similar type.

However, these advantages have to be balanced by the real practical difficulties of establishing a customer database within a conventional retailing context. Most retail information systems are not designed to capture information on individual customers and their related transactions. Indeed, in the vast majority of retail transactions the name of the customer is never known. So a move to database marketing requires a completely new approach to capturing and using customer information, probably extending to a complete rewrite of your database and EPoS systems.

Once you have a customer list it must be *used*. Customers will resent spending time to give information that is not going to be used for their potential benefit, and from a purely practical and economic viewpoint, remember that unused customer data will start to degrade from the day it is collected. Inevitably, people's needs change and with these changes their need to use particular stores will change. People move house as well: as a rough and ready guide, you must assume that 10–15 per cent of your customers will move house every year. The only way you will find out about this is if you use the mailing list. 'Gone aways' will be returned to you by the Post Office, providing you have a clear return address on the envelope (these should always be flagged on your database), and every communication from you should carry a change of address form.

Secondly, you must record the response to every mailing. This will provide vital information to refine your subsequent relationship with each customer. If you obey this rule from the beginning it will also prevent you from sending out mailings that do not request a positive response from your customers. In the end you want people to continue their *trading* relationship with you. Passive mailings that do not allow a customer to respond in some way will deliver neither new business nor new information. Naturally this also means that you must have some form of *response mechanism* built into every customer contact. In practice you will need some form of token or voucher carrying the customer's name and address (or a pre-printed customer code), which the customer returns at the point of sale.

If it moves, measure it!

Direct marketers are mad about figures. They regard guesswork with deep suspicion. In mainstream retailing you may well find managers who subscribe to the 'Don't confuse me with the facts, let's just do it' approach to life, but they are a rare and usually unsuccessful breed in direct marketing. Numeracy is forced upon them. Profits and reputations are made and lost on apparently tiny response rates.

Factual information about the customer becomes the lifeblood of direct marketing companies. This is because they have none of the subjective information available to the shopkeeper despite, perversely, the one-to-one relationship between direct marketers and their customers. They never see their customers; they cannot take account of the questions customers ask, their tone, or the smiles or shrugged shoulders visible as customers examine stock or read price tags. Direct marketers tend to put more weight on specific customer information than on general customer and market research. Research is important, particularly in planning overall strategy, but experience demonstrates that actual, measurable customer behaviour is a more reliable and actionable guide to the future. Consequently mail order and other direct marketing companies expend a great deal of money and effort in building databases of customer information.

Testing, testing!

Direct marketers test their actions constantly. This habit is born of experience: they have discovered that even minor and apparently unimportant changes to advertising and mailings can make the difference between success and failure. So if you decide to experiment with a mail shot to your credit card holders, for example, you must not rely on a single experiment, but be prepared to design and implement a series of tests. Do not assume, if the first attempt either succeeds, that you have found the key to successful direct marketing;

> *Passive mailings that do not allow a customer to respond in some way deliver neither new business nor new information.*

or, if it fails, that you have proved to yourself that the whole idea is inappropriate.

For example, you could test men against women, high versus low credit balances, or test two different response mechanisms. Always measure the results, and then test the most successful result against a new idea. Only repeated trial and error will give you the experience to build up more consistently successful performance.

Mail order for retailers

There are quite a number of retailers who combine mail order and High Street retailing businesses. Among the more well known are Laura Ashley, Habitat, Marks & Spencer and Mothercare. For retailers of this size mail order is usually a secondary business filling niches within their prime market, and allowing scope for range extension where retail space denies them the opportunity to widen ranges in their retail outlets. For niche retailers, often with a small number of shops, mail order offers a wider market and better buying economies.

Would mail order be good for you? The opportunities and advantages to the retailer include:

● access to new geographic markets, both at home and abroad

● a route to national brand recognition ahead of developing a national network of branches

● a way of economic exploitation of niche markets that may not generate adequate revenue in the majority of retail locations

● a way of testing new merchandise and new store brands before committing to the property and shopfitting costs associated with retail expansion

● a potentially self-liquidating source of advertising and promotion

● a basis for developing direct marketing capabilities that could be transferred to the retail business.

Once the 'back-office' facilities are in place to handle orders and fulfilment, mail order offers great flexibility compared to conventional retailing. Expanding the market requires no new shops—just new advertising and an extra catalogue print run. And if you care to, you can totally change the design, style and content of your 'printed shop' every season. Remember each catalogue starts as empty, white paper; its appearance and content can be changed and remains under your total control. Compare this with the inherent inflexibility of shop units, whose interior design may need to be retained for five or six years, and whose site location and shape usually reflect the compromises you have to make in buying new shop units.

Mail order can be a very useful way for smaller retailers to become more prominent. It is very difficult to escape the 'local retailer' tag in the early stages of development, even if you have designs upon a national network of outlets. Mail order gives you both access to customers outside the catchment area of your shops, and an exposure (through customer recruitment advertising) that will be picked up more easily by journalists and other opinion influencers. At a practical level, journalists are more likely to write about your company if, through mail order, you can offer a national distribution. Writers find it difficult to justify telling readers of a national magazine or newspaper about shops located in only a few out-of-the-way towns.

Mail order can be particularly useful for retailers trading in specialist markets: a product has to be very special to draw people living more than an hour's travelling distance, and there will be few locations that can deliver an adequate catchment market. Mail order delivers the opportunity to trade nationally from a single store. Perhaps the best example of this rests not in the UK but in the United States, where the outdoor clothing and equipment store L. L. Bean has just one retail outlet. Nevertheless the company has built up an internationally renowned reputation on the back of a successful and well-run mail order business.

Within an expanding retail business there is useful synergy between the retail and mail order arms. Mail order catalogues, and the associated advertising, raise public awareness of the retailer, so that new branches open into an established market where the brand is already known. Of course some of the mail order sales in the area will be transferred to the retail unit, but USA experience suggests that direct market sales tend to continue at an economic rate.

There are, therefore, some very positive reasons why retailers should also adopt a mail order channel to their customers. Of course, there are also some disadvantages, dangers and difficulties. Some of these are technical or financial, and some are management and attitudinal problems, which are perhaps the most difficult for the retailer to surmount. The problems you will have to face include:

● investing in new prospects and customers

● setting up an effective operational infrastructure

● dealing with conflicting retail and mail order demands

● recognizing the differences in management style and methods.

Investing in new prospects and customers

When you open a new retail branch, the only positive action you have to take is to open the doors. Providing you are sited in a reasonable location, sooner or later customers will walk through the doors and some of them will buy. Often advertising is neither necessary nor economic. Contrast this with mail order. You set up your catalogue, pile copies on your desk, stock the warehouse and sort out the fulfilment system. At nine o'clock on Monday you are ready for business. What happens? Nothing. Absolutely nothing! You have no customers because you have taken no action to tell them who you are or what you offer.

This may seem rather obvious, but it's worth highlighting this vital difference between High Street retailing and mail order. The very existence of a shop publicizes the business and you will attract customers. In the mail order field customers cannot find you; *you* must find *them*. This takes time and money, though at least it is a very controllable investment. In the same way that you must pay for a shop and fit it out before customers can be served, mail order companies must buy customer prospects before they can reap subsequent revenues. Some of the various ways to find customers are listed below.

1 *Advertise to solicit enquiries for your catalogue.* Remember that only a fraction of those who ask for catalogues will subsequently send an order. Similarly, only a fraction of those visiting your shop will buy something while they are there.

2 *Solicit orders directly from your advertisement.* The Sunday supplements are full of these,'direct response' advertisements. In most cases you will receive not only goods, but subsequent catalogues offering you other suggestions.

3 *Rent lists of likely prospects.* An entire industry is building up around list rental. While still in relative infancy in the UK and Europe, list rental and list swopping are totally established in the USA. Lists make good sense because they focus on people who are known to be mail order responsive.

4 *'Piggy back' catalogues with other people's goods despatches.* You won't be able to do this with direct competitors, but often you can find a compatible customer profile; these people, most importantly, are proven mail order buyers and are therefore more likely to respond to *any* appropriate offer.

5 *Ask customers to introduce friends.* Not an easy technique to use
   when you first start (you have no customers to ask) but one of the
   best. It is cheap, even with an incentive, and usually yields very
   high quality prospects. People introduce friends who they think
   have a genuine interest: after all, no one wants to burden their best
   friend with junk mail.

Nobody can tell you with certainty which method will be best. You
can seek advice, and the better the advice the more economic your
initial customer recruitment will become. But in the end there is only
one way to find out. You must *test*.

There are many things you will need to test, all of which can have a
dramatic effect on your profitability. For example:

● advertisement and catalogue creative treatments

● different magazines, newspapers, rented lists, product despatch
  options, introductory incentives

● the size and position of advertisements

● the use of conventional advertisements versus loose inserts in the
  same magazines

● different direct mail letter and even different envelopes

● different days, weeks and seasons.

Each combination represents a unique test—one which, in time, will
need to be repeated—so the number of permutations is enormous.
You cannot test everything at once. In practice it will take years; you
will never stop testing or refining your approach. Thus, when you
start, and you want to keep your programme and budget within
practical limits, there is no substitute for experience. Clearly this is
something you lack, so try to be neither brave nor foolhardy. Go to
one of the specialist direct marketing agencies for help. In the end you
will save a great deal of time, money and heartache.

When I talk of an *investment* in new customers, the word is used
purposely. An example will show you why.

EXAMPLE   Assume that you plan to launch a new, specialist mail order
catalogue—perhaps around 32 pages of outdoor clothing or sporting
goods. It would not be unreasonable to expect the cost of each
catalogue enquiry—i.e. the production and media costs of advertising
in several appropriate national magazines, divided by the number of
catalogue requests received—to average out at around £2.50.

Then let us assume that 15 per cent of these enquirers actually order
something from the catalogue. That means each ordering customer
has cost you £16.67. Add to this the run-on cost of a catalogue at, say,

60p, and enquiry handling and despatch costs of, say, £1.10, and you have a total of £18.37. If your merchandise carries a gross margin of a generous 45 per cent, you are going to need *net* revenue of some £46.00 simply to recover the cost of acquiring that customer. Now remember that some of the goods that you despatch will be returned for refund or exchange. For non-clothing items this might be as low as 10 per cent, and for clothing, upwards of 25 per cent. Hence, your average order values will need to be around £70.00 before you can be confident of making any money.

Not surprisingly, few mail order catalogues make money in their first year. You must understand this if you are to avoid some embarrassing conversations with your banker or finance director, but if you are serious about mail order it should not distress you, because you intend to make long-term profits from each customer. The largest cost of this relationship has been carried 'up front'. Your subsequent costs will be much less, while the revenue stream should continue, if you are careful, for several years.

What conclusions can we draw, therefore, from this brief piece of back-of-envelope analysis?

1 You must be prepared to finance your investment in customers. Using the example above, an initial 15 000 customers will cost you £250 000. But their 'lifetime' revenue over the next four years could be, at an average £60 net sales from each of two seasonal catalogues, some £7 million.

2 Although you *can* 'pull the plug' if sales do not materialize, you should start in the knowledge and expectation of a long-term commitment to individual, customer relationships—because this is where your profits lie.

3 You must look carefully at probable transaction values in relation to the cost of acquiring new customers. In the above example, an active customer should become profitable during the life of your second catalogue. But if the average transaction value were, say, £5.00, few customers would *ever* return a net profit.

You must recognize that the process of recruiting new customers is going to continue indefinitely. This is not to say that your business must *grow* indefinitely. It is merely recognition of the certainty that you will lose customers. You must endeavour to ensure that you do not lose customers carelessly through poor service or an unstable product offer. But inevitably you will lose some customers because their needs change, they have less disposable income, they move away without telling you, or they buy from competitors.

The proportion of your customer base that you will lose will depend on many factors, and only time and experience will give you this information. However, it would be wise to assume that you will lose at least 10 per cent of your active customer base every season. In the early stages of your mail order business development the average attrition rate could be much higher. This is because you are most likely to lose 'new' customers. Once there is an established relationship, the fall-out is much reduced, and more likely to be caused by the customers' changing needs. For example, if you sell children's products, customer losses may be triggered simply by a family growing older and moving out of the children's range.

I do not want to impart nightmare feelings of pedalling hard just to remain stationary, but you must recognize that new customers must be recruited simply to maintain a constant customer base. Positive growth will demand commensurately more recruitment activity and continuing cash investment in the future. Hopefully, you will recognize that there is an economic trade-off between profits today and profits tomorrow. You can always improve the short-term profitability of a mail order business by suspending recruitment, simply because—as you will recall—new customers are almost always unprofitable. I have seen more than one business do this when they have acquired a mail order company. However, this action carries a long-term penalty even if recruitment is subsequently re-started. Each season's cohort of new customers will be with you, albeit diminished steadily through attrition, for several years. The later years will also be the most profitable to you. But if you create a hole in this marching package of profits, you will inevitably reduce the business's overall profitability for the entire lifetime of each missing cohort.

At the core of successful mail order retailing is the principle of maximizing customer lifetimes. The longer you can extend this, the better your profits will be. You must continue to offer products that will be relevant to your customers. Perhaps even more importantly, you must avoid the wanton destruction of customer relationships. Good customer service is vital. It is vital in all sectors of retailing, but the consequences of poor service are more immediate, exposed and measurable in direct marketing relationships. All the advice given elsewhere in this book about careful targeting, customer-orientated business systems, and product and service quality management is just as relevant to mail order marketing as to conventional retailing.

One of the generally accepted principles of total quality management

> *At the core of successful mail order retailing is the principle of maximising customer lifetime. The longer you can extend this, the better your profits will become.*

is 'zero defects'—get it right first time. The goal of all mail order businesses, and the principal source of profit growth, is 'zero defections'.

Setting up an effective operational infrastructure

Effective and timely customer service is the central objective of mail order operations. Keep this firmly in mind as you build and implement systems to run the business, because there will be many opportunities to compromise in favour of apparent operational expedience. In the long run you are not setting up a system for the benefit of the warehouse manager or the computer department: it is being set up for the customer. The essential operational processes are:

● handling catalogue requests

● receiving and processing orders by telephone or post

● order fulfilment and despatch

● handling returns, queries and exchanges.

There are also some 'off line' activities that are essential to mail order business:

● sourcing and selection of merchandise

● catalogue pagination and design

● advertising planning and media analysis

● customer database analysis.

With some excellent direct marketing manuals on the market, a book on retail marketing is not the place to offer detailed procedures for planning and implementing mail order systems, but there are a number of key issues that I would like to address.

Handling catalogue requests

This is the first time that prospective customers will have direct experience of your business. They have already shown interest in what you have to offer, and have taken the trouble to clip and post a coupon or telephone your company. In a retail context this is analogous to customers starting to look more closely at your merchandise, looking round for a sales assistant, or reading labels or pack details. As a retailer, *you know* these are positive signals of interest that need quick and helpful reaction. Treat catalogue enquiries with the same sense of urgency. You will be judged by your reaction. If *you* sent for a catalogue that turned up six weeks later, you would quickly form an opinion, which I suspect would not be very

flattering, about the subsequent level of service you would expect
from that company. Bear in mind recent US research that shows
response rates fall in direct relation to the length of time taken to meet
a catalogue request. Aim to turn round the request within 24 hours.
This might be the start of a long and happy relationship. It is not
worth risking its immediate destruction by your own hand.

Receiving, processing and fulfilling orders

Speed continues to be essential. Mail order is almost always at a
disadvantage to conventional retailing in this respect. Retail
customers can buy and use their purchases on the same day, while
even the most ambitious mail order businesses will not achieve better
than a 24-hour turnround. Most people who are prepared to use mail
order recognize that they sacrifice the instant gratification that the
High Street can deliver, but they will not relish waiting weeks for
delivery. Essentially you must be able to deliver the vast majority of
your range from stock, whether this stock is held on you own
premises or with the manufacturers.

There is a rapid trend away from orders sent by post to telephone
ordering. Less frequent mail order users still accept the idea of using
the postal system, particularly if they prefer or anticipate paying by
cheque of course, but the *cognoscenti* have learned to recognize the
benefits of telephone ordering. Firstly, it is clearly quicker. But more
importantly a telephone call allows them to find out immediately if
the goods they want are in stock, and in turn allows the mail order
company to reserve stock as soon as the order is received. This puts
immediate parameters on the design of your systems: you must have
on-line and preferably real-time stock records. The use of credit card
payments also introduces safeguards for both you and your
customers. However, if you introduce your own credit system you
must either request a written credit application before handling
orders from new customers, or take the higher risk option of
assessing credit risks on-line. This is quite feasible but requires careful
planning and systems that are integrated with credit bureau services.
The need for prior credit assessment is one of the reasons why, in the
UK, you see so many direct response advertisements that say 'send
no money now'. This provides the mail order company with the
opportunity to assess credit risks before accepting your order. But
you can be sure that they are looking for a long-term relationship, and
the despatch of your original order will be followed by subsequent
catalogues.

A telephone ordering system provides you with a rare opportunity
for personal contact with your customers. Take advantage of this by
delivering a friendly, reassuring and reactive response to your

customers. The big mail order companies watch this public face of their systems very carefully, even down to monitoring and managing the time it takes to answer the telephone: anything longer than a few seconds is too long.

The most fundamental advice on systems is simple: don't try to re-invent the wheel. Someone, somewhere has met all the problems you will encounter, and many more. They have designed solutions into computer packages to deal with all the major aspects of enquiry, order handling and fulfilment. If you are starting in this business, it is much better to create your administrative systems around a ready-made computer package, some of which even run on desktop PCs, than to try to design your own solution. After all, you can only design systems for problems you can anticipate, and as a beginner there will be many that you miss.

Exchanges and refunds

These are a fact of mail order life. The customer who sends something back is not being perfidious. The merchandise may not have fitted; the colour may not be quite right; it may not do what was expected. None of these things would have been clear until the goods were received by the customer, who has had no opportunity to see, feel or try goods as he or she would in a shop. So you must learn to accept returns and exchanges in good grace, at higher levels than would have been typical in a retail situation, and plan for their recycling or disposal. You will need to decide who pays for the cost of returning goods. Because returns are such a natural part of the transaction process, and because many consumers are wary of such 'hidden' costs in mail order transactions, my preference is to recommend that the mail order company carries this cost. You will achieve a more relaxed and longer lasting relationship with your customers, and the cost will be redeemed in a longer customer lifetime.

Mail order is an iterative, learning activity

In the mail order world, customer focus is achieved through efficient, integrated internal systems. There is a cycle that begins with customer recruitment, moves through their response to merchandise offers to the analysis of response and consequent refinement of the offer, leading in turn to further orders. At each stage, systems yield not only the essential bureaucratic information to manage throughput, but the analytical capacity to interpret and improve the effectiveness of each part of the cycle. Once you have started the direct marketing process you should never stop learning and never ignore the opportunity to refine and improve the way you do business.

Relevant data and information form the oil that keeps the whole machine running.

Managing retailing and mail order within one firm

When the UK retail giant Sears made its 1988 bid for Freemans, one of the 'big five' mail order companies operating in Britain, its offer document stressed the considerable scope for 'synergy' between the High Street store and mail order arms of the combined business. The exact nature of this synergy was left somewhat undefined beyond some general statements about common merchandise sourcing and the use of retail brands within mail order catalogues. Perhaps this was just as well, because real synergy, though desirable, is difficult to achieve. If you are contemplating the formation of a mail order business to run alongside a retail business, there are a number of issues you will need to resolve.

Sourcing

Manufacturers supplying the mail order market are especially aware of the need for timely deliveries. Not all suppliers share the same sense of urgency that is so important in this business. Suppliers and retailers are both aware that there is some scope within conventional retailing for disguising absent ranges. Retailers do not have to declare their hand quite as publicly as the mail order companies, which publish their total product range offer at the beginning of each catalogue season. With each request for an item that has not been delivered, the mail order firm has publicly to admit failure; the retailer can at least direct customers towards alternative merchandise or suggest a return visit at a later date. Although mail order firms generally maintain back order files for unfulfilled orders, they create a high risk of dissatisfaction and the certainty of additional fulfilment and despatch goods.

Quality standards represent another factor in the choice of supplier. All types of retailer should aim to maintain the highest standards of quality assurance, but the cost of poor quality is probably higher for mail order businesses. Many consumers start from a position of great wariness of mail order quality, and even a single incident of poor quality may serve to support their prejudice, in which case you and the mail order industry will lose a customer for ever. As a mail order trader you also incur direct costs in double handling a replacement, while retailers rarely have to reimburse their customer's extra travel costs. Hence, you must be prepared to use suppliers who have the ability and will to deliver consistent quality. Your internal quality assurance systems are equally important. Consider how quality and consistency might be affected by design specifications, materials and packaging methods. Make sure that you have an effective system for checking incoming stock against samples and specifications. Keep and analyse data on returns so that recurring quality and durability problems are identified.

Stock management

Both retail and mail order businesses ideally like to receive stock just ahead of the relevant sales season, and like to sell the last item of each line of merchandise on the last day of the season. I do not know anyone who has ever achieved this ideal. In practice, retail ranges flow into branches at the beginning of a season over a period extending to several weeks and will sell out progressively, particularly in complex areas such as clothing, so that the whole store range is rarely represented in any branch for very long. Retailers accept that they will sell from broken ranges in the closing weeks of a season, and indeed the customers hardly recognize that this is a problem until they cannot find the right colour or size variant.

Life is very different in mail order. As far as your customers are concerned, your 'shop' is open and fully stocked from the day they receive their catalogues until the day the catalogues are replaced by a new edition. Your customers would be amazed to order something from a new catalogue only to discover it was not in stock. So you have to adjust both your retail management attitudes and your stock management policies. *All* the stock must be available from the first day of trading, as far as is humanly possible. And it must remain in stock throughout the currency of the catalogue. While customers will be more understanding towards the end of a catalogue's life, the absence of stock cover will still generate extra costs in handling refunds.

Mail order companies therefore adopt a different attitude to end of season stocks. While the retailer aims to clear stocks by the end of a season, with a prior rundown period, the mail order operator *expects and intends* to carry terminal stock in order to ensure a reasonable stock cover throughout the season. Stock disposal systems are set up to liquidate this stock after the season has closed. Various methods are used, including sale catalogues, trade 'jobbers' who sell stock

> *As far as your customers are concerned, you mail order 'shop' is open and fully stocked from the day they receive the catalogues until the day you replace the catalogues by a new edition.*

through markets, and the large mail order companies often run a chain of retail outlets that specialize in clearing stock.

Many mail order companies also improve the accuracy of their sales forecasting and stock purchasing by issuing 'preview' catalogues to a sample of their existing customers. The previous catalogue is dispatched some three months ahead of the main launch date, and customers are offered the opportunity to order goods, often at a discount, for delivery when the season actually commences. The resulting ordering patterns enable the mail order company to adjust its order commitments in line with this picture of near real life demand. The system by no means provides a fail-safe forecast, but it usually identifies the season's 'winners and losers', and helps to minimize lost sales and excessive stocks.

Merchandise ranges

My first adventure into mail order started during my time in retail marketing. We already produced a catalogue that was used to promote retail sales and decided to diversify into mail order on the back of this catalogue, reasoning that we could at least amortize the cost of this promotional catalogue. Despite making many mistakes, including developing our own systems instead of buying a package, this venture was quite successful. We learned quickly, though, that the scope of an effective retail catalogue needs to be very different from a mail order catalogue. In a catalogue destined for mail order use, every page must justify its presence with an adequate volume and value of merchandise. Dramatic, full-page shots of one item may look thrilling (especially to its buyer and the catalogue designer), but you must consider whether greater variety of product would increase sales. Pages of low-value items may well reflect the variety of the retail range, but will not encourage high transaction values.

The cost of processing each order will be much the same whatever the value and number of items within that order, and through the design and range content of the catalogue you must encourage customers to want high-value items and to order more than one piece of merchandise. In clothing, for example, colour and style coordinated ranges encourage multiple purchasing.

Management attitudes

Humanity has a disturbing habit of imposing itself on good management principles. In much the same way that customers are said to obstruct the smooth running of the business, managers can obstruct good management! You should accept now, before discovering the hard way, that retail managers can see things in a very different light to mail order managers. If you learn to recognize these different traits, at least you will launch into mail order prepared to understand why there is conflict. While there is an inherent danger in generalizations, a few guidelines may be helpful.

1   Retailers tend to have short-term perspectives. Performance is judged by the Saturday night sales figures. These are analysed against the previous week and the previous year's equivalent. While retailers look at such snapshots, mail order managers probe trends.

2   Retailers make broad judgements and create solutions to implement universally, while mail order people examine detail and implement solutions that can, through database marketing, vary for every customer.

3   Retailers measure branch performance; mail order businesses measure customer performance.

4   Retailers fire buyers who have end of season stock; mail order managers are more likely to fire them if they don't!

5   Retailers distrust statistics, while mail order firms live by them.

6   Retailers revel in 'Monday morning management': instant, reactive decisions combined with immediate implementation. Mail order managers are just as anxious to make decisions, but they may have to wait weeks before decisions can be implemented and months before there is feedback from the market. Once decisions have been made on catalogue design and content, and promotional plans have been set in place, there is little that can be changed—only future catalogues can be adapted.

Such differences are an inevitable result of the differing nature of retail and mail order markets and operations. Neither approach is wrong in its place, but when retail and mail order meet there is a high risk of a culture clash. You must be prepared to recognize that this will happen, and aim not to take sides but to help the process of mutual understanding.

For example, I can assure you that if you launch a mail order business that shares merchandise with an existing retail business you will soon find yourself having to make the Judgement of Solomon.

EXAMPLE   Receiving stock of a new line in August for the new autumn season, you reserve the forecast season's sales through the new mail order catalogue and start to issue the retail allocation. Happily you are surprised by the early retail success of this product, which is selling three times the predicted volume. Your sales manager comes to see you.

'We're going to run out of stock by the end of September. I want some of that mail order that's sitting doing nothing in the warehouse.'

'We need that for the catalogue we're launching next month,' you reply.

'I know that,' he says, 'but how do you know it's going to sell in the catalogue?'

'Well,' you reply, 'I have to rely on their forecasts.' You glance furtively down the corridor in search of a rescue party.

'Rubbish,' he responds. 'You know perfectly well they always have stocks left at the end of the season. Trade's difficult enough already, and you've asked for a 20 per cent sales increase. I can't do that if I haven't got the stock. I get a winner and you're denying me the chance to make my bonus. You know I can sell it and get you the cash in the till inside a month. All you've got from them is a forecast, and you know we can't trust statistics.'

'All right, I'll think about it. Come and see me after the Board meeting.' Your secretary collars you as you leave the meeting. She has the mail order manager in your office, refusing to move until he has seen you.

'You can't steal my stock, you know.' He opens the conversation bluntly.

'Well, I thought you might agree to release it. After all it's only one line', you suggest.

'No way,' he says. 'I'm trying to build you a business and I can't afford to fall down on customer satisfaction. Those customers cost us nearly £20 each. I can't believe you're willing to throw them away for a few pence of short-term profit. I'm looking to keep them for the next five years. What are they going to think if they're told we're out of stock as soon as we launch the catalogue? At least those retail people can try to sell them something else. It shouldn't be difficult if they're so clever at selling.'

The answer, of course, is that both businesses have a right to compete. But they have to fight their battles in the marketplace, not in your head office. Synergy in branding, merchandise sourcing and overall corporate development is a useful and desirable aim, but ultimately you are running two different businesses and they must be managed independently, and utilizing the 'rules of the game' for two quite different distribution trades.

The UK mail order market

This is a market that is full of contradictions. In the UK less than 6 per cent of non-food retail sales is channelled through mail order catalogues, yet at least half the nation's households have recent experience of buying through catalogues. Mail order has a dowdy, down-market image yet pulls fashion sales from young women that would make the managers of some of the high profile fashion chains green with envy. Financial analysts continually forecast the demise of traditional mail order yet promote Great Universal Stores, with over 35 per cent of this traditional market, as an essential and safe component of any investment portfolio.

In this climate of apparent confusion it is all the more difficult for retailers to assess whether a move into mail order would make good sense. This is not the place for an exhaustive analysis of the market, but some guidance for retailers is appropriate.

Both the strength and inherent weakness of the UK mail order market lie in its historical development. The origins of the business stem from the turn of the century, when 'turn clubs' developed in the poor industrial communities of the north of England. Groups of local households pooled small cash contributions, enabling one of the group to buy, in turn, goods for the family that would have been too expensive to fund out of the weekly wage packet. Thus, if 20 households each contributed a shilling (now represented by 5p), one of their number could buy a pound's worth of goods. (Obviously worth much more then than now—in 1917 a man's overcoat could be bought for 85p.) Every 20 weeks one person's turn to buy would occur again. Over the decades that followed, 'turn clubs' grew in sophistication, becoming independent business and buying direct from manufacturers. But the down-market profile and focus on credit purchasing remained. The mail order companies (for they were now large enough to draw customers from a wide area and used the postal system to order and distribute goods) recruited local 'agents' who collected orders, cash, and distributed goods locally to their neighbours.

By the 1960s the business had become both large and lucrative but never succeeded in appealing to the growing and increasingly prosperous middle class. Even today there is considerable resistance among richer communities to the whole concept of mail order. It is not seen as something for 'people like us'. These prejudices have been undermined to some extent, firstly by the arrival of direct response advertisements popularized in the Sunday newspaper colour supplements. Association with up-market newspapers such as *The Sunday Times* helped to dilute the down-market image of mail order, which increasingly was to be re-christened 'home shopping'. But in the early days, product and service were not very reliable and many customers lost their money as direct response advertisers collapsed.

These new mail order customers also learned to associate mail order with long delivery times. 'Delivery within 28 days' became standard small print, perhaps not surprisingly when some advertisers did not confirm purchase orders until the level of response was known. The traditional mail order companies, and their customers, somehow remained silent about the delivery service they had enjoyed and taken for granted for years. Most expected to receive their deliveries well within a week and often within 48 hours. As technology improved, and the household penetration of telephones rose through 80 per cent, mail order groups had introduced telephone ordering and highly sophisticated 'back-office' systems.

History is expected to agree that the next stage of development was triggered by the launch of the 'Directory', the first mail order product to be born of the now dissolved liaison between the British retail group Next and the traditional mail order firm of Grattan. For the first time the Directory promoted the pre-existing benefits of mail order technology—48-hour delivery and credit purchasing over the telephone—to a new breed of customers who considered themselves (rightly or wrongly) more sophisticated than the traditional mail order user. The Directory moved away from the 1000-page printed department store represented by traditional catalogues, utilizing sophisticated graphic design, hard back binding, detailed product descriptions and gummed-in cloth samples. While mail order industry experts would agree that the Directory has had its share of difficulties, there is no doubt that it has created a new respect for mail order (or home shopping) in UK market sectors that previously would have never considered using this retail channel.

European mail order companies have never been subjected to a 'down-market' historical tradition. Home shopping is widely recognized as 'socially acceptable', though only Germany and Austria has a higher proportion of retail sales channelled through mail order. The UK benefits from a compact, highly populated geography that is well served by a sophisticated retail distribution system. In Europe mail order provides a valued service in many areas where access to a full range of shops is not convenient, and in many parts—particularly in Germany—shop opening hours are not yet as generous as is commonplace in the UK.

The £4 billion UK home shopping market remains dominated by the agency arrangement built up by the five companies that control 95 per cent of the market. Because the people who use these catalogues

are generally satisfied by their experience of mail order, they are also
the group most likely to experiment with new catalogues. Even
Next's 'Directory', which is targeted specifically at non-traditional
customers, is well respected and occasionally used by traditional
customers. But equally they see little benefit in moving to direct
catalogues that do not offer the 10 per cent commission they have
become accustomed to receiving, even though the majority no longer
collect orders for friends and neighbours.

Non-users of mail order remain sceptical of the benefits of home
shopping, despite the sociologists' arguments that they should be
impressed by the time-saving factor, which should be so important to
the increasingly cash-rich but time-poor middle class. Their concerns
stem from their view of traditional mail order in the UK: a down-
market image, perceptions and expectations of poor quality, concern
about taking and over-extending credit, a perceived lack of
individuality in catalogue merchandise, and the apparent lack of
immediacy, enjoyment and instant gratification proffered by the High
Street.

Hence, we are left with an interesting paradox for any retailer
contemplating a move into home shopping:

1 Traditional mail order customers are the most active, willing and
   sophisticated users of mail order, but see little reason to switch
   from an established arrangement based primarily on agency mail
   order catalogues.

2 The huge potential customer base of new users remains deeply
   suspicious of mail order, and even trialists will dismiss the channel
   as a whole the moment they encounter an incident of poor quality
   or service. Initially at least, they are also more likely to be sporadic,
   occasional users—buying perhaps once or twice a year compared
   to the traditional user who purchases, on average, more than once
   a month.

Recognizing that mail order economics are based on long-term,
regular relationships between the supplier and the customer, entry
into this market would appear to be fraught with difficulties.

Indeed it is, but they are not insurmountable, providing you are
willing to persevere.

Firstly, you must recognize one of the fundamental rules of direct
marketing. Whatever way you choose to segment your markets, the
difference between those customers who are willing to respond and
those who are not will be greater than any other differences in needs
and habits of your market in general. People who respond to *any* mail
order offer are more likely to respond to a new and even quite

radically different offer than those who have no history of direct market response. This is why list rental and swopping is so prevalent, especially in the mail order sophisticated United States. Someone who buys gardening products by post is more likely to buy wine from a mail order catalogue than a wine buff who has no direct response track record.

So even if you think that your product would never sell to your image of a 'mail order agent' (which is probably inaccurate for the majority of them!), they could still represent your most economic and most profitable prospects if the product and service offer is good enough. You will need to advertise in the media to enable mail order customers to find you. Do not ignore 'popular' media through a misplaced sense of pride; in any case many such magazines will offer, in volume terms, more 'up-market' readers than heavier and more traditional titles.

Secondly, the design of your merchandise, catalogue, fulfilment system and promotional strategy must take into account and counter the prejudices of unsophisticated mail order users. They are looking for reassurance about individuality, quality, risk avoidance, helpfulness and speedy reaction. If there is nothing special about your product, or if you tell them nothing about your service and offer long delivery dates, you will attract neither new users of mail order nor the interest of the more sophisticated and active users of this channel. Current mail order users will be comparing your offer with other mail order products. New users will be comparing your offer with what is available in their local High Street. You must be able to demonstrate differential advantage: the reason why your offer is better.

Do this, and with patience and persistence you can build a valuable business alongside your retail interests. Moreover, the *measurable* insight you can gain uniquely from the analysis of mail order trading can be fed back into your approach to retailing.

Index